"In this deep and rich study, Michael Z⟨ ⟩
capitalist class maintains power by see⟨ ⟩
division along lines of race, gender, nat⟨ ⟩
belief. In examining movements of the past and present, this
work challenges us to understand how only radical liberation
and solidarity can help us overcome the forces that treat us
as 'human capital stock' to achieve a truly just future."
—Sara Nelson, president, Association of Flight Attendants,
Communications Workers of America

"Michael Zweig has produced an important educational resource for
young labor, racial justice, and environmental activists by providing
a clearly written, well-documented account of the economic,
political, and historical forces driving social events. His explanation
of the interrelationships of class and race is especially welcome."
—Bill Fletcher Jr, past president, TransAfrica; former education director
of the AFL-CIO; consultant to union and racial justice strategic
campaigns; coauthor, with Fernando Gapasin, of *Solidarity Divided:
The Crisis in Organized Labor and A New Path Toward Social Justice*

"A new wave of activists against inequality, racism, patriarchy,
environmental destruction, and homophobia is arising in America.
But when mainstream economics informs these struggles, the
cupboard is often bare, the issues seen, if at all, as exceptions. Michael
Zweig presents the problems as parts of a whole that recognizes the
centrality of the productive system and the reality of social class.
Folks across the progressive spectrum should read this book."
—Everett Ehrlich, US under secretary of commerce
for economic affairs (1994–97)

"*Class, Race, and Gender: Challenging the Injuries and Divisions of
Capitalism* is an excellent primer for new and young activists. It
makes difficult concepts accessible and will be a great addition
to the body of information available to folks trying to make
sense of the world we live in and how they can change it."
—Roz Pelles, senior strategic advisor to the Poor People's
Campaign: A National Call for a Moral Revival and
vice president of Repairers of the Breach

Class, Race, and Gender

Challenging the Injuries and Divisions of Capitalism

Michael Zweig

Foreword by Rev. William J. Barber II

Class, Race, and Gender: Challenging the Injuries and Divisions of Capitalism
Michael Zweig © 2023
This edition © PM Press

ISBN: 979–888–744–012–5 (paperback)
ISBN: 979–888–744–013–2 (ebook)
Library of Congress Control Number: 2023930801

Cover design by John Yates / stealworks.com
Interior design by briandesign

10 9 8 7 6 5 4 3 2 1

PM Press
PO Box 23912
Oakland, CA 94623
www.pmpress.org

Printed in the USA.

I dedicate this book to Jack O'Dell, who left a deep legacy of both analytic writings and material advances in the lives of working people. Through his many decades of activism, organizing, and patient mentoring, Jack played foundational roles in the movements for Black freedom, labor rights, peace and international solidarity, as well as for independent progressive media.

Contents

FOREWORD   ix

Introduction   **1**
Who Is Speaking   I
Facing the Reality of the Times   4
Some History   7
Finding Lessons   II

CHAPTER ONE   **Political Practice**   **15**
Independent Working Class Politics   16
Activists and Organizers   25
Movement Values   30

CHAPTER TWO   **Key Questions for Progressive Politics**   **33**
Reform   33
Revolution   41
Where Will the Money Come From?   44
Where Is the Political Will?   50

CHAPTER THREE   **How Do We Know What We Know?**   **55**
Basic Characteristics of History   56
Choosing a Belief System   58
Knowledge Is a Process, Not a State   61
Social Practice   63
The Example of Galileo and the Church   64

Truth in the Imagination   67
Beliefs Are Not Theories   69
Facts and Questions   70
Knowledge and Social Power   71

CHAPTER FOUR   **Production in Capitalism**   **75**
The Centrality of Production   75
Who Depends upon Whom? Surplus and
Exploitation   77
Exploitation in Capitalism   80
Social Production for Private Ends   84

CHAPTER FIVE   **Classes and Surplus in Capitalism**   **90**
Classes in Capitalist Society   90
Productive and Unproductive Labor   101
Where Does the Surplus Go?   106
Slow Growth and Inequality   108
    Table 1. Class Composition of US Labor Force
    in 2019   95
    Table 2. Workers in Alternative Arrangements as
    Percent of Total Employed, 1995–2017   96
    Table 3. Gender, Racial, and Ethnic Composition
    of US Classes in 2019   99
    Table 4. Class Composition of US Racial and
    Ethnic Groups in 2019   100
    Table 5. Value Added by Industry as a Percentage
    of Gross Domestic Product, 1957–2019   109

CHAPTER SIX   **Connecting the Dots across Issues**   **112**
Militarism and Global Reach   112
Environmental Devastation   122
Crises in Capitalist Society   127
Privatization—Everything Becomes a
Commodity   130

CHAPTER SEVEN   **Religion, Values, and Interests**   **136**
Religion   137
Values and Interests   146

CHAPTER EIGHT   **Cultures of Capitalism**   **152**
Individualism and Its Limits   152
Individualism and Education   156
Culture   158

CHAPTER NINE   **Race and Gender in Class Society**   **167**
Race   167
Structural Racism   172
White Supremacy in Other Forms   176
Gender   179

CHAPTER TEN   **Navigating Race and Class**   **189**
Navigating Race and Class   190
A Note to White Readers   199

CHAPTER ELEVEN   **Socialism**   **206**
Different Meanings of Socialism   206
International Labor Solidarity   210
Boundaries to Political Action   214
No Guarantee of a Happy Ending   215

ACKNOWLEDGMENTS   221

INDEX   223

ABOUT THE CONTRIBUTORS   231

Foreword

Whether their interest is academic, practical, or both, any student of social movements knows that there is no formula for planning the action that will change the consciousness of society. Yet, in the history of social change, whenever events have aligned to give rise to movements, there is a tradition of practice that has informed the work of those who were able to bring about genuine change. When Frederick Douglass and Harriet Tubman risked all to gain their own freedom from slavery, they found a movement of abolitionists who already were considering how direct action against human bondage could inform a movement to end chattel slavery. When workers went on strike in the early twentieth century, some of them found their way to the Highlander Folk School, where they were able to learn from and with a labor movement determined to change the conditions of working class people. When Rosa Parks refused to give up her seat on a bus in Montgomery, Alabama, and the Rev. Martin Luther King Jr. agreed to serve as spokesperson for a boycott, they found that they were not alone. E.D. Nixon came. Glen Smiley came. Ella Baker came. Bayard Rustin came. And the Montgomery campaign was informed by decades of movement experience, both in and beyond Alabama.

In 2013, when Moral Mondays began as a form of mass protest against political extremism in North Carolina, those of us who had protested the hijacking of our state government as an act of conscience found ourselves in the midst of a movement, as more people came week after week to demand a government for all of us. It wasn't something we could have orchestrated, and it was bigger than what was happening in our statehouse. It was deeply connected to the growing movement of low-wage workers that would come to call themselves the "Fight for $15." And it was equally bound up with the emerging "Black Lives Matter" movement, as the nation began to face the reality of racial disparities in how everyday people experience twenty-first-century America when a jury in Sanford, Florida, failed to convict George Zimmerman for the murder of Trayvon Martin. We found ourselves within the upsurge of a new movement—a push toward the possibility of a Third Reconstruction in America. And we were not alone.

One of the great gifts of that summer of 2013 in North Carolina was the presence of Rosalyn Woodward Pelles. Though officially retired from her work with the Rainbow Coalition and the AFL-CIO, Roz came. She brought with her a wealth of practical wisdom from decades of movement conversations and work. No, there wasn't a formula for sparking a movement. But once it was moving, it sure was a huge help to have someone who had been thinking for decades about potential pitfalls, strategies for coalition building, and tactics for building real power.

Of course you can never write down everything that someone like Roz brings to a movement. But this book captures a lot of it. Drawing on his own experience spanning America's Second and Third Reconstructions, Michael Zweig offers a framework for understanding the moment we're in and the very practical challenges we face in building a moral fusion coalition for transformative change in America. I hope that people who've been caught up in today's moral movement will take the time to listen to this wisdom and discuss it in their homes and in their communities. This is the sort of practical reflection we should be reading alongside the Scriptures in our churches, synagogues, and mosques, and alongside the newspaper in the community circles where we talk about the change we want to see in our world.

We may not get to choose when and where we have the chance to be part of a social movement, but when the zeitgeist tracks us down and we are in the midst of one, we better listen to the wisdom of those who've carefully considered how we can successfully change the world that is into the world that ought to be. I thank God this book and its wisdom has found its way into your hands.

Rev. Dr. William J. Barber II
President, Repairers of the Breach
Cochair, Poor People's Campaign: A National Call for Moral Revival
Founding Director, Center for Public Theology and Public Policy, Yale Divinity School

Introduction

"If there is any philosophy, it's that those who have walked a certain path should know some things, should remember some things that they can pass on, that others can use to walk the path a little better."
—Ella Baker[1]

This is a book for anyone interested in learning about, thinking more deeply about, or engaging in progressive politics. For me, anything that relieves human suffering is progress. Anything that improves the material conditions, organizational strength, or intellectual capacity of the working class qualifies as progress. Analysis or activity that moves society in these directions is what I mean by progressive politics.

Who Is Speaking

My general orientation to life and politics came from my experiences in an immigrant family that fled Hitler's annihilation to come to America in 1938. I am the first person in my family born in the United States, before my parents had become citizens. English was not my first language, but speaking German on the streets of Detroit in 1946, where my parents had settled, was not a good idea so I picked up this new language before I started kindergarten.

When, after World War II, gasoline stopped being rationed and became generally available, my parents wanted to explore their new country. My older brother and I excitedly looked at maps to see where we might go. When we unthinkingly pointed to the South, my parents were very clear: we will never go to Alabama, South Carolina, or anywhere else where, in the context of Jim Crow, we would have to answer the question "Are we white or are we colored?" in order to choose a seat or get a drink of water. To them, that was not a legitimate question: it was too much like what they had just fled, leaving behind the murderous choice "Are you a Jew or an Aryan?"

In 1955 I saw the shocking magazine pictures of Emmett Till in his open casket after he was lynched in Mississippi.* He was fourteen. I was thirteen. I had heard many stories about the Nazi murders of my grandparents and tortures of other family members and friends of my parents, and realized how lucky my parents and brother were to escape. Now here the horror was in America. In an epiphany, I felt in some important way that I was in the same boat as Emmett Till, that we faced the same evil but in different circumstances. It came to me that I had to help make sure that this racist, murderous condition of US society would end as soon as possible.

That's when I began a long path to the ways of thinking presented in this book, which took a combination of years of practical movement building and study. These two aspects of political work—activism and study—have unfolded in the course of my participation in powerful social movements, principally the peace movements of the Vietnam, Central America, Iraq, and Afghanistan eras, the modern civil rights and Black freedom struggles, and the labor movement.

I grew up in Detroit when its nearly two million residents made it a great manufacturing center, the fourth largest city in the US. I was deeply influenced by its vibrant union movement, rooted in the auto and trucking industries. The influences of that environment later led me to join those helping to organize the faculty and professional staff in the State University of New York system into United University Professions (American Federation of Teachers Local 2190), where I have been for many years a statewide and campus elected officer and executive board member.

As an undergraduate at the University of Michigan in the early 1960s, I was a founding member of Students for a Democratic Society (SDS) and the Ann Arbor chapter of the Congress of Racial Equality (CORE),

---

* Emmett Till lived in Chicago but spent summers in Mississippi where his family was from. When some people believed he had disrespected a white woman, men came to his uncle's house where he was staying, dragged him away, tortured, and murdered him. When his body was returned to his mother in Chicago, she arranged to have an open casket funeral. Her brave and memorable decision meant her son's mutilated body was on display as testimony to the continuing effects of Jim Crow rule, despite the 1954 *Brown v. Board of Education* Supreme Court decision that ended legal segregation of public schools in the US.

organizations that helped build the student, antiwar, and civil rights movements of the time. In the 1970s, with thousands of other activists radicalized in our confrontations with US power abroad and at home, I joined the burgeoning Maoist left of that era through the Revolutionary Union and the Revolutionary Communist Party (RCP), but left the RCP in 1978 when it seemed to me to have become irrelevant, and sometimes antithetical, to real progressive change. Later, bringing together my labor and antiwar experiences, I helped to found and build US Labor Against the War (USLAW) in the run-up to the 2003 US invasion of Iraq, and then continued organizing USLAW to mobilize the labor movement within the broader US peace movement to end the US occupation of Iraq and Afghanistan. Since its founding in 2018, I have been active in the Poor People's Campaign: A National Call for Moral Revival.

In the context of this practical activity, I have undertaken a lifetime of study, reading the work of scholars and practitioners engaged with those movements. I have also done my own research and writing. As an economics graduate student in Ann Arbor, I helped found the Union for Radical Political Economics (URPE). URPE was the organizational support system for those of us who challenged the mainstream economic analysis we were learning. To replace it, URPE has for more than half a century nurtured the radical (going to the root of the problem) economic analysis required to understand the origins of US militarism and the racism and patriarchy so endemic to our society.

In the 1980s, I was impressed by the role churches in the US were playing in protecting Central American refugees coming to the Unites States. Sanctuary churches sheltered thousands fleeing murder and repression imposed by dictators in their home countries who were supported by the US government. These churches also opposed apartheid terror in South Africa and demanded the end of US support for the apartheid regime.

Although I participated in those movements from a secular point of view, the Catholic chaplain at SUNY Stony Brook introduced me to liberation theology. Reading many South American theologians and Black liberation theologians in the US, I came to an appreciation of the importance of the moral aspects of movement building. I saw the possibility of constructive dialogue between liberation theology and radical secular social science. Each could teach the other to stretch its scope of human and social understanding and practice. This process led to the 1991 book *Religion and Economic Justice*, a collection I edited and contributed to. The book in your hands continues that dialogue by presenting both a secular understanding of how capitalism works and a discussion of the values that go hand in hand with that analysis.

For example, liberation theologians articulated "the preferential option for the poor," calling for the church to make the alleviation of poverty its most important social priority. This "option" is a moral choice based in a reading of scripture that foregrounds its many instructions to care for the poor and soothe their suffering. It is also a choice most urgently felt by clergy who are closest to the poor in their ministry, where the poor cry out at close quarters for relief. While secular social scientists (and the religious) should reflect on the moral justice of caring for the poor, the religious (and secular social analysts) would benefit in their practice by understanding that poverty is something that happens to the working class, not to some marginal "other" permanently mired at the bottom of society.

As my movement involvements and studies unfolded, my appreciation of the centrality of class dynamics in shaping our lives, as individuals and as a society, deepened. But it turns out that class is a complicated relationship. As I show in this book, class dynamics percolate through all aspects of society: not just the economy, but culture, politics, religion, climate change, and foreign affairs. And I have found that class cannot be understood without clear attention to the ways in which classes are formed in mutual relation with the operation of race and gender dynamics.

All of these life experiences have shaped me and deeply inform the ideas in this book. They are the experiences of a generation, a generation that came of age in the 1960s and 1970s in the process of building organizations and institutions to challenge capitalism in the fight for human dignity, the dignity that can be found in social and economic justice.

Now, a new generation of activists and leaders carry on that fight with experiences and insights of their own. My hope is that this book will be a useful contribution to a conversation within the generational transition now underway.

Facing the Reality of the Times

The first step in thinking about political strategies for social change is to get as clear a handle as possible on the situation we face—the conditions of life and issues working people experience, and the constellation of forces that offer some openings for progress but that include barriers as well.

The spur to action at the heart of progressive politics is found in the widespread pain, suffering, and enduring dignity among ordinary working people and those living in and on the edges of poverty in the United States. For those directly experiencing these conditions it's a matter of survival. For better-off allies the call to action arises from a moral commitment to right the suffering they know to be so widely present in society.

The last year of the Trump presidency saw a renewal of progressive mass movements in the United States that urged broad social transformations in ways not seen in many decades. At the center were demands for racial justice galvanized by the murder of George Floyd by police in Minneapolis. His murder was captured on video and broadcast throughout the country—with undeniable, grotesque, heart-wrenching, enraging images. They energized mass marches in hundreds of US locations, from the largest cities to the smallest towns across the country.

These marches were remarkable because of their massiveness, geographical reach, and racial and ethnic diversity. With Black people and other people of color leading demonstrations of outrage in the streets across the country, tens of thousands of white people marched as well, all engaged in common determination to put an end to white supremacy. In some cities, demonstrations and marches went on for over one hundred consecutive days. George Floyd's murder was the spark, but the tinder had been prepared by dozens of recent police killings of Black men and women whose names we name as we march: Breonna Taylor, Michael Brown, Tamir Rice, Trayvon Martin, Eric Garner, Rayshard Brooks, Atatiana Jefferson, Stephon Clark, Philando Castille, Sandra Bland, Freddie Gray, Kawaski Trawick, Tyre Nichols. The list is much longer.

Their murders were not a series of isolated incidents generated solely by their own specific circumstances. The rising movement called them out as evidence of a pattern of killings that had common roots in systemic racism and white supremacy. The pattern came with manifestations beyond police killings: it can be seen in mass incarceration, grossly disproportionate poverty rates, and racial inequalities in almost every social measure of well-being from schooling to health, pay, life expectancy, housing, and employment.

Meanwhile, the COVID-19 coronavirus pandemic reinforced our understanding of the signs and consequences of systemic racism. Black and brown people and Native Americans have suffered disproportionate economic hardship, illness, hospitalization, and death. Calls for universal health insurance grew in intensity and breadth of support, challenging the system that private insurance companies, pharmaceutical corporations, and giant hospital networks keep in place as they dominate the current system for their own benefit instead of people's health. Further, as record high temperatures bring about historically destructive fire seasons in the western states, record numbers of hurricanes on the Gulf and Atlantic coasts, and record-breaking tornado volleys, as well as unprecedented flooding across the country, the movement for control of carbon emissions and environmental justice grows bolder.

At the same time, the #MeToo movement was transforming public understanding of sexual harassment, resulting in the disgrace and fall from power of New York's Governor Andrew Cuomo and many high-profile men in political, media, and business worlds. Media reports have exposed the disproportionate hardship women have suffered from the impact of the COVID-19 pandemic, adding energy to demands for gender justice.

We have also seen a flowering of union organizing among Starbucks and Amazon workers that has caught the public's attention. The Fight for $15 campaign to increase the minimum wage has also touched the majority of Americans. Support for unions is at the highest level in decades while actual union membership continues to fall as corporate leaders mobilize every resource to thwart union organizing campaigns.

Joe Biden's 2020 presidential campaign reflected all of these realities. His election and selection of cabinet officials heavily drawn from the Obama administration promised a "return to normalcy" that many voters hoped would come once Trump was defeated and left office.

But going back to the "normal" of recent decades is exactly where we should not go. That "normal" was the set of policies, attitudes, institutions, and power relations that brought Trump to dominance in the first place. The prospect that this "normal" will continue contributes to the continuing disillusion of millions of people, many of whom are drawn to the neofascist blustering of Donald Trump and those who would take political advantage of the base he has inflamed.

Many progressive people in elected office and movement organizers understand this very well. The Congressional Progressive Caucus now numbers nearly one hundred members, better organized and more influential than ever. Progressive organizers across the spectrum of issues have brought movement pressure to bear on members of Congress and President Biden. This has pushed Democratic Party centrists and some of their potential Republican allies somewhat to the left. But the danger of right-wing extremism is far from over.

A progressive agenda is urgently needed to combat the threat of right-wing antidemocratic forces still riding high in US politics and public policy. It cannot become successful in a year's activity, or in one or even three election cycles. To accomplish such an agenda, we will have to challenge and undo decades of political, economic, judicial, and cultural norms that have brought capitalist power to heights not seen for a hundred years. Now is the time to build progressive movements in every arena to increase the pressure we put on the powerful and to become powerful ourselves in numbers, organization, and understanding. With this book, I hope to contribute to that future.

Some History

In the United States and around the world, despite some cracks in its system, we are living in a time of capitalism triumphant, a time of historically small amounts of power in the hands of working people. In the great conflicts of the twentieth century, workers tried mightily and with varying degrees of success to protect themselves from the suffering of capitalist domination. Going back to the beginning of the Industrial Revolution in the eighteenth and nineteenth centuries, workers developed many forms of collective effort to confront their employers: sometimes targeting just the employer, sometimes the industry, sometimes the capitalist system as a whole. They organized strikes, boycotts, and other forms of economic confrontation. They formed or joined political parties, some allied with sections of the capitalist class, some organized for the working class specifically. They followed a variety of ideological paths, among them socialist, anarchist, syndicalist, communist, social democratic, and reformist approaches to politics. They waged struggle with nonviolent means, and sometimes in armed conflict and revolution. But, in the end, the working class lost.

Today capitalism dominates nearly every country in the world and the capitalist class is secure in its power. As the working class has lost power, the fight for racial justice and every other progressive cause and movement have suffered corresponding setbacks. This is the context in which we live, work, and try to build a more just and peaceful world. Successful, long-lasting radical organizing to improve conditions of life must be grounded in this reality, painful as it is to acknowledge and live with, daunting as it is to confront. Throughout history, all successful organizing has had to be grounded in the reality of its times.

Despite the economic and political power currently in the hands of capital, progressive challenges to capitalist domination, as well as to the many social props that hold it up, continue to spring up. The old saying "Where there is oppression, there is resistance" is as true today as it has ever been. We see it in the Movement for Black Lives and #MeToo, in the massive teacher strikes across a number of Republican-controlled states in 2018, in the Fight for $15 an hour minimum wage campaigns, in some of the Democratic Party electoral victories that have increased progressive voices in the US Senate and House of Representatives. Yet, during the Trump presidency and early Biden years, these challenges have had limited positive effect on working people's lives. Congress has been paralyzed by division, and the needs of working people and the poor are not just unattended but undermined.

Despite a growing understanding of intersectionality, most movements have remained too isolated from one another. There is not yet a revival of the pervasive atmosphere of energetic struggle on many fronts that came together in the mid-1960s to create what at the time was called the "Movement." Yet it is nevertheless in the air.

The existence of the Movement meant that as a person entered into whatever particular form of resistance, they experienced being part of something larger, on both intellectual and emotional levels. Each particular movement was a tributary to a torrent of resistance that characterized the time. However many differences and conflicts there were among and within the individual tributaries—antiwar, civil rights, Black power, women's equality, workers' rights, American Indian Movement (AIM) actions, environmental concerns, countercultural expressions, Puerto Rican liberation and Chicano struggles, antinuke, early LGBT demands—we were, together, shaking the country for power, and all knew it. Although there was no overarching coordination, participants recognized one another as allies and comrades in a deep common cause to end oppression and suffering. Activists worked to create institutions and cultures that could do that, while challenging those that could not.

For those who made and took strength from that atmosphere, the Black Lives Matter uprisings of 2020 were very welcome developments. It is hard to recall or imagine now what that movement atmosphere was like and what it brought into being. Yet the upsurge of 2020 brought back a sense of what it was like to have capitalism and its many support props on the run, on the defensive, forced to make significant concessions. Let us develop the understanding, patience, daring, and strength of purpose to create such a powerful intersectional movement again.

Looking back, as the 1950s came to a close, no one imagined what profound changes would come in just a decade, how different the country would become in 1969 compared with 1959. It was Richard Nixon, of all people—a probusiness anticommunist—who in the early 1970s, pushed by pressure from the streets, had to sign such progressive laws as the Clean Water Act, the Clean Air Act, and the Occupational Health and Safety Act (creating OSHA). It was Nixon who opened relations with the People's Republic of China; and who ended the Vietnam War. It was Lyndon Johnson, a Texas politician, who signed the Civil Rights Act and Voting Rights Act in the context of the Black freedom movement, after wrestling them through Congress to get them to his desk. Radical critiques of capitalism flourished in many social science disciplines in universities and colleges. Organizers and activists in Science for the People challenged those who would use science to support the military and other pillars of capitalist power. Under the force of second-wave feminism and the LGBT movement born at Stonewall in 1969, gender relations began to change. Churches took up radical critiques of capitalism in the "War on Poverty."

As early as 1964, the *Wall Street Journal* reported in its lead story on the front page that campus culture had turned hostile to business interests, as was reflected in the difficulty many companies were having in recruiting graduating seniors into management ranks. Readers learned that "one of the toughest obstacles confronting company recruiters on many campuses is a general atmosphere of scorn for business."[2] I remember seeing a full-page ad from the US Chamber of Commerce in the campus newspaper at the University of Michigan around that time that sought to address this obstacle. It read: "Capitalism has brought us this far. Let it finish the job!"

We can get a sense of the atmosphere at that time, and how far removed it is from today's overall reality, by looking at a fascinating private memo that corporate lawyer and future US Supreme Court Justice Lewis Powell wrote in 1971 to guide the US Chamber of Commerce in various methods to turn back the power of the Movement in those turbulent times. It's telling to quote Powell at length as he reveals the power and scope of the antiestablishment protesters at the time that led him to call for a broad corporate response to save the system as a whole.

He began:

No thoughtful person can question that the American economic system is under broad attack. This varies in scope, intensity, in the techniques employed, and in the level of visibility.

There always have been some who opposed the American system, and preferred socialism or some form of statism (communism or fascism). Also, there always have been critics of the system, whose criticism has been wholesome and constructive so long as the objective was to improve rather than to subvert or destroy.

But what now concerns us is quite new in the history of America. We are not dealing with sporadic or isolated attacks from a relatively few extremists or even from the minority socialist cadre. Rather, the assault on the enterprise system is broadly based and consistently pursued. It is gaining momentum and converts....

The sources are varied and diffused. They include, not unexpectedly, the Communists, New Leftists and other revolutionaries who would destroy the entire system, both political and economic. These extremists of the left are far more numerous, better financed, and increasingly are more welcomed and encouraged by other elements of society, than ever before in our history. But they remain a small minority, and are not yet the principal cause for concern.

The most disquieting voices joining the chorus of criticism come from perfectly respectable elements of society: from the college campus, the pulpit, the media, the intellectual and literary journals, the arts and sciences, and from politicians. In most of these groups the movement against the system is participated in only by minorities. Yet these often are the most articulate, the most vocal, the most prolific in their writing and speaking.

Moreover, much of the media—for varying motives and in varying degrees—either voluntarily accords unique publicity to these "attackers," or at least allows them to exploit the media for their purposes. This is especially true of television, which now plays such a predominant role in shaping the thinking, attitudes and emotions of our people.

One of the bewildering paradoxes of our time is the extent to which the enterprise system tolerates, if not participates in, its own destruction.[3]

Vladimir Lenin, leader of the 1917 Russian Revolution, is said to have cheekily remarked that the capitalists, always eager for profit, "will sell us the rope with which we will hang them." Lewis Powell was hoping to prevent this metaphoric circumstance. His memo helped motivate and, perhaps more important, structure a deliberate, broad corporate counteroffensive. This right-wing pushback began taking shape in the 1970s and has gained strength and complexity ever since.[4] In response to Powell's analysis, the corporate elite began to fashion the organizations that have shaped the reactionary environment that we are still living with, such organizations as the Federalist Society, the Cato Institute, the American Legislative Exchange Council (ALEC), and the Heritage Foundation.

It will be no simple matter to eradicate its influence in favor of progressive change. It is my hope that this book will help provide examples of the understanding and method of analysis that can contribute to that process, in which a majority of Americans come once again to be "the most disquieting voices" that Powell feared.

When coming to terms with what we face today, we need knowledge and ways of thinking to judge how we can most effectively challenge current conditions and create more favorable lives for working people. It will help to understand how social conditions today have arisen from the Movement of the 1950s and 1960s, as well as the decades-long capitalist reaction to it. We also need to understand this recent history in the longer past of US economic, political, and cultural developments.

Finding Lessons

In this book, I focus on what I believe are some of the most important lessons of this history, drawing on concrete examples that I hope today's activists and organizers will evaluate as they try once again to recreate a time when, in Lewis Powell's assessment, the "assault on the enterprise system is broadly based and consistently pursued [and will again be] gaining momentum and converts."

I present what I think are among the most important points of orientation that have come from radical movements in the US. I hope that organizers and activists now building a new radical movement will consider them as we confront our own current conditions and set about to build and consolidate the power required to challenge, and ultimately defeat, capital. I draw these ideas and methods from history, as they have been confirmed for me through my own experiences.

I hope that these points of orientation will become common and foundational as we struggle to articulate any particular detailed analysis and practice. Whatever analysis of any concrete situation we may develop, I believe the analysis should incorporate these basic understandings, or "threshold concepts" as I learned the term from Professor Christie Launius at the 2015 annual conference of the Working Class Studies Association at Georgetown University.

Launius quoted educational theorists Jan Meyer and Ray Land's work, in which they explain: "A threshold concept can be considered as akin to a portal, opening up a new and previously inaccessible way of thinking about something. It represents a transformed way of understanding, or interpreting, or viewing something without which the learner cannot progress. As a consequence of comprehending a threshold concept there may thus be a transformed internal view of subject matter, subject landscape, or even worldview."[5]

Threshold concepts provide the analytical categories upon which more detailed and particular work can be built. They are introductory, but not simple.

To draw meaning from concrete experiences, to express the inner logic of an event or campaign or process, requires a process of abstraction from the particulars. *New York Times* music critic Jon Pareles revealed the difficulties of this process in his account of the performances a number of artists contributed to Aretha Franklin's memorial service in September 2018. He wrote: "There's no formula, no simple set of demographics or allegiances or parameters, to create an artist like Aretha Franklin. Imitating the notes she sang—as some of her admirers did on stage [at her public funeral service]—is just technical mimicry, far from her true lesson of creativity."[6]

"Technical mimicry" was the point of a story I heard China scholar William Hinton tell concerning the use of the Dazhai Brigade as a model of communist agriculture, which the Chinese Communist Party put forth for emulation during the Cultural Revolution of the late 1960s and early 1970s. Dazhai was a small commune in the mountains of North China. Through careful analysis of their conditions, its party committee led the peasants to surmount many physical, technical, and organizational obstacles to terrace their mountainside, thereby increasing the land available for planting by creating narrow flat strips in the steep mountainside. Terracing is a traditional agricultural technique in China, but it had never been applied in that area. It worked! But, Hinton reported with amusement, some party leaders, who came from all across China to "Learn from Dazhai," went back home to their own flat plains areas to puzzle over how to build terraces where there were no hills.

Obviously, the point wasn't to mimic the particular activity taken in Dazhai. Rather, to learn from Dazhai, people had to pay close attention to the method of analysis the people of Dazhai had applied in order to understand the difficult conditions they faced in ways that allowed them to formulate an effective policy to transform their own conditions.

Much of the analysis I propose in this book will be familiar to those who know the work of Karl Marx. Two points are important in this regard. First, even though Marx is most closely associated with socialist and communist countries, his work is almost not at all about such societies. Marx wrote almost entirely about capitalism, basing his theories on close observation of Britain and other capitalist economies of the mid-nineteenth century. His focus on capitalism is especially relevant for us now, at a time when capitalism is dominant across the planet.

But no one should approach Marx's writings as some sort of gospel. Not everything Marx wrote was correct. Not everything we need to know about capitalism is covered in Marx's writing. Yet Marx developed ways of thinking and discovered important truths about economies and social systems that remain seriously helpful as we confront today's society and the tasks we face to transform it.

I take it as our shared goal across generations to build a country that treats its workers well and with respect, opposes war, conserves a healthy natural environment, and defeats the many forms of white supremacy and patriarchy that cause suffering among so many scores of millions of people. But as important as action is in moving toward these goals, that action must be guided by understanding based on analysis of the conditions in which our movement operates. We need both sides of movement building: action and analysis. As Rev. Martin Luther King Jr. put it, "Education without social action is a one-sided value because it has no true power potential. Social action without education is a weak expression of pure energy. Deeds uninformed by educated thought can take false directions."[7]

It is natural and easy to be enraged by the circumstances of life in the US if you allow them to register in your awareness. This outrage unleashes "pure energy" that motivates and sustains the urgent call to "do something." I am well aware of the many studies that show that people respond to emotion much more readily than they do to rational analysis. But to transfer emotion into *effective* action, action that avoids "false directions," we need clear analysis of the conditions at hand and the forces at play. Still, in the process of rational analysis it would be well to recall the words of Argentinian doctor and Cuban revolutionary Che Guevara, printed on millions of T-shirts in the 1960s: "A true revolutionary is motivated by feelings of love." Love for the people; love for humanity.

I hope this book will help a new generation of activists and organizers to walk our common path in more effective ways than we of the older generation managed to do. I look forward to learning from and contributing to dialogue across generations as our common struggle and related study continue.

Notes

1   Baker quoted in Barbara Ransby, *Ella Baker and the Black Freedom Movement: A Radical Democratic Vision* (Chapel Hill: University of North Carolina Press, 2003), 357.

2   Roger Ricklefs, "Scorning Business: More College Students Shun Corporate Jobs, Choose Other Fields," *Wall Street Journal*, November 10, 1964.

3   Lewis Powell, "Attack on American Free Enterprise System," confidential memorandum to Eugene B. Snydor Jr., Chairman, Education Committee, U.S. Chamber of Commerce, August 23, 1971, accessed August 28, 2021, https://scholarlycommons.law.wlu.edu/powellmemo.

4   Nancy MacLean, *Democracy in Chains: The Deep History of the Radical Right's Stealth Plan for America* (New York: Penguin Books, 2018); Kim Phillips-Fein, "Conservatism: A State of the Field," *Journal of American History* 98, no.3 (December 2011): 723–43, https://doi.org/10.1093/jahist/jar430.

5   Jan Meyer and Ray Land, *Overcoming Barriers to Student Understanding: Threshold Concepts and Troublesome Knowledge* (London: Routledge, 2006).

6   John Pareles, "In a Hometown Send-Off, Aretha Franklin Belongs to Everyone," *New York Times*, September 3, 2018, https://www.nytimes.com/2018/09/01/arts/music/aretha-franklin-funeral-detroit.html.

7   Martin Luther King Jr., "Guidelines to the Dr. Martin Luther King Jr. 'Word from the Mountaintop' Oratory Contest," accessed April 7, 2023, https://uab.edu/dei/images/engagement/MLK_Oratory_Competition_2019-2020.pdf.

CHAPTER ONE

Political Practice

In my long participation in political life, mostly building social movements but also occasionally immersed in electoral efforts, including once running for local office and losing, I have come to appreciate the overriding importance of building a political force independent of corporate involvement, one that mobilizes the working class majority and organizes and strategizes in tandem with other social justice movements. In the US political system this is a tall order, but progressive people have enough experience to suggest fruitful ways to approach such work, difficult though it is.

As I said in the introduction, for me "progressive" means anything that relieves human suffering or improves the material conditions, organizational strength, or intellectual capacity of the working class. Making sure all children get good care and nourishment is a progressive social norm. Insuring their ability to learn and to flourish in their interests and capacities is another. Universal health care, affordable housing, good jobs at living wages, environmental responsibility—these and other indicators of material well-being are familiar goals of progressive politics. So, too, are demands for democracy and the respectful treatment of all people, to live with dignity at work, in their families and communities, and in their political engagement. Action toward any of these goals leads to conflict with those in power.

Any successful organizing campaign engaged in conflict with corporate or government power has to involve broad social participation of affected and aggrieved people. Ella Baker, guiding light to the civil rights movement of the 1950s and 1960s, stressed a critical feature of political organizing. As her biographer Barbara Ransby put it: "Any viable social change organization had to be built from the bottom up. 'Authentic' leadership could not come from the outside or above; rather, the people who were most oppressed had to take direct action to change their circumstances. At best, national organizations could offer activists the resources they lacked: financial support, media attention, and political education."[1]

Progressive organizing is not a top-down mobilization. In the words of the working class anthem "The Internationale": "We want no condescending saviors." Whatever resources and analysis national groups or knowledgeable individuals from outside a community may bring, they must empower and be answerable to ordinary people on the ground who best know their own experiences and circumstances. The influence of leadership operates only through the internal processes of their communities. This reflects the importance of respect that organizers must show toward the people they propose to organize.

These principles characterize the "pedagogy of the oppressed" that Brazilian educator Paulo Freire championed among the poor.[2] He stressed the importance of engaging peasants in discussions through which they themselves would articulate their needs and discover possibilities for transformative action. The method was central to the practice of liberation theology throughout Latin America in the 1970s and 1980s. And it is central to the work of the Poor People's Campaign: A National Call for Moral Revival, under the leadership of Rev. William J. Barber II and Rev. Liz Theoharis.[3]

To have any chance of effecting progressive change, electoral work must be associated with powerful movements that do three things: (1) articulate programmatic needs; (2) identify leaders who can enter electoral campaigns and win; and (3) hold those elected officials accountable as they assume the responsibilities of elected office.

In this relationship between the "inside" of electoral office and the "outside" of social movements, experience shows that social movements need to be the dominant element. How to maintain that interconnection is the work of activists, organizers, progressive elected officials, and in certain circumstances nonelectoral worker parties.

Independent Working Class Politics

Reforms that improve the lives of working people and marginalized communities—like food stamps or union protections or voting rights—have only come about in response to powerful social movements. To challenge the rules that defend the capitalist class and its interests, it makes sense that the working class should exercise its own power in these movements, independent of the capitalist class.

This principle is already well established in law. Section 8(a)2 of the Wagner Act outlaws any management interference in the processes by which workers organize and operate their unions.[4] Congress enacted this provision in 1935 to prevent the then widespread practice of management establishing "company unions," which employers controlled to keep genuine worker-led unions out of the workplace. The interpretation of Section 8(a)2 by courts and administrative judges continues to be based on the recognition that labor and capital have conflicting interests that must be represented in completely separate and independent organizational forms when they negotiate terms and conditions of employment.*

Although administrative and court rulings subsequent to the passage of the Wagner Act have aided employers by greatly increasing the allowable scope of actions they can deploy to resist workers trying to organize unions and win contract fights, section 8(a)2 remains in force. As one consequence, management still may not give money to the campaign of someone who runs for union president, hoping that person would rein in the workforce and go light on the company once elected.

What's true on the shop floor should also be true in politics. But in the United States we do not have any political party distinctly devoted to advancing the interests of the working class, run by workers, free from the presence of capitalist representatives. Third-party efforts to create a genuine electoral labor party have either failed, as with the Labor Party founded in 1996, or have been short-lived and marginal in the scheme of things, as were the Socialist Party early in the twentieth century, despite it getting one million votes for Eugene Debs as its presidential candidate in 1912, and the Progressive Party that won a half-million votes for Henry Wallace in 1948.

When over 1,400 workers from many industries and unions met in Cleveland to found a new Labor Party in 1996, I was in my union's delegation.[5] The convention declared its independence from both Democratic and Republican parties and asserted itself as the political representative of the working class. In a great intensity of purpose and with joyous energy,

---

* Workers can be on corporate boards or participate in other forms of labor-management cooperation only after the union representing the workers agrees with management to the terms of the cooperation. Management may not establish these forms unilaterally, even when there is no union present.

delegates passed a platform of broad social democratic measures, often after spirited floor debate. To avoid running show campaigns as mere symbolic gestures with no chance of success, delegates voted to limit the Labor Party's electoral work to campaigns that fielded significant committed support from unions.

That requirement proved to be an insurmountable obstacle to success. Unfortunately, almost all unions refused to give up their allegiance to the Democratic Party, which they saw as the only practical chance to influence and draw upon political power. Unwilling to engage in what would be nothing more than campaigns that might draw only 1 or 2% of the vote, the Labor Party, after that initial burst of hope and energy, melted away in the early 2000s.

It is one legacy of Cold War anticommunism that almost all union leadership have tied themselves to an unyielding defense of capitalism as a system. Union leadership sought influence instead, settling into the role of junior partner to capital inside the Democratic Party, hoping that the legacy of the New Deal would continue indefinitely. For over eighty years, the symbiosis of the great majority of labor leadership and the Democratic Party has been unshakable. Despite the clear domination of the party by corporate interests, its embrace of neoliberal trade and social policies, and its repeated marginalization of progressive primary candidates, progressive elected members of Congress, and the movements that successfully put them in office, union leadership for the most part has found neither the will nor the outlook to seek or create a new political home to advance working class interests.

It reminds me of the first time I heard—as a teenager—that the New York *Daily News* was the working class newspaper in New York City, only to discover that it was the paper some capitalists put out for the working class to read. In the early 2020s in the United States, there is no independent working class political party, and no independent mass circulation working class media platform.

To leverage labor influence, some progressive union leaders built the Working Families Party (WFP) in New York in the late 1990s, taking advantage of a law that allows a candidate to run for office on two political party ballot lines at the same time (called "fusion politics"). To exert progressive influence on the Democratic Party, the WFP would endorse the Democratic candidate for governor or other elected office so their name would also appear on the WFP ballot line. The larger the number of votes a candidate got on that line, the more influence the WFP leadership could claim in legislative negotiations.

This strategy resulted in some important moves to the left in state policy decisions, for example increasing the minimum wage and securing paid family leave. The WFP also has had influence in local races. But, mainly, Democratic Party leadership chafed under this pressure and in early 2020 amended the law governing fusion politics in New York to make it more difficult for a political party to sustain its presence on the ballot. Despite that, progressive voters there returned the WFP to the ballot, and it continues in the long tradition of progressive activists and organizers trying to influence the Democratic Party, supposedly the "party of labor," from within.

But fusion politics is allowed in only a handful of states. When organizers for the progressive New Party in Minnesota challenged that state's law prohibiting fusion politics in 1997, the US Supreme Court upheld the law, writing that the Democratic/Republican two-party system promotes political stability, which the court found to be a legitimate state interest. Therefore, the court concluded, state legislatures may bar fusion politics that the court claimed would, by empowering smaller parties, increase political instability.[6]

In this national legal terrain, perhaps the long-run strategy with the greatest potential for success is to directly confront establishment party officeholders in primary contests, in a process that vies for leadership at local, state, and national levels. These have sometimes met with success, as when Alexandria Ocasio-Cortez defeated senior Democratic Party congressional leader Joseph Crowley in a 2018 New York primary in the Bronx and Queens, and when Jamaal Bowman defeated sixteen-term incumbent Eliot Engel, chair of the House Foreign Affairs Committee, in 2020. Still, after decades of occasionally successful challenges from the left, corporate domination of the Democratic Party continues, frustrating efforts to make the party into a genuine workers' political instrument. That frustration has led many working class voters, burned by the Democratic Party's adoption of corporate-friendly practices on trade, taxes, and union protections, to turn away from their traditional Democratic Party association and either vote for Republicans or give up on electoral participation altogether.

Working class politics must take its place as part of a coalition of progressive insurgencies that explicitly assert a social justice and working people's agenda. Given the dominance of the two-party system in US politics and the near impossibility of creating an independent labor party in the foreseeable future, the labor movement, allied with all other progressive movements, must establish itself firmly within an organized camp of primary-election challengers inside the Democratic Party. This needs to be a coherent, long-term, multi-election-cycle force, consciously organized to transform US electoral politics but rooted in ongoing grassroots mass movements. Steady pressure arising from the increasing capacity of the working class with other progressives over time and across the country may reconfigure the Democratic Party into a genuine progressive force independent of capital, or the internal conflicts may become so intense as to contribute to the disintegration of the Democratic Party as part of a general political realignment.

The Republican Party, too, is experiencing, and may not survive, its own deep internal divisions following the Trump presidency. The political instability disrupting US society in the early 2020s, however, suggests opportunities for progressive realignment. Labor and other progressives should take this as an opportunity to be bold in their assertion of deep challenges to capitalist power.

Sociologists Aldon Morris and Dan Clawson have called our attention to the probable process by which working people will organize the insurgency required for a progressive realignment.[7] Writing in 2005, they were doubtful that the historic labor organizations of the AFL-CIO would be able to lead such a process for labor, given the deep cultural acceptance of its status, at best, as junior partner to capital. Rather, they made an analogy with the modern civil rights movement. In a landmark study, Morris had found that new organizations at that time, like the Southern Christian Leadership Conference (SCLC) and Student Nonviolent Coordinating Committee (SNCC), developed the militant program and tactics needed to lead the movement to breakthroughs, while traditional civil rights organizations like the NAACP and the Urban League were drawn into the wake of that militancy.[8] In Morris's view, the older organizations made real contributions but were not able to provide the necessary leadership for success.

Carrying that analysis into the labor movement at the start of this century, Clawson and Morris argued that new forms of worker organizations would have to arise in what Clawson called "the next upsurge,"[9] providing the vision, militancy, and coalition ties required to rekindle an energetic labor movement, at best drawing traditional unions into the new movement's wake once it gained strength. Going into the 2020s, no such labor insurgency has emerged as an organized, articulate presence among working people, despite occasional local battles that have drawn national attention, such as organizing drives among Starbucks and Amazon workers.

Whatever name or form a new insurgency takes, its platform, actions, and political methods must link its electoral work to mass movements of workers and marginalized peoples who challenge capitalism to its roots. Organizationally, coordination between the "inside" of electoral politics and the "outside" of social movements is essential to advance a progressive agenda.

In that relationship, experience has shown that the "outside" must be the most dynamic and leading element. The New Deal arose from mass uprisings of working people. The Civil Rights and Voting Rights Acts of 1964–65 arose from mass uprisings of African Americans. A number of police departments have recently implemented some changes in practice, and criminal justice reform has risen on the political agenda, in response to the power of the Movement for Black Lives.

More important, even a truly independent working class electoral party—should a viable one arise—must for the foreseeable future be involved in reform politics, which necessarily involves compromise with the ruling class. But such close proximity has dangers: endless opportunities for co-optation, both subtle and outright. All the more necessary is it, then, to secure a powerful "outside" political movement to hold its politicians accountable.

Independent working class parties can take nonelectoral forms, too. Communist parties have played important roles in the United States, France, Italy, and other capitalist countries, mainly shaping and building social movements, although sometimes engaging in electoral politics as well. In periods of reform, at their best communists have provided education and consistent leadership in a wide cross section of single-interest movement organizations, helping to draw them together in a common framework that challenges capitalist power from many directions at once. The Communist Party in the United States played such a role in the 1930s, when its members had leading roles in organizing the unemployed, sharecroppers, and unions, while taking up campaigns for racial justice and civil rights that mobilized many whites as well as Black people.

As another example, in the 1950s members of the South African Communist Party (SACP) were involved in the leadership of unions, women's organizations, youth and farmer groups, and others fighting apartheid, as well as in the leadership of the African National Congress, which became the dominant political party opposing apartheid. This widespread presence allowed the SACP to formulate what came to be called the Freedom Charter, adopted in 1955 at a people's assembly of representatives of many anti-apartheid organizations.[10] This charter, only two pages long, set forth the common goals of the majority of the anti-apartheid movement and served as a uniting point of orientation for that movement until its victory over apartheid in 1994.

We have no effective communist party in the US at this time. In the 1970s, I was among thousands of people coming out of the 1960s student movement who formed organizations we called communist—the Revolutionary Communist Party (RCP), the Communist Party Marxist-Leninist, the Communist Workers Party, and others, well-documented by Max Elbaum in his book *Revolution in the Air*.[11] Remnants of these, and others formed since, still exist at this writing.

I joined the Revolutionary Union in 1971 and helped found its successor organization, the RCP, in 1975. I stayed with it until it split at the end of 1977. I and others in the New Communist Movement believed that radical transformation of the US required the coordination of the various elements of the social uprisings of the times—among workers, women, veterans, students, health professionals, Black, Asian, Puerto Rican, Native, and Chicano uprisings, and more. We thought it was important to bring communist understanding to the activists in those movements and recruit them as they accepted our leadership.

In the mid-1970s the RCP had many working class members and considerable influence among Viet Nam veterans and students, as well as in unions in several key industries: auto, mining, steel, garment, and the post office. We immersed ourselves in those movements, to build them as bulwarks of working class power and to bring the message of revolution to the people. We also entered into talks and some common work with the Young Lords, I Wor Kuen, the Black Workers Congress, and other revolutionary organizations rooted in communities of color, seeking to forge a multiracial, multiethnic, working class force.

But that experience taught me the limits of ideological guidance to political work. We and the rest of the New Communist Movement soon isolated ourselves from the people we were trying to organize when we denounced reform efforts and insisted on taking "revolutionary action" that we thought corresponded to "revolutionary times" that in fact had not developed. My favorite example, from the RCP after I and about 40% of the membership had already left the organization because we rejected its dominant analysis and practice, was the call for RCP members in work-places on May Day 1981 to put down their tools at their places of work at noon and get up and shout out support for May Day as the workers' day, and, while they were at it, try to lead a walkout in revolutionary protest of conditions imposed by the employer and life in capitalist society. Those who did so gained no new followers and found only puzzlement, scorn, and isolation from their fellow workers.

Another consequence of that ideological dominance, removed from concrete analysis of the conditions and arrangements of forces we faced, was the inability of the different communist organizations to work together. The slightest difference in understanding of doctrinal questions about class, race, imperialism, or the relationship between ideology and practical work made us enemies of each other. The animosity among us was especially crippling and destructive when we were working in the same union or other organization, pulling it apart for reasons we took seriously but which were utterly opaque to almost everyone else with whom we were working.

It is a serious weakness in US politics that there is no organization with the reach and legitimacy that the CPUSA had in the 1930s (or the South African Communist Party had in the 1950s) that can pull together the disparate strands of social upheaval now coursing through the US into a common, unified anticapitalist force. There is only the most limited capac-ity to create a common "Freedom Charter" for our times, derived from popular deliberation across all parts of the movement, despite the existence of a draft "Democracy Charter," which veteran labor, peace movement, and civil rights leader Jack O'Dell and others crafted in 2010.[12]

As much as it would be good to have such an organization, no one can declare it or create it in name and have it be real just because in principle it is a good idea. It has to grow organically out of constructive movement-building work. That's the context in which people prove themselves as leaders, by showing practical ways forward. In building movements, activ-ists and organizers help to figure out ways of dealing with the immediate problems people have, walking the walk of those ways with the people, and engaging in mutual education and learning in the process.

To be successful in the long run, all political movements and organi-zations require a culture of openness, in which leadership is accountable to members and to the public, in which the arrogance and hubris of power meets its match and more. Communist parties have been notorious for stifling internal dissent and eradicating accountability. One story, possibly apocryphal, summarizes the point perfectly. Nikita Khrushchev, then general secretary of the Communist Party of the Soviet Union (CPSU), famously delivered a denunciation of Joseph Stalin at the 20th Congress of the CPSU in January 1956. The audience of some two thousand high-level party leaders sat in stunned silence as their understanding of Stalin as the hero of Soviet progress was shattered by Khrushchev's revelations of Stalin's many crimes. At one point someone in the audience broke the silence, calling out: "And where were you, Comrade Khrushchev, while all this was going on?" Silence. Khrushchev, the story goes, put his papers down on the podium, looked out and asked: "Who said that?" Silence. "Who said that?" More silence. "Really, who said that? Let's discuss it." Further silence. Khrushchev then replied: "Comrade, I was then where you are now."

All too often in political life, fear keeps people in line: fear of punishment by those with more authority; fear of jail, torture, and death; more modestly, fear of losing a job, of social ostracism, of seeming out of step with the norm. To my lasting shame, I fell into this trap in my RCP days when a leader excoriated a close friend of mine in a meeting, where I, knowing what the leader was saying with such vehemence was completely false and slanderous, said nothing in my friend's defense. Thinking about it later, I admitted to myself (but not to my friend) that I was afraid of being attacked by a leader of the organization I took to be so important to my identity and my aspirations for social change. Later, hoping never to make that mistake again, I did not hesitate to challenge the RCP's leadership in its internal meetings. Ultimately, in great personal upheaval, I quit the RCP but not the struggle.

We do not need to look to communist practices to see fear in operation. In the early 1950s, US Senator Joseph McCarthy got New Deal liberals to quake in fear lest they be called communists, or communist sympathizers, and then hauled before his Senate committee. Others were brought before the House Committee on Un-American Activities (HUAC), or some other state or federal investigation. I once asked a leftist friend who lived through that period why more people did not resist. He replied: "Michael, you have to understand fear." Pete Seeger, Lillian Hellman, Dalton Trumbo, Dashiell Hammett, Lee Grant, Paul Robeson, Virginia Durr, Carl Braden, Frank Wilkinson, and others did resist. But the paralysis that comes from fear held broad sway for several years before the fever broke.

In recent times we've seen Donald Trump wield fear in ways that tied leaders of the Republican Party into knots. After the 2020 presidential election, he got some to abase themselves in appalling ways as they sought Trump's favor by endorsing wild conspiracy theories that supported his ridiculous claims that he had actually won the election. These contorted expressions of fealty to Trump's lies have continued to infect Congress and Republican Party politics more than two years after the January 6, 2021, assault in the Capitol in service to those lies.

A common sentiment among political pundits in the media held that these politicians were afraid of Trump's base. These analysts put the responsibility for the power of Trump's neofascist political culture on the people, especially rural white working class people. Reactionary and white supremacist sentiments are there in some of these communities, and in urban centers as well. But they aren't mainly the people who are responsible. Who appeals to those sentiments, who gives them permission, reinforces, encourages, and welcomes them, funds them, and gives them organizational outlets? Who cynically plays upon these sentiments for personal political advancement? People with power; they, not the powerless, are responsible.

Republican politicians were afraid of Trump, not directly his base. They were afraid that Trump would denounce them on social media, that he would manipulate the base as only a demagogue can do. They were afraid that another politician would challenge them in the next primary, whipping up Trump's base without Trump. Trump's is a politics of fear, typical of authoritarian leaders at every level of society, in every country and social system. It is fear of the leader that we must challenge, however much the leader seeks to shift responsibility down, in the name of right-wing populism. The focused challenge to the authoritarian leader must also include outreach to their base along two tracks: (1) to promote policies that address in constructive ways the real suffering upon which demagogic leaders build their following; and (2) in that context, to break the links of misinformation and lies that demagogues require for success.

Activists and Organizers

In building "outside" movements in any constituency, it is important to have both activists and organizers, and to distinguish between them. Activists show up for what they believe in, participating in demonstrations and other activities they usually find out about on Facebook and other social media platforms. Among activists there is a live-and-let-live approach to the many reasons that move people to come together in shared outrage to engage in a common rally or march. Activism is a vital part of movement building. But activism without organization is necessarily short-lived. Only stable organization can provide the framework required for the long haul that progressive politics must undertake.

Organizers do more than mobilize people to action. Organizers create ongoing frameworks—organizations—to sustain the work and develop leaders from among the activists over time. But, at least since the Occupy Wall Street uprisings in 2011, there is a suspicion among many progressive activists that organization leads to stultifying hierarchy, bureaucracy, and undemocratic control.* Too often, women and people of color have experienced organizational structures as vehicles of repression. There is a wariness that "analysis" leads to sectarianism and factionalism, problems that have crippled many progressive movements in the past. The ease of mobilization using social media, the gratification of self-expression that comes from action itself, the difficulty and riskiness of analysis, and frustrations of organization-building and the decision-making process, lead many on the left to prefer sticking to action while downplaying organization and thinking through strategy.

Yet progressive organizations grew dramatically during the Trump era. As Oluchi Omeoga, a leader of the Minneapolis organization Black Visions, put it in 2020, "It's important to know there's a difference between a protester and an organizer. There's a different skill set.... The biggest lesson we learned from 2013 and 2016 [from when Trayvon Martin was killed, setting off the Black Lives Matter Movement]—we need skills to organize versus just showing up."[13] We see this understanding reflected in the dramatic growth of the Movement for Black Lives, Democratic Socialists of America (DSA), the Poor People's Campaign: A National Call for Moral Revival, #MeToo, Indivisible, Our Revolution, 350.org, the Sunrise Movement, Dream Defenders, Fight for $15, and a host of other mass organizations with local chapters that have grown dramatically in the years since Occupy.

---

* Ironically, movements that reject organization for fear of undemocratic control can become the least democratic movements. They inevitably have leaders, but without organizational structures the leaders rise spontaneously in struggle and cannot be held accountable for their statements or their actions. Democracy requires accountability. Accountability requires structure.

When building the student movement of the 1960s, we learned the importance of organization from the labor movement. Students built SNCC and Students for a Democratic Society (SDS). In addition to unions, our elders built the SCLC, the Southern Conference Education Fund (SCEF), and strengthened long-standing organizations like the NAACP. We learned that organizations are difficult to build and difficult to sustain. Factional differences, egotism among leaders, and quarrels about money inevitably arise. These can only be overcome by conveying the urgency of common goals requiring common action, and developing the skills to navigate the political rapids and personal conflicts that buffet every movement.

As political scientist and Labor Party organizer Adolph Reed has pointed out, organizing for "inside" electoral politics involves a radically different time frame than organizing "outside" popular movements. Movement building takes years of patient work. Electoral campaigns are relatively short and focused on a specific election deadline. Organizing phone banks, door knocking, or get out the vote efforts focus on creating brief contacts with voters to allow the maximum number of contacts in the time allowed. Typically, the time pressure of an electoral campaign requires that the depth of contact required for movement organizing gives way to securing the breadth of contact through many quick encounters with potential voters.[14]

One never knows when some event will tip the political process from the step-by-step quantitative increase in the numbers of people involved into a qualitative explosion of mass activism. We saw that in the explosion of SDS in the mid-1960s, which went from a small number of campus chapters with charters granted by a national office in 1962 to hundreds of thousands of students on hundreds of campuses spontaneously taking up the SDS banner in 1966. These chapters were led by students with very different views and methods of work, most with no connection to the national office. The inability to draw into common purpose the many political tendencies that flourished in SDS after 1966 led to its ultimate disintegration in 1969.

Our ability to organize and lead successful political mobilizations is based on making a careful analysis of the conditions and constellation of forces that are the movement's context. Success requires a clear long-term strategy: a guide to action grounded in an explicit understanding of the basics of the situation, the immediate goals of the movement and their relationship to longer-term goals, and current steps and actions needed to advance toward those goals. There is no general formula for coming to an effective analysis, except the necessity of looking at each situation as it is, taking into account the specific time, place, and conditions in which action is developing. In chapter three we will look more carefully at the methods of dialectics and materialism that can guide our thinking in this process.

But understanding is only one step. The analysis we arrive at becomes the basis for action, the reasoning through which to persuade and motivate and organize others to act. It becomes the basis of educational forums and study groups. As organizers engage others, we have to be open to listening and learning from their experiences and insights as the practice of movement building unfolds.

Education amounts to nothing without thoughtful organization built to exert power. And it is a cardinal principle of organizing practice that you cannot organize people you do not respect. White workers have been looked down upon in movement circles from the days of the Weather Underground in the late 1960s. Weather People declared that white workers were a "labor aristocracy" hopelessly wedded to US imperialism. I refused to support the Weather People, some of whom were my friends from earlier common work in SDS, because of their contempt for white working people. But I soon made the reverse error of attributing immediate revolutionary potential to the working class, white as well as Black, in my dedication for a time to the RCP.

Operating from an understanding that distorts reality extends into mainstream politics as well. Hillary Clinton carried on the tradition of disdain for white American workers when she characterized those who supported Donald Trump in 2016 as "a basket of deplorables." Democratic Party strategists who scolded and dismissed whites in the working class following Trump's 2016 victory continued the tradition. Thomas Frank and J.D. Vance have written best-selling books documenting what they identify as political pathology among white workers, who do not recognize their own interests and defy rational political appeals.[15]

Sociologist Michael Seltzer has written a fierce critique of this thinking,[16] astutely likening it to Edward Said's portrayal of Western condescension in his pathbreaking book *Orientalism*.[17] Sarah Smarsh and Joan Williams have also written powerful rebuttals in their portrayals of real life and politics among working class whites.[18] As Smarsh put it in a 2018 op-ed in the *New York Times*:

This account [of the "aggrieved laborer" as a reactionary white worker at fault for Trump's election] does white supremacy a great service in several ways: it ignores workers of color, along with humane, even progressive white workers. It allows college-educated white liberals to signal superior virtue while denying the sins of their own place and class. And it conceals well-informed, formally educated white conservatives—from middle class suburbia to the highest ranks of influence—who voted for Donald Trump in legions.... Millions of white working class people have refused to be played. They have resisted the traps of racism, sexism, homophobia, xenophobia and nationalism and voted the other way—or, in too many cases, not voted at all. I am far less interested in calls for empathy toward struggling white Americans who spout or abide hatred than I am in tapping into the political power of those who don't.[19]

Following up on this last thought, building organization is a process. There will be people who "get it" first and can join in early organizing efforts. There will be people who stand in hostile opposition at first, perhaps for a long time. Most will be somewhere in between, uninterested, unsure, suspicious, unwilling to act. But these groups are not static. People learn in the course of action, their own and that of others around them. As the conflict unfolds in practical ways, those unsure or nervous can be drawn in, increasingly isolating those who remain hostile. While those with deep disagreement or open hostility deserve basic respect, it's a waste of time in the early stages to focus on them. Start with "tapping into the political power" of those who get it.

Access to money is a perennial problem in sustaining organization. Sometimes a GoFundMe campaign can sustain a local initiative in its early stages. But the budget for staff, communications, travel, office space, supplies, and meetings can quickly rise, even into millions of dollars as an organization grows and takes on more activity. As a result, foundations, NGOs, or government agencies provide most of the money used to mobilize an oppressed people.

As welcome and useful as these funds often are, unfortunately they constitute a fundamental limit on the action and educational programs of the organizations they sponsor. These sources draw all their funds and decision-making leadership from the ranks of capital. Increasingly in recent decades, extremely wealthy individuals have given tens of billions of dollars to various causes with conditions that amount to close supervision through active, hands-on management of how the money will be spent. In the context of sharp budget cuts for social programs, this has the effect of substituting private funds and private control in place of public spending and democratic control.[20] Bill Gates has given hundreds of millions of dollars to public school systems in an effort to shore up education standards, but his efforts have often promoted charter schools and forced the implementation of his personal views on the best ways to fix the schools as a condition of his grants.[21] The ruling class supports reform, but keeps it under their ultimate control by influencing public policy, and increasingly through private philanthropy.

Ruling class tolerance for reforms that limit capitalist power can increase with the independent strength of the movements demanding those reforms, but at the same time resistance to them from other sections of the ruling class can increase. Organizers need to establish the independent power of their base and use all available resources to build on that strength. The more independent and powerful the movement, the more it can maintain negotiating capacity when dealing with funders, and with opposition. In any event, the task is to center the movement among the people affected, not in the technical and political resources of a foundation or an NGO.

Movement Values

As we will see in chapter seven, values have a class stamp. In building a progressive movement, we need to be clear about the values we cherish, and draw a direct connection from them to the policy platform we put forward. These are values of mutual aid, respect for the dignity of each person, individual responsibility toward the public good, and a commitment to minimize the suffering that is now so much a part of working people's lives.

Religious traditions are important carriers of these moral values. But no tradition is unambiguous or uniform. Class dynamics, as we will see in chapter seven, flow through all religious institutions, secular thought, and political practice. The secular left has much in common with people who ground their progressive activism in interpretations of various religious texts and traditions. The secular and the religious, each in their own community, develop their common movement on common understandings of moral principles. These understandings necessarily arise through struggles over moral and ethical norms, which are also reflections of class antagonisms. These struggles must be carried on within each community, religious and secular, in terms and categories inherent to that community.

We also need to champion a respect for evidence-based, reality-based analysis, for speaking in accord with actual conditions and constellations of forces, for telling the truth. French writer Éric Vuillard memorably captured an instance of political cynicism and its catastrophic effects. These arose from a willful disregard for the truth in French Prime Minister Édouard Daladier's public announcement after the famous Munich Conference in September 1938, when British Prime Minister Neville Chamberlain declared that England had secured "peace in our time." France joined England in that disastrous agreement with Hitler's Germany and Mussolini's Italy. Vuillard tells us that Daladier, speaking about that agreement on the radio to the French people, claimed that "he was convinced of having saved peace in Europe: that's what he said. But he didn't believe it for a second. 'Those morons, if only they knew!' he apparently muttered as he got off the plane to the cheering crowds." Vuillard then continues: "*This great jumble of misery, in which horrific events are already taking shape, is dominated by a mysterious respect for lies*. Political maneuvering tramples facts."[22]

As we deal with the political legacy we have inherited, we must interrupt and reverse the "mysterious respect for lies" that has come to characterize much of mainstream politics, in socialist as well as capitalist societies. Donald Trump took this practice to extremes, but there is no cause to relax now that he is gone from office. We need to be clear-eyed about the "horrific events that are [still] taking shape," accept them as they are and tell the truth about them and their origins in order to confront them better. Averting our eyes, or making excuses for cynical political maneuvering in any form, especially within our own ranks or among our allies, can only lead to action that misses the mark, followed by the widespread cynicism and passivity too many politicians are glad to see among the people they govern.

Notes

1   Barbara Ransby, *Ella Baker and the Black Freedom Movement: A Radical Democratic Vision* (Chapel Hill: University of North Carolina Press, 2003), 170.

2   Paulo Freire, *The Pedagogy of the Oppressed* (New York: Penguin Books, 2017).

3   For more information, see Poor People's Campaign, accessed August 31, 2021, https://www.poorpeoplescampaign.org.

4   National Labor Relations Act, accessed June 23, 2023, https://www.nlrb.gov/guidance/key-reference-materials/national-labor-relations-act.

5   The Labor Party, accessed August 31, 2021, http://www.thelaborparty.org.

6 *Timmons v. Twin Cities Area New Party, 520 U.S. 351* (1997), analyzed in Lynn Adelman, "The Misguided Rejection of Fusion Voting by State Legislatures and the Supreme Court," 56 IDAHO L. REV. 0:114-117, accessed November 22, 2021, https://digitalcommons.law. uidaho.edu/idaho-law-review/vol56/iss2/1.

7 Aldon Morris and Dan Clawson, "Lessons of the Civil Rights Movement for Building a Worker Rights Movement," *WorkingUSA* 8, no. 6 (December 2005): 683–704, https://doi. org/10.1111/j.1743-4580.2005.00078.x.

8 Aldon Morris, *The Origins of the Civil Rights Movement: Black Communities Organizing for Change* (New York: Free Press, 1986).

9 Dan Clawson, *The Next Upsurge: Labor and the New Social Movements* (Ithaca, NY: Cornell University Press, 2003).

10 Congress of the People, Kliptown, Johannesburg, South Africa, "The Freedom Charter," June 25–26, 1955, accessed June 19, 2023, https://www.anc1912.org.za/the-freedom-charter-2.

11 Max Elbaum, *Revolution in the Air: Sixties Radicals Turn to Lenin, Mao and Che* (London: Verso, 2018).

12 Jack O'Dell, "To Grasp to Transform American Society," *The Nation,* March 23, 2015, https:// www.thenation.com/article/archive/beginning-see-light.

13 Omeoga quoted in Jenna Wortham, "Ground Work," *New York Times Magazine,* August 30, 2020.

14 Adolph Reed Jr., foreword to *Crashing the Party* by Heather Gautney (New York: Verso, 2018), xii–xiii.

15 Thomas Frank, *What's the Matter with Kansas?* (New York: Picador, 2005); and J.D. Vance, *Hillbilly Elegy: A Memoir of a Family and Culture in Crisis* (New York: Harper Paperbacks, 2018).

16 Michael Seltzer, "The New Savages" (paper presented at the Working-Class Studies Association, University of Kent, England, September 2019).

17 Edward Said, *Orientalism* (New York: Vintage, 1979).

18 Sarah Smarsh, *Heartland: A Memoir of Working Hard and Being Broke in the Richest Country on Earth* (New York: Scribner, 2019); and Joan Williams, *White Working Class: Overcoming Class Cluelessness in America* (Boston: Harvard Business Review Press, 2017).

19 Sarah Smarsh, "Liberal Blind Spots Are Hiding the Truth about 'Trump Country,'" *New York Times,* July 19, 2018, https://www.nytimes.com/2018/07/19/opinion/trump-corporations-white-working-class.html.

20 David Callahan, *The Givers: Wealth, Power, and Philanthropy in a New Gilded Age* (New York: Knopf, 2017).

21 Linsey McGoey, *No Such Thing As a Free Lunch: The Gates Foundation and the Price of Philanthropy* (New York: Verso, 2016).

22 Éric Vuillard, *The Order of the Day,* trans. Mark Polizzotti (New York: Other Press, 2017), 115–16; emphasis added.

CHAPTER TWO

Key Questions for Progressive Politics

As we pursue a progressive agenda, it will help to be clear on a few central questions that have long bedeviled left politics: What's the difference between reform and revolution? How do we generate the political will to effect the changes we seek? Where will the money come from to pay for them? We turn to these matters now.

Reform

Perhaps the most important single statement on reform has come from formerly enslaved abolitionist leader Frederick Douglass, who said in 1857:

> Let me give you a word of the philosophy of reform. The whole history of the progress of human liberty shows that all concessions yet made to her august claims have been borne of earnest struggle. The conflict has been exciting, agitating, all-absorbing, and for the time being, putting all other tumults to silence. It must do this or it does nothing. If there is no struggle there is no progress. Those who profess to favor freedom and yet deprecate agitation are men who want crops without plowing up the ground. They want rain without the thunder and lightning. They want the ocean without the awful roar of its many waters.[1]

For all their thunder, reform efforts shy away from challenges to the basic structure of class power in society. They seek to improve the lives of workers and marginalized people by bending, but not breaking, the fundamental contours of capitalist class power. In one way or another, progressive reform seeks to soften the humiliation and hardship ordinary people suffer. There is no doubt that reform in this sense has had, overall, a long and successful history in the United States.

But reform, by definition, leaves the boss the boss. It seeks only to limit his authority to act alone and in his sole interest. On a social scale, however, it is important to understand that the boss, the ruling class, is rarely a monolithic whole. It is usually divided in its views. One section of the ruling class can support a policy choice and course of action that another section opposes. All reform movements that address deep questions of capitalist power and social organization need to understand and make use of these divisions.

No significant reform has ever succeeded without the active support of at least a part of the ruling class at which the reform is targeted. The fact that reform movements always at some stage involve association with a portion of the ruling class makes them susceptible to cooptation, which is often necessary and unavoidable to some extent because reform by its nature involves compromises with those who maintain ultimate authority.

The New Deal enacted during the Great Depression is an example. Because he championed its reforms, President Franklin D. Roosevelt was denounced by large numbers of capitalists as "a traitor to his class." During the 1936 presidential election, FDR proudly acknowledged this hostility in his announcement of the Second New Deal, which he planned for his second term. He said: "[During the first term] we had to struggle with the old enemies of peace—business and financial monopoly, speculation, reckless banking, class antagonism, sectionalism, war profiteering. They had begun to consider the Government of the United States as a mere appendage to their own affairs. We know now that Government by organized money is just as dangerous as Government by organized mob. Never before in all our history have these forces [of opposition] been so united against one candidate as they stand today. They are unanimous in their hate for me—and I welcome their hatred."[2]

At the start of his first term, in 1933, Roosevelt won passage of the National Industrial Recovery Act (NIRA), which contained important rights for workers to organize unions and to shape national economic and industrial policy. It didn't take long for the Supreme Court to rule the NIRA an unconstitutional assault on private property rights. But after that union rights and protections were strengthened in the 1935 National Labor Relations Act (NLRA, or Wagner Act, named after its principal sponsor, New York Senator Robert Wagner), which won court approval after one justice, by 1937, had changed his mind about the relative constitutional importance of private property and worker rights. Passage of the Wagner Act provides an ideal example of the intersection and accommodation of radical reform with a section of ruling class interests.

The act was bitterly opposed by most corporate leaders and their political representatives, as Roosevelt noted. But the act, like each New Deal victory for reform, contained profound compromises that also bolstered corporate power. While the Wagner Act greatly enhanced workers' capacity to form unions and bring the power of collective action against their employers, it also changed the dynamics of labor-management relations in ways that ultimately consolidated the power of management while weakening the power of the unions it protected.

The act did this mainly by channeling protected collective bargaining between unions and management toward the goal of reaching a contract legally binding on the parties. This deliberately replaced earlier ad hoc arrangements in which workers forced management, when they could, to agree on wages and working conditions through strikes and other job actions, even without unions and without contracts. Gradually, the act had the consequence of resolving disputes over the administration of contracts through legal battles. As a result, administrative proceedings and court fights came to substitute for the conflict of direct action on the shop floor and in the streets. The effect was to give over to the union's legal department powers formerly applied by the organized shop-floor membership. Used less and less frequently as union lawyers came to the fore, member power atrophied and unions weakened. It is now essential to reverse this trend, especially with the anti-union legal climate that President Trump has left us in the federal courts.

Putting the protection of unions in the hands of the courts also made unions vulnerable to changing political circumstances, in which the power of capital could reassert itself as independent union power declined. We have seen exactly this in the past seventy years of legislation, administrative rulings, and court decisions that have rendered the Wagner Act, a hopeful reform in its early implementation, now virtually useless, a dramatic departure from its original pro-union purpose.

While the Wagner Act protected unions in collective bargaining, it limited that protection to "mandatory topics of bargaining" dealing with wages, benefits, seniority, and grievance procedures. But it also allowed for protection of "management prerogatives" to be included in contracts, or preserved implicitly with no reference to them in the contract. These provisions reserve to management alone such critical questions for the workforce as production methods and the implementation of new technologies, choice of product lines, opening and closing of plants and work shifts, and the organization of the supply chain. Unions cannot use the protections of the Wagner Act to compel negotiations on these vital subjects, although management can agree to bargain over them if it wants to or is forced to.

While the act requires "good faith" bargaining, it does not require the sides ever to come to an agreement. Management prerogatives, which are not mandatory subjects of negotiation, are typically off-limits for bargaining if an agreement is to be reached. In many cases, after workers win union representation through an election over management opposition, management refuses to agree to a first contract, sometimes stalling for years until workers give up and vote to end union affiliation.

These long-term dangers inherent in the Wagner Act compromise were well recognized by a few union leaders who opposed the law, fearing that it would subject unions to government control while the government remained untouched as an instrument of capitalist power. But at the time most workers and union leaders downplayed these fears. They thirsted for government protection from stifling corporate power and welcomed the Wagner Act. They greeted Roosevelt as a great leader and savior of the working class. The Communist Party supported Roosevelt's reelection in 1936 and workers in the tens of millions voted for him.

The Wagner Act also divided the capitalist class. While most opposed it, fearing the power ceded to working people, Roosevelt had some ruling class support, ironically also arising from fear of working class power. In 1934, the year before Congress passed the act, the country had been shaken by three extremely powerful displays of working class street power. In San Francisco, longshoremen and other dockworkers won recognition after a general strike shut down Bay Area businesses for days, forcing employers on the docks to recognize the International Longshore and Warehouse Union (ILWU) as the workers' representative. In Minneapolis, truck drivers and warehouse workers led a general strike that ended in the recognition of the Teamsters union by reluctant management. And throughout the East, from Maine to Tennessee and Alabama, over 100,000 workers in the textile industry struck for months seeking union protection. While that strike was crushed in the end, it was nevertheless another wake-up call to employers everywhere that workers had power that had to be reckoned with. This was the context in which the Wagner Act promised employers labor peace.

A second spur to partial corporate support for the Wagner Act came because the law was proposed in the midst of the Great Depression. Businesses everywhere were desperate for customers to buy their products. Some recognized that workers needed higher pay in order to be able to buy, and recognized, too, that unions would be an important institution to win those wages. If unions could secure those wages simultaneously from all employers in an industry, no single employer would suffer a competitive disadvantage from paying it. So some employers, and their representatives in Congress, overcame their hostility to unions out of fear of continuing the ruinous effects of the Depression.

A third factor that drove some in the ruling class to support labor rights was fear that communism would take firmer hold in the United States. The Bolshevik revolution in Russia was less than twenty years in the past. American communists, and others sympathetic to them, were among the leaders of the 1934 uprisings, proving their ability to gain a broad following. The protections of the Wagner Act were accepted as a safety valve needed to avoid further radical unrest if worker demands were not addressed with some sympathy. Throughout the prior history of union organizing, workers trying to organize were typically met with repression, often violent and deadly, rather than reform. The Wagner Act, and the rest of the New Deal, reflected a decision by a section of the ruling class that harsh repression was no longer the most effective response to workers' demands for union rights, workplace dignity, and a better standard of living.

FDR led this change in thinking and approach. Revolution may not have come had the ruling class applied deeper repression at that time, but reform certainly preserved the stability of the system when it was being severely tested. Looking back, almost every historian and corporate leader now rejects the claim that Roosevelt was a traitor to his class. By choosing reform over repression, FDR may have saved the capitalist system.

Similar calculations lay behind the passage of the 1964 Civil Rights Act and the 1965 Voting Rights Act. These great victories for reform came in response to a broad and disruptive mass civil rights movement of African Americans that occurred, significantly, in the context of the Cold War. The US and the Soviet Union were competing for influence in the newly emerging world of African and Asian countries, then in the midst of freeing themselves from colonial rule by France, Portugal, and Britain. Presenting itself as the "leader of the free world" and champion of democracy, the US ruling class faced increasingly embarrassing taunts of hypocrisy from the Soviet Union, which challenged those claims by pointing to the continuing grip of Jim Crow and racist rule in the US.

When Thurgood Marshall argued before the Supreme Court that they should overturn the "separate but equal" doctrine that supported racial segregation in schools in the 1954 *Brown v. Board of Education* case, the US Department of Justice filed a supporting brief in the case, urging the justices to end the doctrine because, "Racial discrimination furnishes grist for the Communist propaganda mills and it raises doubts even among friendly nations as to the intensity of our devotion to the democratic faith."[3]

Nearly a decade later, the *New York Herald Tribune* reflected the same theme when it reported a 1963 speech given by Dean Rusk, then US secretary of state: "Secretary of State Dean Rusk solemnly warned civic leaders yesterday that racial strife is crippling U.S. foreign policy and confronting the nation with the gravest issue since 1865—the end of the Civil War. The 'issue of race relations deeply affects the conduct of our foreign policy relations.... I am speaking of the problem of discrimination.... Our voice is muted, our friends are embarrassed, our enemies are gleeful.... We are running this race [the Cold War] with one of our legs in a cast.'"[4]

As leading sentiments at the highest levels of national power changed, some local governments and business elites in cities across the South also adopted more pragmatic openings on issues of race. The harsh resistance to civil rights in Birmingham began to give way to the attitudes of the "New South," most closely associated with Atlanta.

The legal advances of course rested on the power of organized Black resistance to Jim Crow in the civil rights movement of the 1950s and 1960s. The power and dignity of the thirteen-month Montgomery bus boycott was symbolized by Rosa Parks but rested on the carefully organized campaign that provided volunteer transportation and other forms of support for the people who needed bus travel yet held onto the boycott for over a year. The widespread bravery and steadfastness of 1960s Black protesters in the face of the televised viciousness of Klan bombings and assassinations, police dogs, and high-power fire hoses moved the nation, attracted tens of thousands of allies, especially among students and white liberals, and called Jim Crow injustices to the attention of the world.

But the practical effects of many civil rights reforms all too soon began disappearing into the New Jim Crow, as white supremacy restored its traditional grip in new forms. It is highly significant that some African Americans have been accepted into the halls of corporate, political, media, and academic power. Their visibility conveys the possibility of fuller equality. But, meanwhile, the vast majority of working class African Americans have yet to experience, let alone consolidate, most of the gains promised by the reforms of the 1960s.

In 2020, the militancy of the Movement for Black Lives again put the question of racial justice into the realm of ruling class consideration in foreign policy circles, although with less urgency than Dean Rusk had expressed in the sixties. Writing that year in the policy journal *Foreign Affairs*, two long-time US State Department diplomatic corps veterans put it this way: "It is a depressing fact that today only four of 189 U.S. ambassadors abroad are Black.... The diplomatic corps is becoming increasingly homogeneous and detached, *undercutting the promotion of American interests and values.*... The top four ranks of the Foreign Service are whiter today than they were only two decades ago.... Lower promotion rates for racial and ethnic minorities and the precipitous drop-off in the number of women and minorities in the senior ranks are flashing red lights of structural discrimination."[5]

The radical reforms in South Africa that led to the democratic election of Nelson Mandela as president in 1994 followed a similar track. The changes that brought an end to apartheid were indeed profound. But, as Zwelinzima Vavi, general secretary of the Congress of South African Trade Unions (COSATU), explained in a June 2002 speech, the changes had resulted from negotiations with the white South African ruling class. They had not come from a revolution that altered basic class relations.[6] Isolated in world markets by a broad boycott, finally blocked from access to international finance, the white political establishment, led by president F.W. de Klerk, freed Mandela from prison in 1990. They negotiated the end of apartheid and the entry of Black South Africans into the political process.

But, in exchange, Mandela, his political base in the African National Congress, and the South African Communist Party agreed to leave in place the capitalist economy, and white domination of it. Some Black South Africans have been absorbed into the ranks of top corporate directors and into the halls of political, academic, and cultural power, but economic realms remain dominated by whites. For the great majority of working class Black South Africans, the reforms ending apartheid have had little effect on their standard of living or access to such basic needs as adequate housing and clean water. At the same time, the ruling class has come to include Black members, such as Cyril Ramaphosa, militant president of the South African Union of Miners during apartheid, who himself became a billionaire industry director in the new social order and then president of South Africa. Yet Black government in South Africa has been unable to transform the economy to relieve suffering among the masses of South African workers still embedded in a capitalist order.

A similar dynamic, linking ruling class openness to reform to perceived threats to its system, developed in the United States in the first months of the Biden administration. For example, as the authoritarian agenda of the Republican Party swept across many states in new laws to curtail voting rights, Biden and many other Democrats talked repeatedly about the need to protect democracy. While they no doubt sincerely felt that way, their sense of urgency came explicitly from their desire to "make democracy work" as an international counterweight to China and China's appeal to authoritarian leaders in many countries. Democratic Party leadership also felt the pressure of the Black movement for police and criminal justice reform, a movement that has thrust the question to the forefront of sympathetic public attention, including among large numbers of white people who became active after the murder of George Floyd by police in Minneapolis.

In a similar way, while support for a Green New Deal is spreading among progressives on the ground, many in the corporate elite have caught on to the seriousness of the problem. It was the focus of attention at the international gathering of corporate and government leaders at Davos in January 2019, and in 2020 became a subject of concern for the Business Roundtable, which brings together the CEOs of the two hundred largest corporations in the US. As reported in the *Wall Street Journal*, "The Business Roundtable opposed President Obama's Clean Power Plan to reduce carbon emissions from electricity generation. Still, business is acutely aware that the public is increasingly concerned about the economic impact of global warming.... Even the US Chamber [of Commerce] and the National Association of Manufacturers have become more supportive of action on climate."[7] As Joe Biden was preparing to take office as president, "a broad cross section of big US corporations including Amazon, Citigroup, and Ford Motor Company [called] on Congress to work closely with President-elect Biden to address the threat of climate change."[8]

As the threat of climate change to business interests becomes apparent to sections of the ruling class, and as popular movements rally around the

Green New Deal and other radical solutions that also threaten business interests, we can be sure that the movements will engage with the ruling class in shaping the scope and specific content of the response. The same will be true for voting rights and the rest of the progressive agenda. Only a long and sustained political process will put US representatives and senators in a squeeze that can have the best possible outcome for progressives, and only if the movements remain strong with continuing focus on what truly must be done. Whatever political and policy compromises may be required along the way are for politicians to decide. Movements holding them responsible must keep the pressure on until the problem is well and truly solved.

We will see in practice in coming years how far racial justice, environmental stability, and worker dignity can flourish through reforms in the ways capitalism functions. Returning here to Frederick Douglass, we must understand that these reforms will require militant action in addition to words and petitions. As in the past, deep reform will require real disruption of the machinery of oppression, not just choreographed performative acts of civil disobedience precleared with the police.

Revolution

The necessity of compromise with the ruling class in reform efforts, and the resulting limits in the content of the reforms and their life span, throws shade upon reform politics in the eyes of those advocating revolutionary change. "Revolution" is a term easily bandied about. In ads, a new skin cream can be "revolutionary." Bernie Sanders talked of revolution, effectively picking up on and mobilizing intense desires among young people for radical changes in their life circumstances.

Then there's actual social revolution.

It's worth considering some words of twentieth-century revolutionary leaders to get our bearings on the subject. In the early years of the Chinese Communist Party, founded in 1921, Mao Zedong was in his native rural Hunan Province while party leadership was concentrated in the city of Shanghai. In 1927, Mao, observing the peasant revolts that were shaking the countryside around him, reported back to his urban Shanghai leaders, who tended to have an intellectual approach to improving social conditions. Mao famously wrote: "A revolution is not a dinner party, or writing an essay, or painting a picture, or doing embroidery; it cannot be so refined, so leisurely and gentle, so temperate, kind, courteous, restrained and magnanimous. A revolution is an insurrection, an act of violence in which one class overthrows another."[9]

Echoing the seriousness of these remarks some years later, Chinese writer and cultural leader Lu Xun wrote:

> Although some dream of "food for all," others of a "classless society" or "universal equality," very few indeed dream of what is needed before building such a society: the class struggle, the White Terror, air raids, men tortured to death, boiled capsicum [a pepper plant] poured down the nostrils, electric shocks.... Unless men dream of these things, that better world will never materialize, no matter how brillliantly they write. It will remain a dream. And describing it will simply teach others to dream this empty dream.... Nonetheless there are men who intend to make this dream come true.... They dream of the future and struggle to realize it now.[10]

In short, revolution is deadly serious business. The mass of people do not enter into it lightly, however much they may dream of a better life. Vladimir Lenin, leader of the Russian Revolution, challenged people who championed revolution when the conditions for it were not present. He wrote:

> For a revolution to take place it is not enough for the exploited and oppressed masses to realize the impossibility of living in the old way, and demand changes; for a revolution to take place it is essential that the exploiters should not be able to live and rule in the old way. It is only when the "*lower classes*" *do not want* to live in the old way and the "upper classes" *cannot carry on in the old way* that the revolution can triumph. This truth can be expressed in other words: revolution is impossible without a nation-wide crisis (affecting both the exploited and the exploiters).[11]

We may take those two conditions as necessary for an actual revolution. First, the mass of people cannot continue to live in the old way. Life is too hard—so hard that people are willing to risk their lives and what little remains of their property to overthrow the existing order. But this alone is not enough. For revolution to succeed, the ruling class must not be able to rule in the old way. Their legitimacy and repressive power must crumble. Deep divisions in the ruling class must reduce it to a state of indecision and paralysis. The military and police must become unreliable, unwilling to shoot down their neighbors as they rise in rebellion. The legitimacy of the ruling class, and the system they oversee, vanishes among the people and among the police and military, lending permission to rebellion.

But these two conditions are still not enough for actual revolution. Lenin attached a third: the existence of a political party that could lead the tactical and strategic twists and turns of the revolutionary process to the victory of the rising oppressed class, and then begin to establish a new society.

Unlike Russia in 1917, none of these three conditions is now present in the United States. We are not in a revolutionary moment, or close to it. Even so, some on the left dream of revolution in ways that bring to mind the revolutionaries that the working class Scottish writer Ralph Glasser described in his portrait of life among Russian exiles in 1920s and 1930s Glasgow, where he grew up: "They talked with the certainty and passion of people who saw a bright deliverance within reach, convinced that they were in the van of those who would secure it.... It was possible to believe that at any moment they would compel the world to realize their dreams.... They nourished their souls by fixing their gaze on the far horizon.... Theirs was a desperate optimism. Like storm-tossed navigators they fed their hopes with signs and portents."[12]

We cannot "compel the world to realize [our] dreams." But this doesn't mean that we should not dream the dreams that sustain us, as dreams sustained Emma Goldman, Che Guevara, and countless reformers and revolutionaries who have come before us in countless countries and social circumstances. We are not powerless to advance toward the realization of our dreams of dignity and power for working people, peace, environmental justice, and the end of gender and racial oppression, revolutionary as their achievement almost certainly must become one day. But our dreams cannot be left as dreams. They must be infused with careful analysis in the unified practice of progressive politics.

Politics at this moment is by necessity reform politics. Technical matters are not the stumbling blocks to progressive policies. We know how to deliver education and medical care to all. Detailed plans already exist to expand local and long distance mass transit. There is no mystery to raising wages with minimum wage laws and industry-wide bargaining, sometimes known as sectoral bargaining, which encourage competition through improved products and lower prices while preventing employers from competing with one another by reducing wages for their workers. With concentrated effort and solid financial support, scientists and engineers can almost certainly develop technology for the high-capacity batteries and efficient long-distance transmission of electric power required to move fully away from fossil fuels. We know how to make it easy for people to vote and have their votes honestly and completely counted.

Two things stand in the way of success in achieving these and other progressive goals over the resistance of capitalist power: mobilizing the resources required to finance them, and mobilizing the political will to accomplish and direct this mobilization. Let's consider each in turn.

Where Will the Money Come From?

The first objection elites raise to demands for progressive reforms is that they are too expensive. How often do we hear "there is no money"? Yet that claim is patently ridiculous in a country with the fabulous wealth available to the US economy. *Of course* there is money. Congress threw trillions of dollars into the economy to deal with the financial crisis in 2008–9, and more trillions to address the dislocations caused by the COVID-19 pandemic, taking unprecedented action when it suited their interests. *Of course* there are adequate resources in the US economy to enhance the standard of living of the American people while leveling out the gross inequalities of income and wealth with which we now live and die. We just need the right priorities and the political will to achieve them.

The most common mechanisms progressives identify to get resources for urgent human needs are the following: (1) cut the federal military budget; (2) increase tax rates on very high incomes, and levy those taxes on forms of income more common among the rich, such as capital gains and income generated from hedge funds; (3) impose a sales tax on financial transactions in stock and bond markets; and (4) impose national wealth taxes, including taxes on inherited wealth, which would extend to other forms of wealth the limited form of a wealth tax we already have that is imposed by local governments on real estate property.

Consider a modest tax of 2% applied to the household wealth (net worth, after subtracting any debts) of only the top 1% of households. In 2022, these households held 30% of all household wealth in the US, compared with the 4.5% owned by the bottom half of households.[13] In 2022, the net worth owned by this top 1% amounted to around $4.5 trillion.[14] A 2% tax applied only to this wealthiest 1% of households would generate around $90 billion a year. And that would likely not reduce these super wealthy households' wealth at all because it is entirely reasonable to expect that in a usual year they would experience at least that much gain in the value of their assets.

But we can make more and deeper justifiable claims on wealth by building a movement that asserts the fact that, as we will see in detail in chapters four and five, all wealth has its origins in the labor of working people. We will see that the product of this labor is divided into two parts. One is returned to workers to sustain them at the accepted standard of living. This can come as wages from employment or in what's called the social wage, the portion of output that workers receive from social spending rather than private wages and salaries. The rest of workers' output is surplus. We will see that this surplus is not just the profit of business and the incomes of capitalists as they accumulate great personal wealth; a much greater part of the surplus goes to support finance, commerce, and all other unproductive economic activity.

We know something about what corporations do with their profits. The *New York Times* reported that in 2022 "companies announced plans to buy more than $1.2 trillion of their own stock.... Firms are spending roughly 90% of their earnings on buybacks and dividends and could come close to, or surpass, that [in 2023]." The main argument defenders presented for this practice was that it increased share prices.[15]

Taxing corporate profit is one way to redirect resources toward socially productive uses instead of devoting them to boosting stock prices and high-end income and wealth. But the income and wealth of capitalists and superwealthy individuals hardly begins to tap the vast resources of economic surplus that are available to mobilize for whatever purpose satisfies the interests of those who control that surplus.

As activists and organizers challenge the claim that "there is no money," it is useful to recall that one of the most basic contests in capitalist society centers on control of the economic surplus: the question of where the great bulk of the money goes in advanced capitalist society. Increasing the wages of working people has always involved intense struggles with capitalists to repurpose some of the surplus toward higher living standards for working people. Increasing the social wage is another way in which the surplus has been redirected, by taxing capitalist income and wealth.

These two arenas of struggle have been the basis of increased living standards in the past. As movements today address where the money will come from to fund contemporary reforms, it will help to sustain the political path toward progressive results if more and more people become conscious of what usually remains hidden: that the source of funds is mostly found in the surplus the working class produces.

To access and repurpose that surplus is a challenge to capital that requires a powerful working class movement at its core. We must extend the conflict over resources and budget priorities to contest the basis on which wealth as a whole is allocated. This involves going well beyond the usual debates over the division of corporate revenues between wages and profit, or government policies to tax and spend. The question should be: how should the surplus be used? For the creation of real wealth that can improve the lives of working people and the middle class in the provision of decent housing, education, environmental protection, and health care? Or for unproductive activities like the increasingly arcane filigrees of financial derivatives, currency speculation, and commercial activity that undermine the ability of the economy to improve living standards, while concentrating wealth in the hands of fewer and fewer people?

As we will come to understand in chapter five, the progressive movement can "find the money" by transforming the way we allocate economic resources between productive and unproductive sectors of the economy. This form of wealth allocation operates on a social scale, not just in the context of individual corporate decision-making or wage and benefit settlements in collective bargaining. Nor can the market drive this reallocation. Benefits that can be drawn from this social pool of surplus have to be directed by conscious social policy.

This need not require direct government takeover of private business. We already use government subsidies and tax policy to encourage some kinds of business and discourage others. We encourage private homeownership by allowing homeowners to deduct from their income their interest payments and at least some of their property taxes before arriving at federal taxable income. We encourage oil and natural gas production by offering a host of subsidies to the fossil fuel industry. We impose what are called sumptuary taxes on behaviors we want to discourage for moral reasons, for example heavy taxes on alcohol and tobacco products. These taxes have the dual effect of making it less likely that people will drink too much or smoke, while raising revenue that can be used to fund the public health costs that arise from these destructive behaviors.

In this same vein, with the political will and authority, we could decide that financial and commercial activity is undesirable and destructive if it does not directly support productive activity that raises the standard of living of working people. We could then restrict that activity by imposing a tax on it, like the tax on alcohol and cigarettes. Proposals for a financial transactions tax go in this direction, as does the so-called Tobin tax on currency transactions, named after the Nobel Laureate economist James Tobin who first proposed it.

To shift resources away from unproductive uses, we can also tax the profit from undesirable activity enough to bring its after-tax return below the return earned by unproductive activity that actually enhances productive investment and reduces income inequality. Suppose, for example, the profits made from consulting and finance fees related to mergers and acquisitions were subject to a 95% tax rate. It would raise some revenue, but it would mainly act to shift resources to other, more socially suitable, purposes.

We should not be distracted by the claims raised by big banks, hedge funds, and investment houses that all the fancy financial instruments they invent to buy and sell—derivatives of all sorts—will stabilize markets and reduce risk. The massive financial crisis of 2008–9 gave the lie to that. We should not be distracted by the engaging advertisements corporations put on every media platform to get us to buy their products just because the ads are so cool or fun. They often are. But the resources and intellect going into all that financial manipulation and commercial trickery would be better directed toward productive activity that addresses climate change and improves workers' social conditions and standard of living.

Even direct government interference requiring the reallocation of corporate resources to public purpose would not be a radical departure from existing policy options available to the president of the United States. For example, the Trump administration intervened in the market to order the redirection of economic resources to restore power grids and supply food and water to communities during the storms of 2017, and again in 2020 to generate some needed medical supplies and equipment in the COVID-19 crisis. Other presidents have also intervened, relying on the Defense Production Act (DPA) of 1950, which authorized President Harry Truman to use government decrees to direct the allocation of private resources to meet the needs of the Korean War effort. Other presidents have invoked the DPA for other emergencies.[16] President Biden is continuing in that tradition.

The DPA gives the president broad power to commandeer private business resources for national defense. The act declares:

> The President is authorized (1) to require that performance under contracts or orders (other than contracts of employment) which he

deems necessary or appropriate to promote the national defense shall take priority over performance under any other contract or order, and, for the purpose of assuring such priority, to require acceptance and performance of such contracts or orders in preference to other contracts or orders by any person he finds to be capable of their performance, and (2) to allocate materials, services, and facilities in such manner, upon such conditions, and to such extent as he shall deem necessary or appropriate to promote the national defense.[17]

But what is national defense? What is national security? It is not hard to argue that defending the nation justifies the allocation of resources for adequate housing, education, and health care for our people, or to build functioning infrastructure. For example, a major demand of progressive politics, picked up by Senator Bernie Sanders and other politicians, is free public higher education. To put that demand in the context of our military spending, in 2018 the total cost of tuition, fees, and room and board for all full-time students enrolled in public two-year and four-year colleges and universities in the US was $17.8 billion.[18] The total military budget that year was $648 billion.[19] We could have had free public higher education—no public college or university tuition, no student debt for millions of students and their families—for less than 3% of that year's military budget, what the Pentagon spends in little more than a week.

The National Priorities Project calculates the cost of the military expressed not just in dollars but in what dollars spent for the military could buy if they were spent for other purposes—what economists call the "opportunity cost" of the budget item. In 2021, for example, the total federal military budget was $740 billion. If we would have reduced that by just 15%, or $111 billion, bringing it back down to the level of military spending (in real terms, adjusted for inflation) just before 9/11 and the disastrous US wars in Iraq and Afghanistan, the federal government could instead in 2021 have paid the annual salary of 242,000 elementary school teachers and 198,000 registered nurses, and funded 509,000 Head Start slots for kids for four years, and provided 63 million homes with solar energy, and built 2.6 million new units of public housing.[20] All of that is the annual cost of having increased our military spending after 2001. These improved social conditions that we have given up would surely enhance our security more than another navy carrier group or thousands of modernized nuclear weapons.

The DPA gives the president power to override any and all private contracts to require the reallocation of resources to national defense. Perhaps it is a stretch to imagine such a government intrusion into private markets to defend national security understood in a proper way. Nevertheless, the power is already there in federal legislation, available in principle, and already used in practice, to address a national security emergency. Certainly the conditions of poverty and near poverty so widespread in our country constitute a legitimate emergency, if we look squarely at them.

With any large-scale structural change in the economy, workers' lives will be disrupted as jobs disappear in declining sectors. We already see this problem loom large in plans to move away from fossil fuels to sustainable energy sources, opposed by workers and their unions in the fossil fuel industries. We see it in campaigns to reduce the military budget, when unions representing workers in weapons-producing companies object, or among workers in the private health insurance business who worry about their jobs if a Medicare for All program were to replace private health insurance.

These are legitimate concerns. They will come up in any program to shrink unproductive sectors. In all these cases, government programs will be necessary to retrain and redeploy affected workers into the expanding productive-sector jobs that are the other side of shrinking unproductive sectors. We can think of this as the need for what people call a "just transition." Transitions in any one of these sectors will require coordination across all sectors so that workers in declining industries can be absorbed in an orderly way by growing industries. Ordinary markets cannot accomplish such structural coordination.

New Deal programs such as the Works Progress Administration (WPA) and Civilian Conservation Corps (CCC) are historical precedents for productive economic activity planned and run by the government to provide millions of displaced workers with useful employment. WPA projects built dams that brought electricity for the first time to millions of people in rural areas. Workers engaged in WPA projects paved thousands of miles of streets and highways and built bridges and housing across the country. The WPA employed artists, writers, photographers, musicians, and theater professionals to create, document, preserve, and perform all manner of cultural work. The CCC employed millions of young men and women in natural conservation and rural development projects on federal, state, and local public lands. Thousands of projects from that era were still operating in 2020.[21] There is no technical reason that such programs could not be brought forward again where private markets are unable to provide jobs at living wages.

Where Is the Political Will?

Will is a question of consciousness, understanding, and commitment to act. Class consciousness among workers can be marginalized with the strength of conscious identities concerning other dimensions of their lives—individuality, nationality, religion, race or ethnicity, gender, region of the country (think of pride in being from Texas or the Bronx).

But there identities can coexist with class consciousness. In 2017, 35% of working US adults identified themselves as belonging to the working class.[22] Some working class consciousness is present in over a third of the population, more than half the number of people who actually are in the working class. Not bad as a starting point for working class politics, considering that Bertell Ollman, a leading Marxist political scientist, once remarked to me that when Marx wrote about workers developing class consciousness he did not anticipate that almost every worker would have several talking boxes in their house that flickered for hours on end, flooding their hearing with thoughts, values, theories, and stories that supported capitalist norms. The ever-present intrusions of Facebook posts, Twitter noise, and voices coming at us from so many social media platforms all day long only magnify the problem.

Novelist Abir Mukherjee got at this from a different angle when he had a fictional character explain to a British police detective new to Calcutta in 1919 how it was possible for 150,000 British people living in India to control a population of three hundred million Indians: "The rulers need to project an aura of superiority over the ruled. Not just physical or military superiority, but also *moral* superiority. More importantly, their subjects must in turn *believe* themselves to be inferior; they must need to be ruled for their own benefit."[23]

The main problem progressive politics confronts is the way dominant forms of our media, education system, culture, laws, and politics reinforce the basic power grid of our capitalist society. To achieve progressive ends for working people, politics has to challenge capitalist authority in one way or another, in small steps or big campaigns, in all these domains. The political will and appropriate policies and organizational forms to do this will arise in the political process itself, developing hand in hand with action.

The first requirement in the process to build class consciousness is to recognize and name the working class as a social reality, and as the large majority of the population. That's why I titled my book about this subject *The Working Class Majority: America's Best Kept Secret*.[24] It is a mistake to accept language that characterizes the US as a middle class society, with fringes of rich and poor on the edges. It weakens us to believe that unions have brought American workers into the middle class, as union leaders typically say in defense of the importance of unions. As unions have won benefits and higher wages for their members, allowing them for the first time to own a home, take a vacation, have the security of health insurance and a decent pension, these auto workers, nurses, and flight attendants are no less workers than they were before the union came into their lives. Their unions have not brought them out of the working class; they have helped improve the standard of living that working class people can experience and expect.

Naming the working class is only the beginning of analysis and practice based on class understanding. For example, we need to understand that poverty is something that happens to the working class, not to some marginal "other" stuck at the bottom of the social order. Poverty comes from low wages, unemployment, and the hardships women can experience in divorce. People cycle in and out of poverty, so while the poverty rate fluctuates between 12 and 14% in a given year, during a decade more than half the working class experiences poverty in at least one year.[25]

We cannot solve the problem of poverty without improving the conditions of life for the working class. Thinking of poor people as different from and inferior to working people is another way to divide the working class. All too often this division is mixed up with dysfunctional racial stereotypes that equate poor people with Black people. It is true that poverty afflicts the Black community disproportionately. In 2021, 19.8% of Black people were poor, compared with a national average poverty rate of 11.6%, and 8.1% for non-Hispanic whites. The poverty rate among Hispanics was double that of non-Hispanic whites. But numerically in the US in 2021, there were nearly twice as many non-Hispanic white people in poverty as Blacks in the US, and more than four-fifths of all Black people were not poor.[26] This demonstrates that poverty is a condition shared across the entire working class and needs to be addressed as such.

As with every issue compounded by race and gender, the class confrontation that addresses poverty requires particular consideration for the needs of Blacks, Hispanic people, women, and any marginalized peoples. Their conditions within the working class must be improved through policies that go toward dissolving the grip of white supremacy and patriarchy. Historical experience teaches us clearly that without specific policies to address white supremacy and patriarchy these oppressions will not disappear on their own or automatically.

Yet movements focused exclusively on the needs of marginalized people, sometimes called "identity politics," can raise analysis and demands that ignore or minimize the class foundations of the problems. Without an explicit attention to class, these movements tend to be led by and benefit professional middle class people and those rising to positions of power, as happened in South Africa after apartheid and the US after the 1960s civil rights and second-wave feminist movements. This tension between class and "identity politics" is perhaps the most important and most difficult dynamic that progressive politics has to navigate. We will turn to this issue in detail in chapters nine and ten.

Clarity about class involves more than recognizing the working class. We need to be clear about the other pole of the class system, too. The will to engage in confrontation with the ruling class requires that we look at the rich through the lens of class, as we do with the poor. If the target of our political campaigns is "the rich," or even "the billionaire class" without further explanation, we reinforce the false understanding of class as a question of degrees of income and wealth only. Although it might seem counterintuitive, given that billionaires can make attractive targets, especially those who engage in ridiculous degrees of conspicuous consumption and tax avoidance, this approach actually misses the proper focus of struggle: the capitalist class and its ruling elites.

Just as our current political language has increasingly come to accept the term "working class," first as an adjective and more recently as a noun, we have to popularize the term "capitalist class" as its opposite, but interconnected, partner. The working class confronts the capitalist class, not "the rich," although capitalists are certainly rich. But in major US cities, a "rich" couple might also be a doctor married to a senior programmer. If they are not the people who run their city, or their company or a hospital, or the country, targeting them as "the rich" misses the reality of power and alienates potential allies. It keeps people from learning how things actually work. Going into the resulting dead-end battles leads to confusion and undermines the will to fight. We need a politics that names and keeps track of the system we face and the actual class forces operating in it.

Notes

1   Frederick Douglass, "West India Emancipation," speech at Canandaigua, New York, August 3, 1857, Blackpast, January 7, 2005, https://www.blackpast.org/african-american-history/1857-frederick-douglass-if-there-no-struggle-there-no-progress.

2   "Franklin Roosevelt's Address Announcing the Second New Deal," October 31, 1936, Our Documents: The Second New Deal, accessed August 29, 2021, http://docs.fdrlibrary.marist.edu/od2ndst.html.

3   US Department of Justice quoted in Charles King, "The Fulbright Paradox: Race and the Road to a New American Internationalism," *Foreign Affairs* (July–August 2021): 101.

4   Marguerite Higgins, "Rusk Bemoans Racial Crisis, Gravest Problem Since 1865," *New York Herald Tribune*, May 27, 1963, introduced into the Congressional Record by Emanuel Cellar, Chair of House of Representatives Subcommittee #5 of the Committee on the Judiciary, May 28, 1963, quoted in Gary Younge, "What Black America Means to Europe," *New York Review of Books*, July 23, 2020, 9.

5   William J. Burns and Linda Thomas-Greenfield, "The Transformation of Diplomacy: How to Save the State Department," *Foreign Affairs* 99, no. 6 (November–December 2020): 102, 106, 107; emphasis added.

6   Zwelinzima Vavi, "Class Analysis of the Situation in South Africa," (paper presented at How Class Works—2002 Conference, State University of New York at Stony Brook, June 2002).

7   Greg Ip, "Business Roundtable Shifts Climate Stance," *Wall Street Journal*, September 17, 2020.

8   Timothy Puko, "Action Urged on Climate Change," *Wall Street Journal*, December 2, 2020.

9   Mao Tse-tung, "Report on an Investigation of the Peasant Movement in Hunan," in *Selected Works of Mao Tse-tung*, vol. 1 (Peking: Foreign Languages Press, 1965), 28.

10   Lu Xun, "Listening to Dreams," in *Selected Works of Lu Xun*, vol. 3, trans. Yang Xianyi and Gladys Yang (Beijing: Foreign Languages Press, 2003), 218.

11   V.I. Lenin, "'Left-Wing Communism': An Infantile Disorder," *Selected Works*, vol. 3 (Moscow: Progress Publishers, 1971), 401–2, accessed August 29, 2021, https://www.marxists.org/archive/lenin/works/1920/lwc/ch09.htm; emphasis in original.

12   Ralph Glasser, *Growing Up in the Gorbals* (Thirsk, North Yorkshire, UK: House of Stratus, 2001), 8.

13   Board of Governors of the Federal Reserve System, "Distribution of Household Wealth in the U.S. since 1989," accessed March 17, 2023, https://www.federalreserve.gov/releases/z1/dataviz/dfa/distribute/table.

14   Board of Governors of the Federal Reserve System, "Recent Developments," accessed March 17, 2023, https://www.federalreserve.gov/releases/z1/20220609/html/recent_developments.htm.

15   Andrew Ross Sorkin, et al., "Buffet Makes His Case in Trillion-Dollar Debate Over Stock Buybacks," *New York Times*, March 6, 2023, https://www.nytimes.com/2023/03/04/business/biden-buffett-debate-share-buybacks.html.

16   Noah Weiland and Emily Cochrane, "War Powers May Be Used to Meet [Coronavirus] Outbreak Needs," *New York Times*, February 29, 2020, https://www.nytimes.com/2020/02/28/us/politics/trump-coronavirus.html; and Zolan Kanno-Youngs and Ana Swanson, "Wartime Production Law Has Been Used Routinely, but Not With Coronavirus," *New York Times*, March 31, 2020, https://www.nytimes.com/2020/03/31/us/politics/coronavirus-defense-production-act.html.

17   Defense Procurement Act 1950, as amended, [50 U.S.C. App. § 2061 et seq.] Section 101(a), accessed August 29, 2021, https://uscode.house.gov/view.xhtml?path=/prelim@title50/chapter55&edition=prelim.

18   National Center for Education Statistics, "Tuition Costs of Colleges and Universities," accessed August 29, 2021, https://nces.ed.gov/fastfacts/display.asp?id=76.

19 "U.S. Military Budget/Defense Budget, 1960–2021," Macrotrends, accessed August 29, 2021, https://www.macrotrends.net/countries/USA/united-states/military-spending-defense-budget.

20 Calculated from data presented by the National Priorities Project, "Trade-Offs: Your Money, Your Choices," accessed March 18, 2023, https://www.nationalpriorities.org/interactive-data/trade-offs.

21 For details of the many continuing sites of New Deal projects, see "The Living New Deal," https://livingnewdeal.org, accessed August 29, 2021.

22 Frank Newport, "Looking into What Americans Mean by 'Working Class,'" *Gallup Polling Matters*, August 3, 2018, https://news.gallup.com/opinion/polling-matters/239195/looking-americans-mean-working-class.aspx.

23 Abir Mukherjee, *A Rising Man* (New York: Penguin Books, 2017), 152; original emphasis.

24 Michael Zweig, *The Working Class Majority: America's Best Kept Secret*, 2nd ed. (Ithaca, NY: Cornell University Press, 2012).

25 Zweig, *Working Class Majority*, 90.

26 John Creamer, Emily A. Shrider, Kalee Burns, and Frances Chen, "Poverty in the United States: 2021," US Census Bureau, September 13, 2022, https://www.census.gov/library/publications/2022/demo/p60-277.html.

CHAPTER THREE

How Do We Know What We Know?

When I think back on my lifetime of activism, I admit I made some pretty stupid mistakes along the way. Some arose from relying on incorrect information, but the most difficult ones arose from not thinking right. We got excited about schemes for power that seemed to make sense because we wanted them to, but led us nowhere except to isolation and frustration. We treated people who agreed with us on almost everything as bitter enemies because we disagreed about *something*. We were stubborn in the face of problems, refusing to accept reality for far too long.

This history, no doubt shared to some degree by people in progressive social movements everywhere, leads me to conclude that it is critical for activists and organizers to become conscious of their thinking processes as a first step toward developing our ability to discern reality and act in ways appropriate to changing it. Too often we are unaware of the assumptions that guide our thinking, failing to rise above the limitations that lead us into theoretical and practical dead ends. In particular, I have come to appreciate the power of dialectical thinking, which is almost never taught as a method of analysis. And I have learned that the materialism that grounds science and technology can also ground social analysis and movement practice. That's why I start this chapter with what are sometimes considered philosophical questions, but in terms related to social practice.

It is hugely important that we question whether we are in touch with reality or off in some dream of wishful thinking, which is why I ground our social analysis with the question: how do we know when we're right? How do we reset our course in the face of errors of analysis or judgment? How can we learn more quickly about the world and what to do to change it?

Basic Characteristics of History

When I was in college I thought the point of studying history was to avoid the mistakes people had made in the past, and to discover positive historical examples that one might try to repeat. Only years later did I came to understand that history is not solely in the past, to read about, look at, and pick and choose from. History flows directly into the present. History is a palpable force that continues to shape current events. As American novelist William Faulkner put it, "The past is never dead. It's not even past." Faulkner's focus was the American Civil War, but the point applies more broadly.

The institutions, cultural norms, and social dynamics at any given time don't just happen. They don't arise arbitrarily or at the whim of some powerful person. And they can't be changed arbitrarily, or at will. As the saying goes, "Wishing doesn't make it so." As we confront the present and seek to shape the future that arises from it, we have to have as clear a picture as we can muster of the dynamic processes involved in creating the present, processes that will bring into being a new future from the present.

I believe it is essential to be explicit about the method and approach used in this book. An explicit awareness makes it easier to follow and understand the arguments—and also to challenge them—and will make it easier for anyone reading this book to do their own thinking, research, and social activism in ways that are more closely connected with reality.

I have found four basic characteristics of historical development especially useful to keep in mind: (1) change is the basic state of affairs; (2) change is driven by internal dynamics of what is changing, through which external forces must operate to have an effect; (3) these internal dynamics are powered by contradictions operating as unities of opposites; and (4) relatively slow quantitative changes lead to abrupt qualitative changes. These propositions characterize the method of thinking called dialectics.

First is the recognition that *change is the basic state of nature and society*. Society is in motion. Stability is transitory and always pregnant with change. The most important problem in social analysis and practice is to understand the processes that drive the changes, to see inside the apparent stability of the moment the dynamics that can transform it in one way or another.

Second, *the basis of change is internal to what is changing*. External forces can be important, but they operate by affecting internal dynamics, which are determinative. This is true in personal life as well as in social conflict. No "outside agitator" can come into a workplace to organize a union, go into a town to organize a civil rights movement, travel to Russia's Finland Station in St. Petersburg to organize a revolution, or, for that matter, enter into another's personal relationship to bust it up, without an appreciation of the internal conditions of the shop, town, country, or marriage. And no manager, sheriff, czar, or bullying partner can long hold the status quo while blind to the dynamic conditions in which they are enmeshed except, for a time, through brute force. Effective organizing for social change always requires focused attention to the internal processes at play in the arena in which one is organizing.

Third, *the internal dynamics that guide change are best understood as contradictions.* These are sometimes called unities of opposites, suggesting something different from the colloquial use of "contradiction" to mean opposite and irreconcilable states or propositions like cold and hot, or good and bad. We would do well to turn away from such dualisms that are so common, like mind and body, politics and economics, nature and nurture, theory and practice, which can easily lead to overly simplistic "either/or" thinking. Each of these pairings, apparently involving separate and opposite elements, is instead best understood as a mutually interacting unity of opposites that constitute a dynamic whole.

Many phenomena are complex, involving several contradictions operating simultaneously. One or another may be dominant in driving development at any particular time, depending on conditions and their relationships. We should explore the complex dynamics that unite these opposite, yet not fully independent, elements into processes of change, and be alert to identifying which of the contradictions provides the most immediate energy to shape change.

A final characteristic of dialectics suggests that *change is not a smooth process but one of periodic leaps that follow relatively long periods of more subtle change.* We know this from such colloquial phrases as "the straw that broke the camel's back," or the enraged "That's it! I'm leaving" that marks a sharp break in a personal or employment relationship after a gradual accumulation of grievances. Someone may suffer physical and psychological torment from a parent or partner or boss for years and then, one day, finally summon the strength to rebel and escape.

In so many aspects of life and nature we see that quantitative changes lead at a certain point to a qualitative change in the basic situation. We see it in the change of water into steam, a qualitative change from a liquid state after the incremental heating of the water to 100 degrees centigrade. Urban rebellions in African American communities across the US, going far back into US history, from Harlem in 1964 to Watts in 1965, Newark and Detroit in 1967, to recent uprisings in Ferguson and Minneapolis, and dozens of other locales, arose in a flash after an accumulation of bitter experiences with local police brutality, long borne largely in silence before the explosion.

This is of course not limited to the US. Iranian writer Azadeh Moaveni, reporting on the massive uprising of women that swept Iran in 2022–23 after Mahsa Amini died in police custody after being arrested for failing to wear her hijab properly in public, observed that "mass protest is often provoked by a specific humiliation, but the underlying oppression explains why the unrest races through society."[1] As we will see in chapter six, capitalist economic crises are sharp breaks that reverse economic growth, arising from gradually accumulating changes in underlying conditions that, as they gather, may not be apparent.

The insights of dialectical thinking go back over two thousand five hundred years to ancient Greek philosophy. This is not the place to explore the intellectual history of the dialectical method. But I hope its wisdom and usefulness will become evident as our exploration proceeds.

Choosing a Belief System

Dialectics is a belief system. There are many other belief systems that people use to structure their thinking and their understandings of society, psychology, and the physical and natural world. As with any belief system, those who believe in it take it "on faith." This has led many people to assert that Marxism, based as it is on dialectics, and reaching, as it does, specific conclusions about capitalism, is in essence like a religion, or "just another belief system." The same is often said about science by those who wish to put religion and science on equal footing. "You believe that. Well, I believe this."

As the saying goes, however, "Everyone is entitled to their own beliefs, but not to their own facts." We will return to the question of facts, but first let's look at the claim that everyone is entitled to their own beliefs, as though Marxism, nationalism, racism, liberalism, anarchism, conservatism, nativism, science, creationism, and what have you, are all beliefs of equal standing, matters of personal choice that cannot legitimately be challenged as such. This begs the question: is it possible to evaluate one belief system against another and decide which to accept, which is best to use to deepen our understanding and guide our actions?

To answer, we need to be clear what our point of reference will be when making our evaluation. Do we accept the belief system that makes us most comfortable? Is comfort then our point of reference? Do we accept beliefs that conform to what we've already been taught, so tradition becomes the point of reference? Do we refer to ideas in a religious text we've read and liked, to see if a proposition is consistent with those ideas? Or do we refer to the material world as a guide? Where do we look, what is our point of reference, to test whether we should accept a belief?

Of the several alternatives, I think reference to the material world through a "test of practice" is key to the process by which we can best evaluate propositions, theories, or beliefs. In this test, we put the theory into practice in the material world to see if the result is as expected. We evaluate a proposition in its relationship to the material world, revealed through experiments to check predictions. This is the method of the physical and natural sciences. The scientific method reveals the material basis of dialectics, whose principles are shown to be correct when they correspond to the realities in which we live. Being a materialist leads to dialectical thinking because that's the way the world works.

Before looking at this test more closely, let's consider the proposition that lies at its heart: the claim that there is a material world outside our thoughts and sensations, a material world that exists independent of our own thoughts (but is not necessarily unaffected by them). This material world, being independent of our thoughts, can then serve as the point of reference to which we turn to evaluate whether to believe our thoughts, or not. The question becomes: how well do our beliefs stack up in relation to the material world?

The belief in a material world outside our minds, a reality that exists independent of what we think of it, or even if we think about it at all, is the principal claim of materialism, another philosophical tradition reaching back to the ancient Greeks. Materialists need not deny the existence of ideas or refuse to recognize the importance of ideas in shaping events. Rather, materialists assert that we can ask about the validity of ideas and evaluate one idea or theory against another by checking its conformity with the objective world that the idea seeks to represent or the theory seeks to explain.

The world outside our thoughts is of course hugely complicated and diverse. It has physical features and relationships over a vast expanse; it has social relationships from the personal to the global; it has culture in complex forms and means of expression. We cannot know it all. It is almost incomprehensible. Yet it is there. We always do better when we act as best we can in ways that conform to how reality works.

To take an example, a healthy newborn infant often cries soon after birth. This cry is a practical act, usually undertaken spontaneously, perhaps with a gentle slap to the behind, and without conscious direction by the infant. When crying results in a human response from the mother or other caregiver, typically involving milk from breast or bottle, and other physical comforts that are pleasurable for the infant, these actions are repeated, at first without deliberate planning by the infant. Over time, the infant's brain and mental capacity develop to the point where the child can begin to become conscious of the process and begin to learn to have some control over it—when to cry, what responses different types of crying and various actions will likely elicit from people nearby, what to expect from the world.

We also know from psychology that the patterns of behavior and expectations that a child develops to cope with its early experiences might harden into behaviors that in later life are dysfunctional when the grown child encounters the wider world. These disconnects and the pain they generate can be alleviated by therapy and reflection to make conscious the sources of the behavior and find alternative paths to more appropriate ways of being in the world.

Our mental expectations arise from practical experiences; the ideas have a material basis in interactions with the world, and in the processes of the brain. The ideas arise first as a jumble of observations and impressions we get from our different senses. But the human mind seeks to order these observations and impressions by developing theories that try to explain what is happening. With this understanding we can predict the likely future result of what we do now and choose the action that has what we consider the most desirable expected outcome. If the unexpected happens, we rethink our understanding.

In this process, ideas are not theories. Theories arise in the mind when the ideas, based directly in practical experience, observation, and sense impressions, are linked together in some relation of cause and effect. We have an experience that it is hot outdoors and we have no air conditioning indoors. After acting on this experience by drinking water and finding some relief, we develop a theory and formulate a hypothesis that when it is hot we should drink water.

How do we test the hypothesis that connects hot weather to dehydration, and asserts the positive effect of drinking more water? We test it in practice. We look to see what happens to people who follow this behavior, and compare it with what happens to people in the same circumstances who don't drink much. We learn that "stay hydrated" is good advice on hot days.

To take another example, we might think that it is good protection from hypothermia (dangerously low body temperature) to take a stiff drink of brandy because it feels warm going down. That theory, relating the warm feeling of the alcoholic drink to the process of warming the body, is wrong, despite the image of the trusty St. Bernard dog going up the mountain with a keg of brandy around its neck to rescue someone stranded in the snow. Drinking liquor actually lowers the body's defense from cold by drawing blood away from the body's core. The adverse practical consequences that come from drinking alcohol to relieve cold eventually require us to change the original theory: it fails the test of practice.

Knowledge Is a Process, Not a State

We will avoid many problems when we understand that knowledge is not a fixed binary choice in which we know, or we do not know. Rather, we gain flexibility in our thinking when we recognize that knowledge is a process, not a state. It is best understood and pursued in a dialectical fashion, as a dynamic unity of the opposites: "theory" and "practice." This is the basic contradiction that is internal to "learning" and that guides the creation of knowledge. As we saw with the example of the infant above, all understanding arises from this dynamic process in which theory and practice interact, shape one another, and unfold into knowledge. All knowledge is tentative and transitory, subject to elaboration or radical change depending on future turns in the process.

Knowledge arises from a process that combines activity and thinking. First comes activity, practice, forming the basis of direct experience and observation. Our sense impressions of this action and its consequences, gained either directly or with the help of observational equipment, give rise to ideas. Our mind connects these ideas and impressions together into theories.

We find out if the theories are correct, if the relationships we propose are true (reflect reality), through the test of practice. We put the theory into practice; if the outcome is as expected, we have tentative support for the theory. If the outcome is contrary to what is expected, we have to go back and adjust the theory to account for the new observations. A theory that gains support from a test of practice may later be challenged when it meets observations in new circumstances that it cannot adequately explain, or cannot be reproduced in the same circumstances when repeated.

There is an old saying that "we learn by trial and error." Successful practice may consolidate knowledge, corroborate and strengthen one's prior beliefs. But it does not lead to new learning. We learn something new, come to a fresh understanding, when there is an error, when facts arise or observations are made that ultimately cannot be reconciled with the theories we hold to be true and the expectations we form from them. Our mistakes can help us. Making mistakes and being open to observing discrepancies between expectation and results are central requirements for learning. But, unfortunately, learning is hard when discerning and accepting reality requires giving up firmly held beliefs that offer great psychological comfort or monetary advantage.

Incorporating new observations into a new or more refined theory is one definition of what it means to learn. English professor Mina Shaughnessy applied this method to her approach to teaching writing to urban adult students who had few writing skills. In the introduction to her influential 1979 book *Errors and Expectations*, she writes:

> Students write the way they do, not because they are slow or non-verbal, indifferent to or incapable of academic excellence, but because they are beginners and must, like all beginners, learn by making mistakes. These they make aplenty and for such a variety of reasons that the inexperienced teacher is almost certain to see nothing but a chaos of error when he first encounters their papers. Yet a closer look will reveal very little that is random or "illogical" in what they have written.... [Learning] must be informed by an understanding not only of what is missing or awry but of why this is so.[2]

This observation is central to productive approaches to political education in social movements, far beyond the specific circumstances of a writing classroom. When we make mistakes, we need to analyze their origins carefully. We need to look at the patterns of thought that lead us to our misjudgments. We need to learn political skills in the patient self-critical evaluation of practice.

Everything we know is pregnant with new knowledge. More important than our knowledge at any point is our commitment to the process by which knowledge accumulates. This is what we know as the scientific method, which is highly developed and broadly accepted, at least in its own realm.

A closely related area of human activity where materialism and the test of practice have great acceptance is in the development of technology and engineering principles, and production more generally. Here again we often find the old adage about learning through "trial and error." Try something, fail, adjust, act again, fail again, adjust once more, keep that going until reaching success, where "success" means having something that works, that accords with the operation of the real world and has the effect one predicts and desires. And even a successful trial has to be confirmed through repetition. Repeating experiments to confirm a result is difficult when the experiment is expensive, or technically or socially difficult to re-create, as is the case in high-energy physics or social change. But the principle remains.

Of course we cannot each have our own opportunity to test in practice all the theories we accept and live by. We learn from our education, our cultural traditions, our work experiences. We learn from family. We read books and articles or hear talks and podcasts by authors who report the results of such tests performed by others. We must rely on scientific literature and its popular interpreters to guide us in our understanding. That requires us to decide which sources to trust: Uncle Fred when he's had too much to drink after dinner, peer-reviewed scientific journals, or upstart websites? The *New York Times* and *Democracy Now!*, or *Infowars* and the *National Inquirer*? Here again, the test of practice helps—over time we find out which sources have proven reliable, which sources admit and correct errors when new evidence emerges, which sources help us to choose actions that prove successful when compared with our own expectations in taking them.

Social Practice

Science, technology, and production are not the only realms of practice from which we draw theory and develop knowledge. Our social experiences, both as individuals in families and communities, and among groups at society-wide levels, affect us deeply and call on each of us to develop some understanding of what's going on. As with the example of the newborn infant, we all start with social activity from which impressions and ideas emerge. From these in turn we develop theories that lead to further activity, and so on in a continuum of practice, theory, expectation and prediction, further practice, and more refined theory.

But in the realm of social experience and theory, we cannot control the circumstances of action as physical and natural scientists do. We usually cannot isolate particular suspected causes or link them to specific suspected effects while holding almost everything else in the social and physical environment unchanged, as we would have to do to reliably test a theory in a fully scientific sense. Beyond that, social circumstances and relationships change over time, whereas gravity, the speed of light and the charge on an electron do not. Social reality is a moving target, making it difficult to test social theories over time.

Furthermore, in society objective reality is shaped in part by the subjective understanding of people within it, so the social world changes with the articulation of theories about it. The social world also changes with the tests those theories stimulate in the realm of policy, social activism, and methods of governance and rule. And to complicate matters still further, social reality involves conflicting interests that can lead people in powerful positions to intervene in social practice to suppress outcomes, and related knowledge, that challenge their interests. For example, tobacco company lies about the dangers of smoking and fossil fuel industry denial of their impact on the climate came with vigorous industry attacks on the knowledge science had developed. Such people shape the ideas presented in textbooks, media, and in the culture in ways that promote those interests while isolating, denigrating, and undermining processes and ideas that challenge those interests.

All these complications explain why social knowledge can only be very loosely considered scientific, whether it is expressed in mathematical or narrative form. Yet the ambiguities and complexities of the social world should not lead us to conclude that we cannot really know anything about it, so we can believe whatever we want. Applying the dialectical method and the test of practice to evaluate our social experiences, discern reality as best we can, and distinguish among competing claims provides the best chance of making sense of society.

The Example of Galileo and the Church

This way of thinking helps unravel one of the oldest, most famous conflicts between religion and science: the controversy between the astronomer Galileo Galilei and the Roman Catholic Church in the first part of the seventeenth century. Galileo challenged then-current church doctrine that the earth is stationary while the sun and planets revolve around it, in accordance with the words of the Bible (for example, "God fixed the Earth upon its foundation, not to be moved forever").[3] Galileo, basing his views on detailed observation of the motions of the planets and the moons of Jupiter, made possible by the recent invention of the telescope, proposed that the planets revolve around the sun. In 1633, after severe criticism from the church hierarchy and threats of torture and execution, Galileo recanted, his teachings were banned, and Pope Urban VIII approved his punishment of house arrest for the remaining eight years of his life.

In 1981, nearing the 350th anniversary of the triumph of the church over Galileo and reflecting on the recent one-hundredth anniversary in 1979 of the birth of Albert Einstein, Pope John Paul II convened a commission to evaluate the Galileo controversy. In a rare reversal, they concluded that the church had been wrong to condemn Galileo and, in 1992, he was rehabilitated. As Pope John Paul II expressed it in an address to the Pontifical Academy of Sciences that had completed the study: "Since the cosmos, as it was then known, was contained within the solar system alone, this reference point could only be situated in the Earth or in the Sun. Today, after Einstein and within the perspective of contemporary cosmology, neither of these two reference points has the importance they once had. This observation, it goes without saying, is not directed against the validity of Galileo's position in the debate; it is only meant to show that often, beyond two partial and contrasting perceptions, *there exists a wider perception which includes them and goes beyond both of them.*"[4]

We find a more explicitly hedged statement in a text written in the last months of Pope John Paul II's life when Cardinal Joseph Ratzinger, then soon-to-be Pope Benedict XVI, led the Congregation of the Doctrine of the Faith that approved this 2004 version of the assessment: "Galileo did not prove [his] theory by the Aristotelian standards of science in his day.... As more recent science has shown, both Galileo *and* his opponents were partly right and partly wrong. Galileo was right in asserting the mobility of the earth and wrong in asserting the immobility of the sun. His opponents were right in asserting the mobility of the sun and wrong in asserting the immobility of the earth. Had the Catholic Church rushed to endorse Galileo's views ... the Church would have embraced what modern science has disproved."[5]

Understanding that knowledge is a process, not a state, throws a new light on such equivocal judgments as "they were both right while they were both wrong because each had a part of the truth." The question is more useful if we don't ask "who was right" but instead ask: "Who had the best way that existed at the time to find out what is right?"

In this regard, the church and Galileo had irreconcilably different points of reference to test a proposition. For Galileo the point of reference was the actual, observable motion of the planets and moons of Jupiter. He had a test of practice, oriented toward the material world. For the church the point of reference was the received doctrine of the faith, a test that compared a proposition with biblical text and church teaching to seek consistency of belief. There is no way to fudge this difference.

In choosing between these points of reference, Galileo's method was the way to move through a process to deeper understanding of the universe, despite the fact that his original proposition was later shown to be incorrect. The method of the church was a dead-end path to knowledge. In its approach and treatment of Galileo, the church was fully wrong; Galileo was fully correct.

Works of fiction can illuminate the process of knowing by looking into human emotions. The novelist John Williams, for example, wrote a novel in the form of a biography of a fictional character, William Stoner, a University of Missouri professor of English. Set in the first half of the twentieth century, the book describes the development of its main character, including the ways in which Stoner comes to experience love. Williams sums up his character's process in these words:

> In his extreme youth Stoner had thought of love as an absolute state of being to which, if one were lucky, one might find access. In his maturity he had decided it was the heaven of a false religion, toward which one ought to gaze with an amused disbelief, a gently familiar contempt, and an embarrassed nostalgia. Now in his middle age he began to know that it was neither a state of grace nor an illusion; he saw it as a human act of becoming, a condition that was invented and modified moment by moment and day by day, by the will and the intelligence and the heart.[6]

The insight that knowledge is a process, not a state, allows us to evaluate historical figures in a nuanced way. During the broad rebellion that broke out after the murder of George Floyd in 2020, many activists and politicians called for the removal of memorials erected to honor Confederate leaders such as Robert E. Lee and Jefferson Davis. Some activists extended the call to target George Washington, who owned two hundred enslaved people, and Abraham Lincoln, who initially fought the Civil War to prevent the spread of slavery without seeking its abolition.

We now know that Washington was wrong on slavery, but he was right in helping to lead a revolution against British rule. We now know that he was wrong about such antidemocratic features of the US Constitution as the counting of enslaved individuals as three-fifths of a person to give slaveholders more representation and power in Congress, or having state legislatures select senators, and assigning two senators to each state regardless of population. Washington was wrong, but in the main he was right, because he asserted an overall method of governance that has unfolded toward greater freedom and democracy, not less. Washington was on the right side of history, King George III on the wrong side.

Lincoln, too, was wrong in his embrace of "colonization," the proposed policy of sending Black people back to Africa as the solution to racial divisions in the US. He did not seek the full abolition of slavery at the start of the Civil War, only its restriction from the Western territories and states. Even his 1863 Emancipation Proclamation only affected slavery in areas not yet occupied by the Union Army, leaving untouched slavery in those parts of the Confederacy already under Union Army control, and border slave states like Kentucky and Maryland that had remained in the Union. But there is no proper equating of Lincoln with Jefferson Davis who was treasonously trying to break up the country to preserve slavery. Lincoln, who led forward, helping to bend the moral arc of the universe toward justice, was on the right side of history. Jefferson Davis was on the wrong side.

Understanding knowledge as a process allows us to see that it is right to honor Lincoln with statues, and right to pull down statues of Jefferson Davis, Robert E. Lee, and "Stonewall" Jackson. It is right to leave statues of Washington standing but to remove statues of King George III and take his and all statues of such reactionaries to museums of history where their roles can be presented in context.

But just as we can know that Galileo was wrong from the modern scientific point of view, and study how and why he made what we now recognize as mistakes, we should study carefully how and why Washington and Lincoln were wrong, even as they were right. And, 150 years from now, who knows how people will look back at our incomplete understanding of society and the universe and argue over how much forgiveness they should show toward the failings that will surely arise in our current understanding.

Truth in the Imagination

Imagination and ideas that guide artistic creation do not have the same test as those operating in the physical and natural sciences, or in the study of society and human behavior. Creative dance, music, film, painting, and literature arise from the imagination. They are accepted, or not, by any person based on subjective taste rather than material conditions existing outside of personal opinion, although culturally determined norms on a social level can strongly influence an individual's subjective taste.

Yet even in the arts there are objective limits to successful creative work. Music heard in the imagination of the composer must be executed through the physical properties of instruments, including the human voice, and the physical capacities of the musicians. Every composer knows and works within these tests of practice. We can say the same for choreographers and dancers, or painters and sculptors who are restricted by properties of the people or materials with which they work. Every architect who imagines and sketches a strikingly beautiful design for a building must accept the limits structural engineers impose, resulting from their knowledge of properties of the materials to be used in executing the design so that the building can actually stand up.

Over time, engineers discover new ways to use materials that allow previously impossible structures; skilled craft workers create new musical instruments or pigments, or extend the capacities of existing ones; trainers develop techniques to extend the physical capacity of dancers and musicians. As the material circumstances of artistic expression develop, creative imagination in the arts can extend its scope.

Artistic expression itself, however, is similar to knowledge arising in other areas of life. It, too, is a unity of opposites drawn together into a single process. There is the imaginative, creative spirit. And there is the structured discipline of the art itself—playing the instrument, applying the paint, writing the sentence. In a creative work, these opposites are united into a whole that is neither the raw creative spirit nor the discipline alone, nor some average of the two. It is its own experience, in which the opposites of spirit and discipline, theory and practice, combine to form something that has the character of each but is neither spirit nor discipline, neither theory nor practice.

Creative spirit without discipline is the wild painting of a two-year-old; cute and cherished by its parents, perhaps, but not art. Just playing scales on the piano is not art. It is practice to develop the discipline that can take an imaginative passage of music in the artist's mind and play it, in the world, as art, without having to think about how to make the music as a conscious effort. A creative writer can imagine all kinds of fantastic worlds or situations. These imaginings and evocations of a mood or scene can be expressed in literature, as art, only if they can be molded with the discipline of writing sentences and structuring story. In this sense, art and science share their nature as processes uniting the opposites of theory and practice, imagination and discipline.

Materialism is completely open to the defining importance of ideas and imagination. Far from ignoring or downplaying or denying the centrality of ideas and imagination in the living of life and the formulation of theories, materialism requires them. And, if done well, fiction in a novel or short story, or meaning in a poem, can be true, in that it captures and expresses some aspect of human experience that a reader can recognize.

Beliefs Are Not Theories

As we seek knowledge about society and the physical world, it is important to consider that beliefs are not theories, although these concepts are often conflated. Darwin's writings on the evolution of species, and the work of his followers, constitute evolution as a theory that continues to develop, based on detailed observations of living and fossil records that continue to emerge over time. On the other hand, creationism, based in a literal interpretation of the Bible, is a belief, without observation. Evolution and creationism are not of equal standing or equivalent intellectual or explanatory power, distinguished only by what one chooses to believe. They have different points of reference. Believers in evolution recognize it as a developing theory based in repeated observation of the material world. Believers in creationism recognize it as the word of God as revealed in the Bible, to be taken as truth on that account alone. One is a theory in which people believe as long as material evidence supports it; the other is a belief without requiring material evidence, sustained by faith alone, as long as that faith lasts for the believer.

The controversy in the United States over climate change is another example of differences in points of reference. Careful observations of the planet Earth have led a vast majority of scientists to conclude that human activity, especially the release of carbon dioxide and methane into the atmosphere, is resulting in rising temperatures and climate changes that threaten profound disruption of human society and the extinction of myriad plants and animals. Many executives and workers in carbon fuel industries reject this theory and propose beliefs that are less challenging to their livelihoods and short-term profit. They turn away from what Al Gore aptly termed "an inconvenient truth," beliefs that political representatives of these industries champion in public policy.

But the material world keeps providing evidence that bolsters the science. "More and more of the predicted impacts of global warming are now becoming reality," as the *New York Times* summed it up in late 2017. These include coastal city flooding, ocean warming, disrupted fisheries, longer and more intense storms and fire seasons, and disrupted global supply chains.[7] Today the material evidence has only gathered clarity, revealing ever more destructive effects.

President Trump confronted science with baseless belief in many policy areas. When the most devastating fires in recorded California history ravaged the state in November 2018, Trump blamed it on bad forest management. Scott Austin, president of the Pasadena Fire Fighters Association, responded: "Mr. President, with all due respect, you are wrong. The fires in So. Cal [Southern California] are urban interface fires [where urban development encroaches on forest] and have NOTHING to do with forest management. Come to SoCal and learn the facts & help the victims." Harold Schaitberger, general president of the International Association of Fire Fighters, called Trump's remarks "reckless and insulting."[8]

Facts and Questions

Given the importance of facts in learning how to fight fires, and in the materialist method more generally, it is tempting to be satisfied with the idea that facts can be referenced without regard to the questions they may address—the idea that facts are facts, theories are theories, and the two are wholly distinct. This is the kind of dualism that separates opposites in a way that obscures what is going on in the dynamic interaction of the two parts.

Of course there are facts—elements of reality existing outside and independent of the human mind. And there are ideas and theories that are the product of the human mind. But these completely different elements of knowledge are intimately bound in the dialectic of practice and theory. The sharp separation that poses "fact" and "theory" only as opposites misses their interaction. There are billions of facts. How many exits are there in the room? How many people need a flu shot this year? At what altitude from the earth's surface does human life without external sources of oxygen become impossible for more than three minutes? How many ears of corn typically grow on a single stalk?

These all have facts for answers. But which facts among the billions available should we consider? Which facts are important for us to know? That depends entirely on what the question is. How many exits in the room?

Who cares except if you want to know how quickly the room can empty if there is a fire. Who cares about that? Only if you care whether people die trapped in the fire. That caring, or not, reflects the values and interests of the investigator, whose questions seek to elaborate theories of fire spread and human movement through space. Outside such questions, facts become isolated curiosities, answers in games of trivia. No fact is important or irrelevant in its own right. Every fact requires a theoretical context in which we consider its significance.[9] This reflects the dialectical unity of opposites: theory and fact.

Facts encountered in practice shape theory—theory does not exist without them—but theory can result in practice that not only verifies the facts but discovers or creates new facts, new circumstances, new material conditions, especially in the study of society. We need to recognize and take into account the unity of these two opposites as they drive the spirals of greater understanding.

Knowledge and Social Power

Philosopher Thomas Kuhn demonstrated the history of intense resistance to revising accepted theories.[10] He focused on physics, but his findings are relevant more generally. Believers in existing theory naturally dominate their area of study. They establish their professional prestige, their ability to raise money for research, and their value as consultants and media pundits on the basis of their work within the generally accepted existing theoretical framework. Any deep challenge to that framework is a threat to its advocates, many of whom are in positions of power from which they can marginalize those who disagree, by denigrating their credentials and by casting doubt on the new observations that support the challenge.

Right-wing politicians, pundits, and media figures regularly complain that universities in the US are dominated by liberal or leftist elites who eliminate conservative thinking from academic debate and keep students from access to conservative beliefs. These complaints can resemble what Kuhn was warning about, but they are usually of a very different order. Yes, it is essential to learning that every discipline and theory be subject to critical investigation. But no legitimate claim for that purpose can be made by demanding that the academy open its doors to conspiracy-mongering, junk science with no evidence backing its assertions, or outright lies.

The dynamic Kuhn addresses operates with special force in the social sciences, where theories may challenge the structures of power in society, not just in an area of study. Right-wing claims of universities as hotbeds of closed-minded radicals sound particularly misplaced when reflecting on the experience of Marxism in both communist and capitalist societies through the twentieth century. Kuhn's approach explains why Marxist theory is still quite undeveloped, both in the West and in formerly communist countries, without the deepening and greater sophistication that would have come from unrestricted intellectual and practical work along Marxist lines.

In capitalist countries, Marxism was reviled as a revolutionary challenge to the capitalist system itself. Marx was broadly dismissed in all social sciences. Scholars in the Marxist tradition were often marginalized, denied funding for research, denied publication in mainstream academic journals, and denied tenure at major universities. The Taft-Hartley Act of 1947 stripped government protection from any union that had an officer who refused to swear they were not a member of the Communist Party. The Supreme Court later declared this provision unconstitutional, but the damage was already done. Union organizers oriented toward a Marxist class analysis, not just communists, were hounded out of most unions during the 1950s Cold War era, while unions that continued to protect them were driven out of the AFL-CIO, the principal union federation and center of organized labor after 1955. The anticommunist dragnet that Senators Joseph McCarthy, James Eastland, and other federal and state legislators threw over academic, cultural, political, and public service professionals created a general social climate in which expressions of interest in Marx became intensely dangerous, both to the individual and the institution employing them.

Perhaps surprisingly, in countries dominated by communist parties, Marxism often fared even worse. Academic work, including Marxist analysis, was subject to rigid political control, in these cases to insure that theories and policy proposals matched the thinking of party leaders at the time. The Russian Marxist economist Nikolai Kondratiev, for example, was executed in 1938 after proposing a theory that the Great Depression, beginning in 1929, was another example of "long waves" in capitalist economic activity.[11] Kondratiev had found evidence of such 50–60 year cycles of depression and recovery in historical data from capitalist countries going back into the mid-nineteenth century. But leaders of the Communist Party of the Soviet Union (CPSU) at the time asserted that this view contradicted Marx's theory of economic crisis and undermined the party's claim that the Great Depression was the last gasp of capitalism and would lead to revolution. They could not accept the possibility that capitalist economic recovery could follow the Depression in an upswing of another long wave.

While the CPSU rehabilitated Kondratiev in 1987, as late as 1970 the *Great Soviet Encyclopedia* repeated the view that his long-wave analysis was "one of the vulgar bourgeois theories of crisis and economic cycles … directed against the basic Marxist thesis concerning the inevitability of economic crisis under capitalism, and it conceals the unsolvable contradictions of capitalist society."[12] It's impossible to do serious research and writing under such circumstances of censorship and deliberate misinformation.

The tradition of subjecting academic research to party discipline continues in China, where the practice threatens China's standing in the international community. As professor Priscilla Roberts has noted: "China's avowed objective of developing internationally respected think tanks to boost its soft power and global standing may well be seriously undercut by expectations that these organizations should give policymakers only the advice that they wish to hear, mandates often enforced by the government's ingrained habit of harassing or arresting such institutions' personnel when they deviate from prevailing dictates. Even private think tanks in China are now under pressure to toe the party line, facing closure should they fail to do so, a fate that befell the liberal Beijing-based Unirule Institute of Economics in January 2017."[13]

As we move into an analysis of US social organization appropriate to the tasks of changing it, it is important to pay attention to what the twentieth-century British mathematician and philosopher Bertrand Russell wrote about the relationship between knowledge and authority: "The triumphs of science are due to the substitution of observation and inference for authority. Every attempt to revive authority in intellectual matters is a retrograde step. And it is part of the scientific attitude that the pronouncements of science do not claim to be certain, but only to be the most probable on present evidence. *One of the greatest benefits that science confers upon those who understand its spirit is that it enables them to live without the delusive support of subjective certainty. That is why science cannot favor persecution.*"[14]

I present the ideas in this book without subjective certainty but with confidence that they are reliable assessments, on present evidence, of the conditions in which we live. As we make the road of progressive social change by walking it, we will surely learn more.

Notes

1 Azadeh Moaveni, "Diary: Two Weeks in Tehran," *London Review of Books* 44, no. 21 (November 3, 2022): 45, https://www.lrb.co.uk/the-paper/v44/n21/azadeh-moaveni/diary.

2 Mina P. Shaughnessy, *Errors and Expectations: A Guide for the Teacher of Basic Writing* (Oxford: Oxford University Press, 1979).

3 Psalm 104:5.

4 "Allocution of the Holy Father Pope John Paul II," October 31, 1992, para. 11, accessed August 28, 2021, http://bertie.ccsu.edu/naturesci/Cosmology/GalileoPope.html; original emphasis.

5 "The Galileo Controversy," *Catholic Answers*, August 10, 2004, https://www.catholic.com/tract/the-galileo-controversy; original emphasis.

6 John Williams, *Stoner* (New York: New York Review Books, 2003), 193.

7 Henry Fountain and Brad Plumer, "Damaging Floods, Filthier Air and Political Instability," *New York Times*, November 4, 2017, https://www.nytimes.com/2017/11/03/climate/climate-change-impacts.html.

8 Nicole Rojas, "Donald Trump Should Visit California and 'Learn the Facts' about Wildfires, California Firefighter Association Says," *Newsweek,* November 3, 2017, https://www.newsweek.com/california-firefighter-association-invites-president-trump-learn-facts-about-1211088; original emphasis.

9 E.H. Carr, "The Historian and His Facts," in *What Is History?* (New York: Vintage, 1961), 3–35.

10 Thomas Kuhn, *The Structure of Scientific Revolutions* (Chicago: University of Chicago Press, 1962).

11 Erik Buyst, "Kondratiev, Nikolai (1892–1938)," in *Europe Since 1914: Encyclopedia of the Age of War and Reconstruction*, ed. John Merriman and Jay Winter (New York: Charles Scribner, 2006), 3:1580–81.

12 "Long Cycles, Theory of," in *The Great Soviet Encyclopedia*, 3rd ed. (New York: Macmillan, 1973), 718–19.

13 Priscilla Roberts, "New Perspectives on Cold War History from China," *Diplomatic History* 41, no. 2 (April 2017): 241–304.

14 Bertrand Russell, *The Impact of Science on Society* (New York: Simon and Schuster, 1953), 89; emphasis added.

CHAPTER FOUR

Production in Capitalism

The movements we build address the suffering and injustices people face every day. These arise in the context of the capitalist economic system now dominant the world over. We need to understand why and how economic relations are central to all aspects of social life. This is not a simple set of issues. But understanding them is an essential first step for activists and organizers to be able to ground their work in reality.

Because these matters are not taught in mainstream high school or college economics or political science courses, they remain invisible to most of us. To make matters worse, many people find studying economics a difficult slog. When I have told people I've met that I'm an economist and taught economics at a university, the most common response has been "That was my hardest course! I just couldn't understand it." Don't worry as you read this chapter and the next! This is not the usual economics. You will find that as new concepts become clear, new learning becomes accessible. A new door opens. This chapter lays the foundation for that understanding in the context of the movement issues we face.

The Centrality of Production

To survive, every society must develop a way to produce and distribute what its people need to live, and to raise a new generation of young people. These arrangements constitute the society's economy. Throughout human history, people have created a host of ways to carry out these basic functions.

Societies are obviously enormously complex structures that involve far more than the economy. People create cultures, religious beliefs, and political procedures, as well as institutions to organize and perpetuate them.

All these deeply influence human experience, far beyond the methods of economic life. But, whatever the specifics, economies are at the core of all societies.

The centrality of economic arrangements flows from their necessity to basic survival. In one way or another, people have to produce and distribute what they need to live. If that doesn't happen, nothing else can happen. The society will collapse. In one way or another, culture, religion, and politics need to facilitate, or at least not significantly disrupt, the economic arrangements characteristic of the society. That is what I mean by stressing the central importance of economic organization in any society. In this chapter, our focus will be understanding the economy.

Production is a process with two distinct but completely intertwined aspects, a unity of opposites that are together central in constituting an economy. In one way, production is technical, in that it involves means and methods people use to make and distribute goods and services. These are embodied in society's available technology, tools, and equipment. They are also manifest in the skills of the working population. These are what Karl Marx referred to as "forces of production" or "productive forces." These have developed and become ever more sophisticated over time, especially in recent centuries in countries characterized by capitalism.

But production is also social in that it involves people working in relationships with one another. No society exists on the basis of people working alone to make what they need, in isolation from others around them. A proper study of an economy must recognize and look into both its aspects, the technical and the social. And it must look into the mutual determination of the two by investigating how the technical and the social interact, are interdependent as they shape one another. The dynamic process arising from this mutual determination, this unity of the opposites—the technical and the social—underlies the historical development of economies and societies over time.

Economies differ according to their various technical and social characteristics. Capitalism is only one of many ways people have structured economic activity. It has not always existed in the past. It will not always exist in the future. Like any social structure, capitalism is best understood as a process, a dynamic unfolding rather than as a stable state. It is distinguished from past economic systems—feudalism, slavery, tributary systems, so-called primitive societies—by the relations and forces of production particular to it, relations and forces that in any previous economic system existed in only the most marginal ways, if at all, and that have interacted in ways to create a new history, specific to capitalism.

Who Depends upon Whom? Surplus and Exploitation

If the producing population, whether serfs or enslaved people or workers, can make more than their required needs, the excess can be called "surplus." Every society beyond the most economically primitive has in this sense produced a surplus, and every society has rules for the distribution and use of this surplus. Among North American Northwest Coast First Nations peoples, in what is now Washington State and British Columbia, the surplus was often redistributed to the producers in annual potlatch ceremonies, engaging the entire community in celebrations during which the year's surplus was joyously consumed by all. When the British discovered these societies in the early nineteenth century and came to dominate them, the British forbade such redistributions, thinking them incomprehensible challenges to private property and the good order of society.[1] In what is now New England, the settlers acted similarly in suppressing communal stewardship of the land practiced by the Native peoples.[2]

In most societies, however, the continued presence of a surplus has become the material foundation for exploitation, which is the systematic, forcible taking of what one group of people has produced by another group. These different groups constitute classes—enslaved people and their masters, serfs and the aristocracy, and workers and capitalists. Power dynamics define these classes: the dominant class sets the rules and political and cultural norms required to capture from the subordinate class of producers what the dominant class takes through exploitation. This taking is often invisible, justified by property rules and cultural norms that are internalized by the exploited, who think: "Well, that's just the way things are." And the dynamics tend to exalt the takers and minimize the humanity of the producers.

One of the first and most important uses to which exploiters put the surplus they take is the creation of a military. Because oppression generates resistance, exploiters require police or military forces to impose and secure exploitative relationships against the resistance that producers, the creators of the surplus, mount.

The process by which exploitation takes place varies among different economic systems, as do the political and moral justifications the exploiters present to defend their taking, and the legal arrangements that enforce it. We can distinguish among economic systems by the ways in which exploitation is structured and then justified, always imposed and perpetuated by force, often invisible, but naked when challenged. One of the most powerful and effective means to sustain exploitation has always been to get the exploited to accept their own subordination, to internalize it as natural and appropriate, making resistance to it seem inconceivable. Only when this internalized acceptance breaks down do military force and repressive policing come into the open.

I have found that it is enormously controversial to ask the question whether exploitation exists in capitalism. Exploring that concept is threatening to those who profit by it but also to those who have internalized its naturalness. I've found it helpful to start the discussion with societies that existed largely in the past. We can observe them more easily with some objectivity and then reason forward to the capitalist system.

In slave society, for example, the people who produce are the property of others. They may be sold or traded, and their children become the property of their owners, who exercise complete control over their work, and take the entire product of their labor as their own. The enslaved people of course require food, clothing, and shelter to survive, and the owner has an interest in providing minimum requirements for survival so the working population can continue to work. It can appear that the slave owner is responsible for the enslaved persons' survival since he (it was almost always a man who was the owner) provides them with their necessities. But these are the very products the enslaved people have produced in the first place! They produce everything. The owner only returns a portion of that product to the enslaved people, just enough for their survival, and keeps the change. This is the process of exploitation in slavery, the particular way in which producers (enslaved people in this example) create a surplus that is taken by another group of people (their owners). In providing for his slaves, the owner gives them nothing of his own making. Whatever he provides he has first taken from them.

In feudalism the process is different. The producing population of peasants are no longer themselves the direct property of others. They cannot be sold. They are, however, tied to the land that belongs to others. They have access to the land on which they grow food, raise livestock, and engage in handicraft production. They are required to surrender a portion of their product to the owner of the land in the form of some sort of rent or tax obligation, but may keep for themselves the remainder for their survival. However, the immediate feudal lord, like the slave owner, does not keep the entire surplus for himself. Some is given in taxes or other transfers to higher levels of ruling authority to whom local lords pay tribute, including to religious institutions.

Once again, the producers (the peasants) create more than what they need. This is the surplus taken by the feudal lord for himself, and for those who protect his power. The great Irish Potato Famine of the 1840s resulted from English aristocracy demanding full rent from their Irish serfs, despite failing production because of a potato blight that ruined much of the crop. As a result, millions of Irish peasants emigrated or died of starvation from the operation of a feudal system, at that time subordinated to capitalist England.

It may appear that the serf is beholden to the lord for his survival by permission from the lord to use the land, which is supported by feudal legal arrangements, customs, and traditions. But it is the lord who is beholden to the serf in the material reality of surplus production and its taking. American farmer and UN agricultural advisor William Hinton described a scene he observed in the feudal Chinese village of Long Bow that directly reflected the confusion that can arise about this dynamic. When the Chinese Communist Party first entered Long Bow Village in 1946, as the revolution was spreading through the country, party leaders called local peasants together for a meeting, the first such meeting in the village in twenty years. One urgent question was: "Who depends upon whom for a living?" Hinton tells us that one of the central tasks the party undertook to bring the peasants to power in that village, and across the country, was to get them to understand the material reality that the landlord in fact depended entirely upon them for his wealth and position, while they did not need the landlord at all in order to work and produce; they just needed the land. Many initially held the view that "if the landlords did not let us rent their land we would starve." The peasants came to understand things differently through political education that explained the underlying economic relationships of exploitation in their village.[3]

Slave and feudal societies were of course far more complex than these simple renditions suggest. Each had people in them who were neither enslaved people nor owners, neither serfs nor landed aristocracy. But the characteristic features of the two forms of society that distinguish them are found in the different ways the production of surplus and the process of exploitation were organized in the dominant form of production that involved the great majority of the population in each society.

If we consider society as a whole without reference to the particular forms of economic organization, we can see that everything that is produced comes from the labor of a subset of the population, those who actually create goods and services through their direct labor. This excludes another subset of the population, those who organize, supervise, and control the producers. Today, looking back to these earlier economies, few people would deny that serfs were exploited or that enslaved people didn't create what their owners provided for them.

Yet it remains a central task of the left in today's world to make the analogous but highly controversial case that workers in capitalist economies also create surplus and are exploited through the taking of that surplus by the capitalist class. We will see in later chapters how this process requires engagement in the realms of culture and religion, as well as in direct economic and political conflict. But for the moment, let's focus on the material basis for exploitation in capitalism, which is different from, and more complicated than, the basis of exploitation in earlier societies.[4]

Exploitation in Capitalism

Just as enslaved people made everything, and serfs made everything, so workers today make everything. In capitalism, as in earlier societies, surplus is what is produced beyond what the producing population requires to live and raise a new generation of producers.* These requirements are based in part on physical needs, in part on social norms and traditions. To survive, everyone needs a minimum amount of food, shelter, and clothing. The minimum depends on the climate and the physical intensity of the work. But the required amounts also depend on what we sometimes call the "standard of living," by which we mean the conditions of life we accept as reasonable and proper for working people to experience in a particular place and time. Obviously this can vary widely and can be the subject of intense conflict.

As worker productivity has improved with capitalist development, working people have been able to secure for themselves and their families

---

* In addition to maintaining workers, necessary production involves replacement of tools, equipment, and buildings used up in the production process. If this capital stock is not replaced, those lost resources appear to be surplus, but they actually reflect an unsustainable economy. In accounting terms, we need to focus on net production, after subtracting from gross levels the extent to which equipment and buildings are used up in the production process. We will see in chapter six how this reappears in capitalist degradation of the environment, which in capitalism is treated as a resource that need not be replenished.

a higher standard of living, in which such former luxuries as health care, an array of clothing, and weatherproof housing have come to be the social norm. But these norms are not written in stone, nor are they a biological necessity. Capitalists do not automatically grant these improvements to their workers. They result from often-sharp battles in which workers have demanded from their employers, and from public policy, greater reward for their labor as they have become more productive. These battles continue. Workers' experiences of austerity in recent decades—in the form of wage cuts, erosion of pension benefits, and government cuts in social safety net programs—reflect the power of capital to reduce the expected standard of living, thereby increasing the share of production that capitalists can take as surplus.

With the wages they receive, workers go into the market and claim, through their purchases, a part of what they have created by buying it from businesses the capitalists run. But everything that workers produce belongs at first to the business where the production takes place. When workers build vehicles for General Motors or Toyota, the cars and trucks belong to the company. When workers grow and slaughter hogs for Smithfield Foods, the pork products belong to Smithfield. Of course the owners and managers of these companies do not want the cars, or the bacon, or pork chops. They want the money that can come from the sale of these products in the market.

Since the entire product of the workers starts as the property of business, what is left over after the workers buy what they need continues to belong to the businesses and through them to the capitalists who run them. No less a person than Adam Smith, the original architect of capitalist economics, recognized this fact when he wrote in the eighteenth century: "The value the workmen add to the materials, therefore, resolves itself ... into two parts, of which the one pays their wages, the other the profits of their employer.... He would have no interest to employ them unless he expected from the sale of their work something more than what is sufficient to replace his stock."[5] This leftover portion after the producers—the workers—have claimed their sustenance is the surplus taken by capitalists from them. That is the process of exploitation distinct to capitalist economies.*

---

* Greater exploitation does not necessarily mean greater poverty. More productive workers can demand and receive a higher standard of living even as capitalists can take a greater share of total production as surplus. A steel worker in a US mill is far more exploited than a peasant laborer in rural Guatemala, yet also much better off.

The surplus takes the form of money profits, not hogs or cars. But as we will see below, surplus appears in many other forms in the economy as well.

Beyond wages paid by the employer to support these purchases, some portion of what workers need can be returned to them through government programs like Medicaid and food stamps. These are often derided as signs of "the welfare state" or "entitlements," or termed more neutrally as parts of a "social safety net." But it is far more accurate to understand these programs as part of the "social wage," a channel for providing compensation to the working class that supplements the private wage paid by the employer.

Labor standards change over time as economies develop. Each standard has been the focus of intense conflict in capitalist societies. In US history we have seen this battle play out in the long struggle for the eight-hour day, which became a worldwide rallying cry after the 1886 Haymarket demonstration in Chicago that has ever since been marked each year on May 1 as May Day, "the international workers' day." The long fight against child labor is another example. The conflict continues into our day in efforts to secure mandatory paid sick leave and organizing to increase wages, whether by raising the minimum wage, the Fight for $15, or union contract battles. Recent efforts to defend public education against its privatization into charter schools, as well as efforts to preserve for working class children access to classes in civics, history, and the arts, are examples of the fight over the social wage. We see it also in the determination of some to repeal the Affordable Care Act and to weaken and ultimately abolish Social Security, or at least to raise the standard retirement age to qualify for Social Security benefits—and in the broad popular resistance to these efforts. All these examples bear on the basic question: What does the producing population get back from what they produce, either from the wages they receive from employment or through access to social programs provided by government? All that workers produce beyond these two sources supporting their standard of living is surplus.

Understanding the standard of living solely in terms of goods and services consumed can easily lead to the proposition that "more is better." But this way of thinking drives the consumerism that raises production to levels with catastrophic effects on the environment. And it ignores the wisdom that tells us that, after meeting basic physical requirements for a healthy life, gaining greater wealth does not necessarily lead to greater happiness.[6] Driving people to consume more and more, and more again, leads to closets, basements, and attics full of stuff that people have cast away after the purchases fail to deliver the promised, expected relief from unhappy or stressful lives. We will look at how capitalism requires this extension of commodities in chapter six.

Returning to the question of wages, we have seen that Adam Smith already understood seventy-five years before Karl Marx wrote *Das Kapital* (*Capital*) that it is labor and labor alone that creates value. What Marx added was an understanding of the mechanism by which capitalist exploitation operates, in which the wage plays a central role. The key is to recognize that wages pay the cost of producing and reproducing the worker's ability to work, what Marx called "labor power." *Wages do not correspond to or reflect what workers produce. Wages correspond to what it takes to produce workers.* Surplus arises in the difference between these two: the amount by which what workers produce exceeds what the workers need to go on working and raise children to take their place, at the socially acceptable standard of living, provided either by wages from an employer or government programs.

If this is true, we would expect to find that working class families pass on to their children little or no inheritance at death because they have not been able to accumulate more than what was needed to reach the end of their life. We find evidence of this in data reporting the pattern of inheritance in the US population. As expected, working class families leave little or nothing in inheritance. A 2017 Federal Reserve Board study found that only "twenty-three percent of white families (heads aged 30 to 59) have ever received an inheritance, compared to nine percent of Black families and just five percent of Hispanic families."[7] As expected if wages pay only enough to reproduce the worker, over three-quarters of white families and over 90% of Black families have nothing at the end of their lives to leave to their children.

Unsurprisingly, when money does pass down through inheritance, racial and wealth inequalities increase across generations. A 2018 Brookings Institution study found that: "among households receiving an inheritance in 2020, those with economic income over $1 million are, on average, expected to inherit $3 million, while those with economic income under $50,000 are expected to inherit only $62,000.... Inheritances also magnify wealth disparities by race. White households are twice as likely as black households to receive an inheritance. Moreover, receipt of an inheritance is associated with a $104,000 increase in median wealth among white families, but only a $4,000 increase among black families."[8]

This understanding of wages is completely different from the understanding mainstream economics presents. We usually learn in school that wages buy the worker's time at work, whether as an hourly wage, a weekly or annual salary, or by piece rate or commission. In focusing on these methods of payment for time or effort, mainstream approaches render exploitation a meaningless concept. They hide the relationship between labor and capital that creates surplus in capitalist economies, surplus that is the material foundation of profit.

In economics and the popular culture, we tend to think of "capital" as either a sum of money people invest to make a profit, or physical capital goods like machinery and factory buildings. There is some truth in these definitions, but they are one-sided. They see capital only as things, or an amount of money, but neglect the foundation of all capital, which lies in the *social relationships* from which all capital arises. These relationships operate between workers and their business employers, and between the working class as a whole and the capitalist class as a whole. They are the social forms of the technical aspects of the capitalist production process.

Social Production for Private Ends

In the US, and in Western capitalist societies generally, people are taught that their destiny is in their own hands, that we are responsible as individuals for our own situation. We learn that capitalists are wealthy because they have taken risks, because they have been clever enough and entrepreneurial enough to stake out a market niche and satisfy it with a product or service people want to buy. On the other end of social experience, poor people are supposedly poor because of some personal failing. They are lazy. They are not very bright. They have poor skills and attitudes that employers find repellent. All along the social spectrum, we are given to understand that people find themselves more or less in accordance with their own doing.

We cannot build movements of collective action unless we get to the heart of why these ways of thinking are wrong, how they do not match the material reality of society. Of course capitalists take risks in their decisions (although almost always mainly with other people's money). Of course poor people often lack marketable skills and are sometimes resentful of close supervision at work. But these individual conditions exist in a social network that shapes those conditions and establishes power relationships among us. If we are to challenge that structure of power, we have to put our understanding of private circumstances in the context of social structures. That requires looking more deeply into how capitalism works.

The system in which producers are paid with money wages differs in important ways from slave and feudal orders. Producers—workers—in capitalism get almost nothing of their needs from retaining or having returned to them the immediate products of their labor from their immediate masters, as was the method of support for serfs or enslaved people. One consequence of this is that, whereas serfs or slaves survived on the basis of what they produced locally, workers survive on the basis of what the entire working class produces. To understand how workers survive, how surplus is created in capitalism, and how it ends up in the hands of the capitalists, we have to look at the way the entire system operates as an integrated whole, rather than focusing on the local terms of labor that formed the basis of earlier societies.

While workers produce in specific businesses run by particular capitalists, workers produce their sustenance, and all surplus, literally as a class. A worker making jet engines does not directly consume any part of those engines. A worker making furniture may buy a sofa every ten years, but she gets sustenance from the food, clothing, and other goods made by workers she does not know or work with. As Adam Smith put it, "In civilized society, [a person] stands in need at all times of the cooperation and assistance of great multitudes, while his whole life is scarce sufficient to gain the friendship of a few persons."[9] This was not true in precapitalist societies because such a large network of mutual dependence required for production did not yet exist.

In capitalism, for the first time in history, production is a process that integrates the entire society. Historians and economists often recognize this in the ways capitalist development opens national and global markets and leads to the formation of nation-states and international trading regimes like the World Trade Organization and the European Union. These social and economic institutions were unheard-of and impossible before capitalism developed.

When compared with the immediate and directly personal exploitation enslaved people and serfs encountered in their local environments, the social character of capitalist production results in the exploitative character and processes of capitalist economies being more hidden. Workers in a given business enter into an exploitative relationship that extends far beyond their immediate employers. Capitalism involves classwide dynamics invisible at the immediate workplace, unseen in the production of surplus before it can become visible when embodied in products, activities, and money.

Even though workers often face more or less hostile relations with their immediate employers over the pace of work, wages, benefits, and other conditions of employment, they are, together with all other workers, exploited not so much by their own employer as by an entire other class, the capitalist class, which extends far beyond their own employer. And they share with workers they do not know, in other industries and places, the need to identify and respond, as a class, to the class they face in common. Yet workers enter into this system as individuals, apparently separated from other workers and the production process as a whole, which appears alien and external to them. This alienation causes each of us to lose touch with our very real and substantial ties to the common humanity that, in fact, is engaged in production.

The social character of capitalist production is embedded in the production process itself. It shapes the ways in which the working and capitalist classes come into existence and engage one another. This relationship shows up as another basic contradiction in capitalist society: the interactions of social and private forces forming a unity of opposites inherent to capitalism itself.

Capitalist production is social in several different ways. First, the division of labor in a business means that no individual worker makes the entire product. The firm's work force as a whole produces its output as a social network coordinated by managers who represent capitalist owners. Second, workers in the enterprise use materials produced in other businesses by other workers, often in faraway places, sometimes linked in global supply chains. So capitalist production leads workers as a class into social relationships with capitalists as a class. Finally, the economy is social even in the competition among individual capitalists because each capitalist relates to all other capitalists while seeking to capture the largest possible part of the total surplus.

The other side of this social production is the need, in capitalism, for the total product that working people create socially to be distributed into many individual private hands. We've seen that workers get their share of the socially produced output returned to them as individuals when they take their wages into the market to buy what they need to live and bring up a new generation of workers. Capitalists get their share in the form of private profits. Through market competition, the relatively more efficient or powerful businesses receive in money profit a relatively greater part of the total surplus produced.

We have seen that production in general is a unity of opposites involving its technical and social aspects. Capitalist production in particular is also driven by the unity of opposites, those involving its social and private character. We will return to look at the implications of this contradiction in chapter six.

In their consumption, workers compete with each other for access to means of survival. Those with higher incomes are able to take a greater part of what the class has made than people with lower incomes can. Workers also compete with each other in the distribution of the social wage. Government programs that provide Medicaid, public education, subsidized housing, and other goods and services go to some working class families more than others. Workers with incomes higher than the cutoff to receive benefits like food stamps or Section 8 housing support sometimes resent their taxes going to those poorer than themselves.

Workers also give prominence to their personal competitive position in relation to other workers who are competing for work. We see this in the ways workers in construction trades have long resisted opening the trades to new racial and ethnic groups, or in the more general resistance of native-born workers to the inclusion of immigrants on equal terms, or the resistance of men to the employment of women to work beside them. The fact that the social process of capitalist exploitation is hidden in market operations too often leads workers to embrace what can seem on the surface like an entirely rational individualism. To confront the system as a whole, every organizer has to understand the necessity and complexity of portraying the power of collective action with other workers across the divisions of race, gender, ethnicity, and industry.

The contradiction of the social and private aspects of capitalism, this unity of opposites at the heart of capitalism, is easily obscured by the one-sided centrality of markets and private property in capitalist society. Almost everything in capitalist culture and society's teachings stresses the value, significance, and righteousness of individual responsibility, entrepreneurship, market discipline, and initiative. Every captain of industry, finance, or commerce likes to claim their place at the top is a result of their own efforts and skill. Every worker scraping by paycheck to paycheck supposedly needs to work harder or get training for skills "the market" requires. Poor people are supposed to pull themselves up by their bootstraps. The examples are endless. While it is true that individuals are responsible for their actions, propositions that leave it at that share the effect of erasing the social character of production by making every individual's situation strictly a personal matter. They all blunt workers' understanding of the social structures that constrain and shape their individual lives and prospects. When times get hard, this often results in unwarranted self-blame as well as resentment toward other workers.

When President Barack Obama pointed out during his 2012 presidential campaign that "if you've got a business, you didn't build that," Republicans jumped all over him for denigrating Apple's founder Steven Jobs and business leaders everywhere. Defenders of the president pointed out that the quote was taken out of context, in that critics ignored his shout-out to teachers, builders of infrastructure, and government programs that contributed to the development of the internet, all increasing the ability of the individual business leader to be successful. The *Washington Post* fact-checker column analyzing Republican presidential candidate Mitt Romney's attack on Obama for this comment gave Romney a shameful three "Pinocchios" for his seriously false characterization. But even with this rebuke, and in the supporting quotes provided by the *Washington Post* from Andrew Carnegie, Franklin D. Roosevelt, and Elizabeth Warren, the fact-checker's description of the social context of private wealth accumulation missed the main point. It did not include any reference to the workers who did the actual production that created what the business brought to market.[10]

Without understanding the social character of production and exploitation, workers are left to believe in the overwhelming importance of the competitive position of their own particular company. They make concessions to management to save their jobs, too often in vain. Companies can even get workers to compete with one another on a plant-specific basis, in which workers in the same company outbid each other to take lower wages and suffer worse conditions in their own plant so it can remain open while the company shuts other plants in the self-defeating (from the workers' point of view) downward spiral of wages and benefits that we have seen in recent decades.

To be sure, the capitalist class claims the surplus in the form of profits on the basis of property rights encoded in law and legitimized through long-standing (capitalist) custom. But slaveholders and feudal aristocrats had their own versions of property rights and customs which, to modern eyes accustomed to seeing the world in capitalist terms, now seem antiquated and oppressive. Modern eyes can and must come to see and challenge this same dynamic of exploitation in its modern capitalist form.

Notes

1   Rene R. Cadacz, "Potlatch," *The Canadian Encyclopedia*, October 24, 2019, accessed August 28, 2021, https://thecanadianencyclopedia.ca/en/article/potlatch#:~:text=and%20 fishing%20territories.-,History,and%20wasteful%20of%20personal%20property.

2   William Cronon, *Changes in the Land: Indians, Colonists, and the Ecology of New England* (New York: Hill and Wang, 1983).

3   William Hinton, *Fanshen* (New York: Monthly Review Press, 1966), 128–30.

4   For an excellent presentation, see Robert Heilbroner, *The Nature and Logic of Capitalism* (New York: W.W. Norton, 1986).

5   Adam Smith, *An Inquiry into the Nature and Causes of the Wealth of Nations* (New York: Modern Library, 1937 [1776]), 48.

6   Elizabeth Bruenig, "Wealth Doesn't Make the Rich Happier, But Poverty Makes the Poor Sadder," *New Republic*, January 27, 2015, https://newrepublic.com/article/120859/ money-doesnt-buy-happiness-poverty-increases-sadness-study.

7   Jeffrey P. Thompson and Gustavo A. Suarez, "Updating the Racial Wealth Gap," Finance and Economics Discussion Series 2015-076. (Washington, DC: Board of Governors of the Federal Reserve System, November 7, 2017), 15, http://dx.doi.org/10.17016/FEDS.2015.076r1.

8   Lily L. Batchelder, "Leveling the Playing Field between Inherited Income and Income from Work through an Inheritance Tax," in *Tackling the Tax Code: Efficient and Equitable Ways to Raise Tax Revenue*, ed. Jay Shambaugh and Ryan Nunn (Washington, DC: Hamilton Project, Brookings Institution, 2018), accessed March 28, 2023, https://www.hamiltonproject.org/ assets/files/Batchelder_LO_FINAL.pdf.

9   Smith, *Wealth*, 14.

10   Glenn Kessler, "An Unoriginal Obama Quote—Taken Out of Context," *Washington Post*, July 23, 2012, https://www.washingtonpost.com/blogs/fact-checker/post/an-unoriginal- obama-quote-taken-out-of-context/2012/07/20/gJQAdG7hyW_blog.html?utm_term=. db27d65d6a22.

CHAPTER FIVE

Classes and Surplus in Capitalism

Now that we've looked at the broad meaning of class in various economic structures, it's time to look at what class means in the practical functioning of capitalist society, using the US as our example. Activists and organizers need to know in some detail the class structure that underpins our economy because it clarifies the source of the structures of social power. This knowledge will be helpful in guiding our struggles over the size and priorities of government budgets and finding ways to alleviate the suffering of the poor and near poor who number nearly half of all our people. It will help direct an effective challenge to gross economic and social inequality. It will help us to understand and reverse the slowdown in economic growth over recent decades and deal with the many other issues that hang in the balance of power in society.

In chapter four we saw where surplus comes from. In this chapter, we'll see how important it is to trace surplus in capitalist society and challenge the distribution of that surplus, to redirect the surplus to socially productive uses.

Classes in Capitalist Society

Discussions of class in the US often rest on measures of income to distinguish a broad "middle class" from smaller groups of "rich" and "poor" people at its margins. Even though politicians, journalists, media pundits, and academics often refer to "the middle class" to represent the typical person and the object of their concerns, this way of thinking leads to confused understanding and misdirected politics.

The focus on income and wealth obscures the most important feature of class, that *class is a question of power*. Power is by its nature a relationship—a person has power only if someone or something else has less, or none. Enslaved person and master, serf and lord, worker and capitalist: these are classes defined by the relative power of one over the other. In our language about class, when the working class disappears into the middle class and the capitalist class disappears into the rich, we lose sight of the contours of power in society. Then the key players appear to vanish from the dynamic economic, political, and cultural conflicts we see all around us, and we lose orientation in political work.

To measure the class structure of the US, I use a person's occupation to approximate the power the person holds in the scheme of economic activity. I have found that occupation is the best single indicator of class position, more reliable than income, wealth, or education, although these measures are certainly related to occupation and class.

Working class people have little control over the pace and content of their work and are subject to more or less close supervision by management. They are factory and construction workers, but also tens of millions of people in service industries working as nurses, home health aides, call center workers, technicians, truck drivers, security guards, and sales people. The capitalist class—senior corporate executives and board members—are the opposite pole to the working class. They are the people who have ultimate authority over a business, and the power to direct the activities of the workers they employ.

There is also a middle class, operating in economic spaces between labor and capital. It is composed of three broad groups: managers and supervisors who ultimately report to the most senior executives, small-business owners, and professionals. People in these occupations share some characteristics and attitudes with capitalists, while exhibiting some characteristics and attitudes more aligned with workers. They tend to champion private property and value their authority over others, but they also chafe under the power of those above them in the economic power structure. For example, small-business owners can have difficulty in obtaining credit for their businesses, they suffer relatively heavier costs of government regulation compared with what larger corporations must pay, and they suffer more from the effects of government austerity programs. They are upwardly mobile, but many have grown up in working class families and retain some cultural and political allegiances to that personal history.

Corporate personnel departments often misclassify workers as "managers" to avoid paying overtime normally due working people. A *New*

York Times report highlighted an academic study that found that "the practice of mislabeling workers as managers to deny them overtime, which often relies on such dubious titles as 'lead reservationist' and 'food cart manager,' cost the workers more than $4 billion per year, or more than $3,000 per mislabeled employee." These "managers" are paid a salary independent of the number of hours they work. "The tactic is especially common in low-wage industries like retail, dining, and janitorial services."[1] The US Department of Labor does not follow that deceptive practice in the data I report here.

Middle class professionals, managers, and small-business owners whose work is most closely tied to the lives of workers have suffered economic reverses over the last forty years, along with the class they serve. Those whose work is most closely linked with the capitalist class, on the other hand, have done very well over time, as has the class that they serve. This pattern is revealed, for example, in the different experiences of lawyers in top corporate law firms, whose incomes have increased dramatically, contrasted with lawyers in small practices serving the basic needs of working people in matters of divorce, wills, and claiming unemployment and disability benefits.

We also see evidence of this bifurcation, this hollowing out in the middle class, in personal consumption spending. Luca Solca, chief luxury goods analyst at Wall Street firm Bernstein, found in 2023 that "more people are flocking to spending on luxury goods after having survived Covid lockdowns.... The middle class did suffer and is hollowing out. But the wealthy were untouched, and the upper middle class is spending on all fronts."[2]

Power and autonomy are not precise concepts when applied to people's work environment. A long-haul truck driver may have the ability to decide whether to drive from New York City to Cleveland across Pennsylvania via I-80 or on the Pennsylvania Turnpike. But that power of choice pales in comparison with the power of his boss to order him to make the trip, or to monitor electronically the time of every stop for food or a bathroom break. Some occupations include both people with considerable authority and others with rather little. Schoolteachers, for example, can have a fair amount of control over what and how they teach, especially when their students are children of senior corporate, cultural, political, or academic elites. They are middle class professionals. Other teachers are skilled workers with relatively little autonomy. They teach in schools where the students come from poor and working class families, where school district management tightly controls classroom instruction to meet the needs of standardized tests. Medical doctors, who until recently had ownership and substantial autonomy in their own practices or partnerships, have increasingly been absorbed into the employed, highly skilled, labor force of large hospital and health care behemoths.

In this new environment, doctors are finding unions increasingly attractive for the collective power they require to protect their incomes and working conditions in giant medical complexes. But like university professors who also have turned to union representation, doctors retain enough control over their work, and the work of nurses and other medical providers under their supervision, to be in the professional middle class.

Keeping to the idea of class as a question of power, it is best to consider as capitalists those who have the most senior authority in their companies. They give strategic direction to the firm while their employees do the actual work of the business under the supervision of middle class managers. The senior executives and board of directors—members of the capitalist class—decide what the company's workers produce, what technology they use, how and where the business sells its products, how it structures its finances, and how it relates to government agencies.*

In our highly developed economy, the traditional idea of the capitalist as the personal owner of the company is no longer relevant. Millions of people own all the major corporations in the economy through stocks that are distributed far beyond those who actually have power over corporate decisions. Even though senior executives and corporate board members often own significant amounts of company shares (yet almost always a tiny fraction of all outstanding shares), those shares are not what give them power. Their power comes from their positions of authority in the corporate decision-making process. While in a few cases a single shareholder dominates a major company, as Tesla is dominated by Elon Musk, that is not the typical situation.

The US Department of Labor publishes data on the number of people employed in nearly six hundred detailed occupations, as well as the racial,

---

* We can distinguish between small-business owners in the middle class, who generally employ fewer than twenty people and work side by side with their employees while running the business, from the top executives of larger corporations who are in the capitalist class, who are removed from the production process, run the work force through an intermediate layer of management, and limit their work to giving strategic guidance to the firm.

gender, and ethnic composition of each. I sorted through each of those occupations, assigning the employees in each to the working class or middle class depending on the degree of autonomy they can exercise in their work.

Reflecting this method, Table 1 reports the class composition of the US labor force in 2019, the last year before the COVID-19 pandemic disrupted, at least temporarily, large sections of the employment picture. Truck drivers, for example, are in the "transportation and material moving" category. They are all in the working class. Supervisors in that category, and all other supervisors, enter the data as middle class managers.

Table 1 shows that the working class in 2019 was about 62% of the labor force. This ratio has been stable since at least the mid-1980s, as reported in the two editions of my book *The Working Class Majority: America's Best Kept Secret,*[3] and my earlier essay "Class and Poverty in the United States."[4] Data indicate that the working class suffered a disproportionate share of the jobs lost at the height of the COVID-19 pandemic, but we cannot yet know what long-term impact COVID-19 disruptions may have on US class structure.[5]

Because of the way the Department of Labor reports occupational data, the middle class counted in Table 1 includes some people I would count separately as the capitalist class—senior executives not limited to CEOs, and members of the boards of directors of corporations with at least one layer of management between the senior executives and the workforce. Adding up people with these functions, the capitalist class is about 2% of the labor force, while the middle class of supervisors, managers, small-business owners, and professional people are about 36%.

Unemployed people are in the class of their most recent occupation. Teachers, nurses, college adjunct instructors, and some other occupations divide between working and middle class life along fuzzy boundaries that make numerical precision impossible. For example, as rough approximations I counted 60% of K–12 teachers as skilled working class people and 40% as professional middle class, corresponding to the class composition of their students' families. Based on a close study of nursing jobs, I counted three-quarters of all nurses as skilled workers and one-quarter in the managerial and professional middle class.

But these ambiguities, though worthwhile to analyze closely, are relatively small in the overall picture. Despite the usual story, the US is not a middle class society. It is a society whose great majority are working class people, what I've called "America's best kept secret."

Table 1. Class Composition of US Labor Force in 2019

Employment by Occupation, 2019 (in thousands)

Occupational Group	Total	Middle Class	Middle Class (% of total)	Working Class	Working Class (% of total)
Managerial occupations*	18,985	18,985	100.0	0	0.0
Business and financial operations occupations	7,997	5,707	71.4	2,290	28.6
Professions and related occupations	37,234	25,654	68.9	11,580	31.1
Service (including health support)	26,977	2,379	8.8	24,598	91.2
Sales and related occupations	15,583	4,514	29.0	11,069	71.0
Office and administrative support	17,788	1,306	7.3	16,482	92.7
Farming, fishing, and forestry	1,156	51	4.4	1,105	95.6
Construction, extraction, maintenance, installation, and repair	13,190	954	7.2	12,236	92.8
Production	8,566	844	9.8	7,722	90.2
Transportation and material moving	10,061	435	4.3	9,626	95.7
Total employed	**157,537**	**60,829**	**38.6**	**96,708**	**61.4**
Unemployed	5,888	1,472	25.0	4,416	75.0
Total	**163,425**	**62,301**	**38.1**	**101,124**	**61.9**

* Includes 1,602,000 CEOs and other senior executives who are in the capitalist class, not shown separately.

Sources: US Department of Labor, Bureau of Labor Statistics, "Household Data Annual Averages 11. Employed Persons by Detailed Occupation, Sex, Race, and Hispanic or Latino Ethnicity (Numbers in Thousands)," accessed January 2, 2021, https://www.bls.gov/cps/cpsaat11.htm. Data on unemployed from US Department of Labor, Bureau of Labor Statistics, Employment Situation News Release, June 7, 2019. https://www.bls.gov/news.release/archives/empsit_06072019.htm.

Table 2. Workers in Alternative Arrangements as Percent of Total Employed, 1995–2017

Type of worker	Feb 1995	Feb 1997	Feb 1999	Feb 2001	Feb 2005	May 2017
Independent contractors	6.7	6.7	6.3	6.4	7.4	6.9
On-call workers	1.7	1.6	1.5	1.6	1.8	1.7
Temporary help agency workers	1.0	1.0	0.9	0.9	0.9	0.9
Workers provided by contract firms	0.5	0.6	0.6	0.5	0.6	0.6
Total	**9.9**	**9.9**	**9.3**	**9.4**	**10.7**	**10.1**

Source: US Department of Labor, Bureau of Labor Statistics, "Independent Contractors Made Up 6.9 Percent of Employment in May 2017," *TED: The Economics Daily*, https://www.bls.gov/opub/ted/2018/independent-contractors-made-up-6-point-9-percent-of-employment-in-may-2017.htm.

Most workers have regular full-time jobs. In recent years, with greater attention paid to the gig economy, contingent employment has drawn special scrutiny. But, as Table 2 shows, from 1995 to 2017 the fraction of the workforce in all forms of contingent employment has remained remarkably stable, at around 10%.

This surprising finding may indicate that contingent employment, while growing no more extensive over these twenty-two years, is getting more public attention because of the aggressive organizing among these workers in the Fight for $15 campaigns, among adjunct teachers in higher education, and among Uber and other gig workers. Or the data in Table 2 may underestimate the possibly greater recent prevalence of these work arrangements because the table reflects only a person's primary job, with no accounting for side employment that may have increased the numbers of people in the gig economy. In this regard, it's worth noting that in 2022, "the majority of gig economy participants have a full time position in addition to their gig work."[6] These forms of more tenuous attachment to employment are not characteristic of working class experience as a whole.

Capitalism emerged with the creation of its two defining classes: the working class and the capitalist class. Together they constitute capitalism's basic power grid, in which capital dominates labor. The middle class is in the middle of this power grid, often caught in the cross fire. But these are not the only classes. Remnants of the old landed aristocracy may continue to wield power, especially where agricultural practices are not yet modernized as capitalism emerges in towns and cities. Slavery was an integral part of the early development of capitalism, whether in the cotton it provided to the early English textile mills and those in America's New England, or in the profits the slave trade generated for British merchants in Liverpool and Bristol, and Americans in Charleston and Mobile.

Workers rely on wage labor, no longer tied to the land as a serf, no longer the property of an owner/master. Workers have the freedom to quit a job to break the power relation with a particular employer. This is the freedom capitalism promises its workforce. But, after quitting one job, in almost all cases the worker needs to find another in the same basic class position. Capitalists have workers working for them no matter in which job, and fire them when they are no longer a source of profit.

In the lead-up to the Civil War, one of the most influential apologists for slavery, George Fitzhugh of Virginia, taunted abolitionists on exactly this point. In his 1857 book *Cannibals All*, he mocked the idea of freedom in Northern capitalist society.[7] Slave owners, Fitzhugh claimed, had to treat their property well and make sure they were healthy enough to work. Capitalists, he derisively argued, just threw their workers out when they were no longer wanted, paying no attention to their needs, leaving them to starve.

The individual freedom of wage labor soon runs up against the constraints imposed on the individual by capitalist structures of surplus creation and associated property rules. While it is true that an *individual* worker may escape his class position and rise to capitalist status, or self-employment in a small business, this is obviously not possible on a broad social scale, since that would involve and require the disappearance of the working class from the economy. In capitalism, there must continue to be a population of producers, that is a working class that does the work of creating and capturing the surplus on behalf of the capitalist class that employs it.

The US Department of Labor each year estimates the number of new jobs it expects will come into the labor market in the coming decade, specified by job category. They forecast that for the eighteen categories they expect will add over 100,000 positions in the decade ending in 2031, 67% will be working class jobs. Some middle class jobs will also add over 100,000 positions, such as financial managers and management analysts. But the single largest growth will be among home health and personal care aids (expected to add 924,000 jobs in the decade). The list also includes such jobs as fast food workers, stockers and order fillers, light truck drivers, and laborers.[8] So, according to these estimates, we can expect that the class composition of the US labor force will be only marginally changed by 2031 compared with its composition in 2019.

One important implication of this structural feature of the economy is that it imposes a limit on the so-called American Dream of upward mobility. Middle class professionals tend to think their social position should be taken as the standard of personal success. But as we have just seen, nearly seven out of ten new jobs in the ten years running to 2031 will not afford professional standing. As long as "upward mobility" into professional and managerial life is the norm by which society judges personal success, the majority of the workforce is consigned to a supposedly unsuccessful life.

This may not be the conscious thought of liberals who wish the best for working people, but because the wish is divorced from reality it necessarily creates a dominant culture of imagined inferiority and failure among working class people who do not achieve the standard. This culture leads to resentment among working class people toward the liberals who have declared such aspirations on their behalf. A better path is to accept the legitimacy of all honest work and the fact that there's nothing unsuccessful in the life of a janitor or home health worker or truck driver who enjoys respect on the job while aspiring to a loving family, stable work, good health, reliable friends, a vacation every year, and good rest in retirement.

These three basic classes in capitalist society—capitalist and working classes, with the middle class in between—are not the end of the story. There is above them all a ruling class.[9] This class is composed of the most influential people in the country, who participate in the networks of power that shape society. While the capitalist class is composed of those with strategic power in their own business, the ruling class operates at a different level, providing overall strategic direction for broad swaths of society. It involves a small number of capitalists, and it includes some people who are not capitalists. Its members are people who are in positions to coordinate activity across industries and establish political and cultural norms. These are people who sit on multiple corporate boards, comprising what is sometimes called an interlocking network of directors, and senior corporate executives who meet together in private policy groups like the Business Roundtable, which includes the CEOs of the two hundred largest corporations in the country. The ruling class also includes top government officials—members of Congress, the Supreme Court, the president and top cabinet officers.

Table 3. Gender, Racial, and Ethnic Composition of US Classes in 2019

Percentages of Employed Labor Force by Gender, Race, and Ethnicity*

	Women	Men	Black	Asian	Hispanic[†]	White
Employed labor force	47.0	53.0	12.3	6.5	17.6	77.7
Working class	47.8	52.2	14.0	4.8	21.5	74.4
Middle class[‡]	44.6	55.4	8.9	8.7	10.6	77.9

* Racial totals here do not add to 100% since they do not include Native Americans, Native Alaskans, and Native Hawaiians and Pacific Islanders.
† *Hispanic* is an ethnic category of any race.
‡ Includes CEOs and other senior executives in the capitalist class.

Source: US Department of Labor, Bureau of Labor Statistics, "Labor Force Statistics from the Current Population Survey," Table 11, Employed Persons by Detailed Occupation, Sex, Race, and Hispanic or Latino Ethnicity, January 22, 2020, https://www.bls.gov/cps/cpsaat11.htm.

These people are typically not capitalists themselves, although many are. The ruling class also includes senior media executives governing the content of leading platforms, and education figures at top universities (public as well as private). They are not capitalists, but they help shape political expectations, intellectual standards, and cultural norms for the country. The total is a small number of people. Altogether, I've figured that the entire US ruling class could fit into the seats of New York's Yankee Stadium, around 55,000 people.

Classes are not homogeneous groups. They are all complicated amalgams of people of different races, genders, and ethnicities. Table 3 shows that in 2019 women were nearly half of employed people (47%), but they were overrepresented in the working class (47.8%) and underrepresented in the middle and capitalist classes (44.6%). Blacks and Hispanics were also overrepresented in the working class, while white and Asian people were overrepresented in the middle and capitalist classes. Whites, 77.7% of the employed labor force, were underrepresented in the working class, where they were 74.4% of the class.

While Asians were somewhat overrepresented in the middle class, there were nevertheless millions of poor and working class people of Asian heritage in the US. We cannot conclude from these data that Asian people are a "model minority" who live in affluent conditions. In the 2020 COVID-19

Table 4. Class Composition of US Racial and Ethnic Groups in 2019

	Total Employed in Millions	Percent in Working Class	Percent in Middle Class*	Percent Chief Executives
Women	73.4	63.0	36.4	0.6
Men	84.1	60.0	38.6	1.4
Total employed	**157.5**			
Black	18.9	71.6	28.1	0.3
Asian	10.1	46.4	52.7	0.9
Hispanic	27.2	76.4	23.2	0.4
White	119.3	60.3	38.5	1.2
Total %†		**61.4**	**37.6**	**1.0**

* Includes senior executives in the capitalist class other than CEOs.

† Unlike Table 1, unemployed persons are not included here.

Source: US Department of Labor, Bureau of Labor Statistics, "Labor Force Statistics from the Current Population Survey," Table 11, Employed Persons by Detailed Occupation, Sex, Race, and Hispanic or Latino Ethnicity, January 22, 2020, https://www.bls.gov/cps/cpsaat11.htm.

economic crisis, Asian renters faced the second most prevalent threat of eviction (20%), closely behind 22% of African American renters, compared with 9% of whites with rent past due.[10] And as Brian Chen reported in the *New York Times*: "The Asian-American story has been a complicated narrative. There are the restaurant workers and massage therapists nested in metropolitan enclaves, but there are also the high achievers attending elite schools who end up in well-compensated careers.... Asian-Americans are becoming the most economically divided demographic in the country. In 2016, their incomes ranged from about $12,000 at the 10th percentile to roughly $133,500 at the 90th percentile, with a median of about $51,000, according to the Pew Research Center. That compares with [a range of] about $15,100 and $118,000 for whites."[11]

While the working class was 61.4% of all employees (not counting the unemployed), Table 4 shows that 63% of all women employed in 2019 were in the working class. Hispanic and Black people were most heavily present in the working class (76.4% and 71.6%, respectively), while less than half of all Asians were part of the working class.

Tables 3 and 4 together show that neither classes nor races nor ethnic groups are homogeneous in their social positions and experiences. This situation reflects and generates complicated social dynamics that we will explore in later chapters.

The impersonal and systemic quality of capitalist exploitation has an important and perhaps surprising consequence: no matter how fair, reasonable, and respectful a particular individual employer may be with their workforce, it does nothing to free those workers from the exploitation arising from capitalism as an entire system. Wage workers continue to be caught in a structure of economic activity that places them, together with all other workers, in a subordinate class within a social process that exploits a surplus from it, a surplus taken by a class of others in society who are not producers but who direct them.

I've defined classes here in terms of the position people occupy in the power relationships embedded in production. But classes are produced and reproduced as well in a much more complex network of cultural and political relationships that tend to reflect relative power in production but are not directly tied to it. We got a sense of this as it relates to politics in chapter two. We will return to these aspects of class in later chapters as well.

Productive and Unproductive Labor

The distinction between productive and unproductive labor is another example of a critical issue almost entirely absent from mainstream economics and media attention. Yet the distinction has a long history in economic analysis going back to Adam Smith, David Ricardo, and other economists in the era of early capitalist development. Marx made a detailed analysis of this question, evaluating its many formulations in that literature.[12] More recently, Paul Baran and Paul Sweezy made the distinction a centerpiece of their analysis of modern capitalism.[13]

Because it is today unfamiliar territory, some will find what follows hard to understand. But it's worth persevering for a vital reason. This distinction explains the material foundation and legitimacy of the claim the working class and its allies have for a greater share of the wealth now so highly concentrated in the upper echelons of our society. Furthermore, understanding this distinction is essential for us to understand one of the most important and troubling aspects of modern capitalism—the slowdown in economic growth and great increases in inequality of income and wealth in recent decades. This distinction is central to understanding the process of capital accumulation and the uses to which surplus is put. It's a distinction that explains the justice and fairness of the demand that a part of the surplus workers produce ought to be diverted from capitalist control and subject instead to social control devoted to raising the working class standard of living.

The terms, unfortunately, can be confusing. The distinction between productive and unproductive activity has several different meanings in colloquial discussions of economic matters, all of which lead away from reality. In ordinary speech, "productive" sometimes means useful, while "unproductive" means useless or wasted activity. Sometimes people think of productive activity as limited to the private sector, while all government activity is characterized as inherently unproductive. The word "productive" can suggest necessary; "unproductive" the opposite. Or "productive" can mean desirable, "unproductive" taken as unwanted. We need to set aside these often-pejorative colloquial senses of the word "unproductive." We need to get at the meaning of these terms in a way that will allow us to understand their significance for the political and economic issues we face.

This requires us to link our understanding of these terms to the most fundamental question in capitalism: What does it take to create surplus that can become capital? In this sense, productive means productive of surplus. Any work that creates surplus from which capital arises is called productive. Any work that does not create surplus is called unproductive.

Recognizing the importance of the distinction between productive and unproductive labor in capitalist markets challenges a standard claim in mainstream economics. Economists usually say that any activity that generates a market transaction, and is therefore included in gross domestic product (GDP: the sum of all final goods and services produced in the economy, measured using their market prices*), counts as productive activity, no matter what sort of economic activity is involved. It's enough that it generates a market transaction. So even the market value of financial services is included in GDP.

When the financial sector grows as a share of the economy, it looks like the economy is growing with it. This is misleading, however, because

---

* "Final" means that we include the value of aluminum production, for example, in the value of the cars and other products containing aluminum that are sold to final purchasers. This avoids counting the value of aluminum twice, when it is first produced and again when its cost is included in the price of the products containing it.

our measure of GDP doesn't recognize the difference between productive activity that creates wealth and unproductive activity that draws upon that wealth. Finance and commerce, however necessary they might be in a capitalist system, should not count in the same measure with productive activity when we consider the creation of wealth in society.

We need to understand that markets are an essential institution in capitalism, but markets are not the same thing as the economy. They are necessary for the conduct of business; therefore, economists study markets, and rightly so. But if we remain at the level of market exchange, we ignore, and therefore fail to reach or understand, the underlying dynamics that drive capitalist economies—the production and distribution of surplus in ways that are distinct to capitalism. This omission is a fundamental failure of mainstream economics, which I have written about in the academic field of working class studies.[14]

Productive work is sometimes identified exclusively with the creation of material goods in the manufacturing, mining, and construction sectors of the economy, assigning intangible services to the unproductive part of the economy. This way of thinking misses the most important relationship in the creation of surplus: the relation between what the producing population requires for its physical and mental reproduction at society's accepted standard of living and what that producing population produces. Most service work—financial and legal services, retail and wholesale trade, police and private security—is unproductive. However, the work of those supplying the medical and education services that producers need is productive because it directly helps to produce their labor power, their mental and physical capacity to work. The same can be said of the work of barbers, for example, who contribute to the ability of productive workers to continue to work according to the social standards of the time.

Every population is divided into these two broad categories of people: those who produce what is required so that the people who produce surplus can survive and reproduce at the standard of living socially accepted at the time; and those who do not produce surplus, unproductive workers in the sense that we are using the term here. Unproductive workers in capitalist economies do two important things: they facilitate productive workers by helping to finance companies where productive work goes on and sell their products; and, by doing the work of unproductive companies, they capture for those businesses the share of surplus, produced elsewhere, that sustains the unproductive sectors. Even within companies in the productive sector we find unproductive activity in management and supervision, sustained from the surplus created by the productive workforce.

This is a key question for the ability of the system to generate real economic growth. The more the economy is engaged in its unproductive sectors, the less it has available as the foundation of new wealth. As progressive movements deal with the problem of slow growth and government austerity, this insight takes on practical significance, suggesting ways in which policy might help to reallocate resources from unproductive to productive uses. We saw this when answering the question "Where will the money come from?" in chapter one.

The shaman performing incantations in a prehistoric tribe to bless the hunters about to depart the settlement is unproductive (if he or she has no other role); the hunters are productive. The feudal lord is unproductive in his activities that direct the productive labor of the serfs on the land, and in his political maneuverings with the king and other nobility. The slave owner ordering the overseer to push enslaved people to harvest the crop or make the furniture produces nothing, nor does the overseer. Similarly in capitalist economies, the owners and managers facilitate production, but they do not produce. Capitalists may be necessary to production in a capitalist system, and managers will always be needed in complex production systems, but, the point is, capitalists and managers do not create wealth.

To see this, we need to differentiate between activity that creates surplus and that which either facilitates its creation or distributes the surplus once it has been created. Think about a basketball coach who shapes the play of each member of the team and gets the individual players to work together on the court as a team. Without doubt, the coach is essential to the team's victory. But the coach doesn't play the game, doesn't win the championship. The team does, with the facilitation of the coach.

People who sell products in the market fill a necessary function in the process of getting products to buyers. By engaging in market competition, merchants also guide the process that distributes the surplus across the economy. But merchants do not produce the output, or the surplus. Banks that lend money to businesses for investment facilitate production in critical ways, but they produce nothing. All of these activities—management, sales, finance—are unproductive in the sense I have used the term here, even though they are critically important in various ways that facilitate production. The police and military also produce nothing, but they have the critical function to protect the institutions and social conditions capital requires for its own safety ("law and order") and to suppress any serious threat to them.

Productive work, on the other hand, involves only the creation of goods and services that directly sustain the productive workforce, including creating the machinery, equipment, and other capital goods required for that production. Everything beyond that is surplus.

It may drive the point home to observe that we can imagine a society in which the only economic activity is the production of necessities of life for the direct use of the producers, and a small surplus taken and consumed by a dominant class linked personally to them. In such a society there are no banks or financial institutions; there are no stores to buy things. Military personnel may be fed only by the pillage of their victims, if not by the locally produced surplus. Such societies existed earlier in human history, and still do in isolated areas of the world, before productive workers could create enough to support very many unproductive people.

But there can be no society that can survive if everyone is a merchant, or a banker, or a manager, or a soldier. No society can exist for long if the entire labor force is divided only among these unproductive activities while no one makes the products required for material survival.

The more productive the labor force becomes, the more unproductive activity it can support with the greater surplus it creates. No matter how sophisticated, widespread, and central the financial, commercial, management, and military functions become in an economy, they are all completely dependent upon and paid for out of surplus created by the productive workforce.

But the distinction between productive and unproductive activity need not be a significant dividing line within the working class, which is employed in both activities. Those in productive sectors *create* the surplus for the entire society. Workers in the unproductive sectors do the functions necessary to *capture* that part of the surplus that goes to the businesses in those sectors. Their employers—the capitalists in the financial, commercial, and management sectors—rely on the workers they employ to do the work that brings in their profits, just as employers in productive industries do.

In a technical sense, only productive workers are exploited since they alone produce surplus. But workers in unproductive sectors, who make it possible for capitalists to capture part of the surplus produced elsewhere, endure the same workplace pressures from their employers as do productive workers. They, too, fight against longer hours, less pay, fewer benefits, precarious employment, and lower living standards. Workers in unproductive sectors face the same challenges in public policy as do their productive class-mates when it comes to defending elements of the social wage that are equally available (or not) to all workers who meet eligibility standards. Even though workers and capitalists alike in unproductive sectors depend on surplus created by workers elsewhere, unproductive workers have no more common interest with their employers than do workers and capitalists in productive sectors. The working class extends across both parts of the capitalist economy in a common confrontation with capital in all its forms and uses.

The unproductive part of society extends also to those who are out of the labor force, including children younger than working age, the sick and infirm who cannot work, and people who are able to produce but are retired from paid employment according to the standards of the time. How these populations are treated is also a question for class struggle in the determination of the acceptable living standard, against child labor, for paid sick leave and health coverage, and for economic security in the years when a person is "too old to work but too young to die," in the words of the old labor saying.

Where Does the Surplus Go?

Capitalism differs from all previous economic systems in the form surplus takes, as well as the mechanism by which it is created and taken. In slave and feudal societies the surplus took the form of produced things that the exploiting class consumed—such as food, dwellings, handicrafts, and clothing. To the extent that their productivity allowed producers to be taken from such mundane pursuits and mobilized to build castles, cathedrals, and fortresses, and to write music or paint for the amusement of the rulers, those products, too, were forms of surplus. These all continue in advanced capitalist countries.

Beyond the capitalists' personal consumption, corporate profits are another manifestation of surplus in capitalist society. For the first time in human history, the surplus is not at first an item of consumption or direct use—it takes the form of money. Surplus as a castle is just a castle. Surplus as money can be turned into anything. In particular, surplus as money profits can for the first time be plowed back into expanding production, which explains why capitalism has been an engine of economic growth and technical progress unknown in prior human history. Part of the total product should be used to replace the stock of capital used up in production; if not, production becomes unsustainable, as we have seen in companies going bankrupt when venture capitalists simply strip their assets for short-run profit. Beyond replacement of used up machinery, equipment, and buildings, surplus in capitalism becomes available for expanding production, for economic growth.

But surplus goes to support much more than capitalist consumption and profit that fuels business investment. The entire financial, commercial, management, and military functions of the economy, those sectors that facilitate the creation and distribution of the surplus but do not produce it, are supported by the surplus. This includes all wages paid to the workers in those sectors. As we saw in chapter two, redirecting substantial parts of the surplus, and the labor it employs, to productive use will go a long way toward finding the resources required to realize the progressive agenda.

Since the end of World War II, the US economy and other industrialized societies have experienced rapid growth in their financial sectors. As corporations have increased in size and complexity, their management structures have increased relative to the numbers of people doing the work. And the military-industrial complex President Dwight Eisenhower warned against has grown to outsized proportions in the US as well. The relative expansion of these functions, all of them unproductive, has required the production of ever-greater amounts of surplus by workers who have remained in productive activities. This follows from the simple fact that that there can be no surplus distributed that has not first been produced.

Surplus is at first entirely in the hands of the capitalists who run companies in the productive sectors of the economy. But they require the services of the unproductive sectors to stay in business. They need layers of management to keep their operations going. They need merchants to sell their products. They need banks and financial services to fund their operations. They need lawyers and political institutions and security forces to protect their interests.

Conflicts among leaders in the productive and unproductive sectors as capitalism has developed have resulted in accepted mechanisms that transfer part of the total surplus from productive sectors to sustain all of these unproductive activities. Managers are either paid directly by the productive firm employing them, or the firm pays some contractor to do that work. Merchants get their resources by obtaining the products they sell at discounted wholesale prices, allowing them to obtain greater revenues from retail sales that pay their costs, beyond the cost of goods sold, including the wages of their employees, and allow for some profit as well. Financial institutions receive their revenues from interest and fees paid for their services, and returns on their investments. To the degree that businesses in the unproductive sectors deal with productive firms, there is a transfer of surplus from the productive. To the degree that the unproductive firms are dealing with each other—banks loaning money to merchants, for example, or private equity firms and hedge funds investing people's money—the transactions just redistribute surplus among unproductive sectors and firms.

Government is not just another business. Although private interests may influence or control parts of it, governments are public entities, presumably subject to democratic accountability. Some government functions, like the provision of education, health care, and, in some places, transportation and electricity, to the productive population as part of the social wage are part of the productive economy. But most government functions, like its regulatory apparatus or security forces, are not.

Slow Growth and Inequality

Table 5 gives a rough indication of how US economic activity has been divided between productive and unproductive work. We can see clearly that since 1957 unproductive activity has substantially increased as a share of the whole economy. While wholesale and retail sales have gone down some as a percent of the economy, the finance, insurance, and real estate (FIRE) sector has increased its share by 50%, going from 13.1% to 21.1% of the economy. The service sector has also grown, from 49.4% to 70.4% of the economy, much of it in unproductive activity. Meanwhile, the share going to private goods production (manufacturing, mining, and construction) has been cut more than in half, falling from 38% to 17.3% of the economy, comparing 1957 with 2019. Contrary to the alarmist cries of opponents of "big government," government at all levels (federal, state, and local) has remained essentially unchanged in its share of the economy over the last sixty-five years.

As unproductive sectors have grown in importance and scale in recent decades, manufacturing and other goods producing sectors have lost leverage, especially in their relations with finance. With that, the latter have gained economic and political influence and the ability to demand and receive a greater cut of the surplus.

Table 5. Value Added by Industry as a Percentage of Gross Domestic Product, 1957–2019

Sector	1957*	1967*	1977*	1987[†]	1997[†]	2007[‡]	2017[‡]	2019[‡]
Finance, insurance, real estate, rental, and leasing	13.1%	14.2%	15.0%	17.7%	19.2%	19.6%	20.6%	21.1%
Wholesale/ retail trade	14.1%	14.3%	14.4%	13.4%	13.2%	11.8%	11.0%	11.3%
Private goods	38.0%	34.0%	30.9%	24.9%	21.9%	20.8%	17.9%	17.3%
Private services	49.4%	51.8%	54.7%	61.2%	65.3%	66.1%	69.6%	70.4%
Government	12.6%	14.2%	14.4%	13.9%	12.7%	13.1%	12.5%	12.3%

Sources:
* Robert E. Yuskavage and Mahnaz Fahim-Nader, "Gross Domestic Product by Industry for1947–86: New Estimates Based on the North American Industry Classification System," *Survey of Current Business* (December 2005), Washington, DC: Bureau of Economic Analysis, https://apps.bea.gov/scb/pdf/2005/12December/1205_GDP-NAICS.pdf.
† Robert E. Yuskavage and Yvon H. Pho, "Gross Domestic Product by Industry for 1987–2000: New Estimates on the North American Industry Classification System," *Survey of Current Business* (November 2004), Washington, DC: Bureau of Economic Analysis, https://apps.bea.gov/scb/pdf/2004/11November/1104GDP_by_Indy.pdf.
‡ Federal Reserve Bank of St. Louis, "Value Added by Industry as a Percentage of Gross Domestic Product," *FRED Economic Data*, accessed July 19, 2023, https://fred.stlouisfed.org/release/tables?rid=331&eid=211&od=2019-12-01#.

As finance has increasingly drawn resources away from the productive sector, the basis of economic growth has shrunk. Even the great changes in digital technology we have seen since the 1990s haven't helped that much. While some advances have impacted productive sectors, these innovations have been concentrated in communications, finance, and commerce, where productivity increases contribute nothing to the increase in available wealth.

The relative growth of unproductive sectors has required the intensification of exploitation of workers in the productive sectors, who are after all the sole source of surplus. In the 1980s, US steel manufacturers needed 10.1 labor hours to produce a ton of steel. By 2018, that had fallen to 1.5 labor hours.[15]

As productive businesses have shrunk in relative proportion to the total economy, sharing greater fractions of the surplus with finance, commerce, and management, the foundation for economic growth has diminished because productive sectors retain fewer resources to fund productive investments that yield them profit. In the face of the slowing growth of surplus applied to productive purpose and the resulting reduced rates of economic growth since the 1970s, capital has used its power to accrue a greater share of wealth to itself by driving the ever-increasing income inequality we have seen for the last fifty years in the United States. In the presence of slower real economic growth the ruling class has continued to accumulate riches for itself through redistribution, driving downward pressure on private and social wages alike.

In the years right after World War II, workers, including supervisors and managers, received 66% of total US output. By 1997 it had fallen to 60% and, after a brief increase in the full-employment years of the late 1990s, the share of output going to workers fell to 56% by 2012, with a slight increase since then.[16] These changes have come with direct assaults on any and all forms of power the working class can exert to defend and improve its standard of living.

Notes

1   Noam Scheiber, "You're Now a 'Manager.' Forget About Overtime Pay," *New York Times*, March 6, 2023, https://www.nytimes.com/2023/03/06/business/economy/managers-overtime-pay.html.

2   Liz Alderman, "France Leads the List of the Global Ultrarich," *New York Times*, April 6, 2023, https://www.nytimes.com/2023/04/05/business/forbes-richest-list-france.html.

3   Michael Zweig, *The Working Class Majority: America's Best Kept Secret*, 2nd ed. (Ithaca, NY: Cornell University Press, 2012).

4   Michael Zweig, "Class and Poverty in the United States," in *Religion and Economic Justice*, ed. Michael Zweig (Philadelphia: Temple University Press, 1990).

5   Elise Gould and Melat Kassa, "Low-Wage and Low-Hours Workers Were Hit Hardest by COVID-19 Recession," Economic Policy Institute, May 20, 2021, https://www.epi.org/publication/swa-2020-employment-report.

6   Statistica Research Department, "Gig Economy in the US—Statistics and Facts," September 30, 2022, https://www.statista.com/topics/4891/gig-economy-in-the-us/#topicOverview.

7   George Fitzhugh, *Cannibals All! Or, Slaves without Masters* (VB Publishing Group, 2012 [1857]).

8   US Bureau of Labor Statistics, "Employment Projections: Occupations with the Most Growth," September 8, 2022, https://www.bls.gov/emp/tables/occupations-most-job-growth.htm.

9   G. William Domhoff, *Who Rules America? The Triumph of the Corporate Rich*, 7th ed. (New York: McGraw Hill, 2014).

10   Will Parker, "Mounting Unpaid Rent Risks US Tidal Wave of Evictions," *Wall Street Journal*, October 28, 2020.

11   Brian X. Chen, "Will Asian-Americans Unite Across Class Divides?" *New York Times*, March 21, 2021, https://www.nytimes.com/2021/03/20/technology/personaltech/asian-american-wealth-gap.html?searchResultPosition=1.

12 Karl Marx, *Theories of Surplus Value*, pt. 1, ch. 4 (Moscow: Progress Publishers, 1962), 152–304.

13 Paul Baran and Paul M. Sweezy, *Monopoly Capital* (New York: Monthly Review Press, 1966).

14 Michael Zweig, "Class As a Question in Economics," in *New Working-Class Studies*, ed. Sherry Lee Linkon and John Russo (Ithaca, NY: Cornell University Press, 2005).

15 Paul Wiseman, "As Trump Weighs Tariff, US Steelmakers Enjoy Rising Profits," Associated Press, March 13, 2018, https://apnews.com/cae426730cd74e64932e4be7fa5cdebc#/pq=FGkzCo.

16 Michael D. Giandrea and Shawn Sprague, "Estimating the U.S. Labor Share," *Monthly Labor Review* (US Bureau of Labor Statistics, February 2017), accessed August 28, 2021, https://doi.org/10.21916/mlr.2017.7.

CHAPTER SIX

Connecting the Dots across Issues

Understanding the basic features of our capitalist economy helps to ground and put into context the urgent progressive social movements we are building, well beyond addressing the vital questions of wages and working conditions on the job. In this chapter we will look at four focal points of progressive movements. For each, we will see why it is that, to address them effectively and for the long term, we need to confront and transform the underlying characteristics of capitalist society that give rise to these problems, while also working to ameliorate their immediate effects. People who challenge the effects of capitalism need to understand, and address in their organizing, the links between capital accumulation and the immediate issues that are the focus of their concerns.

In this chapter we'll look in turn at: (1) capitalism's global reach and consequent militarism; (2) environmental devastation, ultimately involving the now-fast-approaching ruination of the earth itself; (3) repeated crises, in which economic growth is interrupted by the periodic reversals of recessions and depressions; and (4) the impulse to turn the result of every kind of human creativity into a commodity, including privatization of such vital public services as education, transportation, prisons, and even the military.

Militarism and Global Reach

People have waged war since as far back as we have records. These wars have had many origins. While it may be an aspect of human nature to fight, those impulses are shaped and channeled by the particular social circumstances of the times. In our era of capitalist development, wars have arisen from conditions specific to capitalism. Anyone opposing war in this era needs to confront these specific conditions.

The globalization that has been so much in the news in recent decades is not new, although the creation of complex global supply chains only recently became possible with the creation of high-speed computer systems that can support sophisticated financial, communications, and logistical operations. But capitalism has had a global reach from its earliest beginnings in Europe. As far back as the start of the fourteenth century, in the predawn of capitalism, the Venetian merchant Marco Polo explored trade routes to China, documenting his hopes and experiences in his journal, published in English as *The Travels of Marco Polo*.[1] As merchant capital grew in importance and power within feudal societies, the kings and queens of Spain, Portugal, the Netherlands, France, and England worked with merchants to raise money for their militaries while extending their domains to places and peoples far removed from Europe. Merchants pulled in enormous profit through trade by outright plunder and exercising economic domination enforced by the military power of the crown, which fought off merchants from other countries and in turn drew its resources from the crown's taxing a share of the merchants' profits.

Meanwhile, early merchant capital set the preconditions for the start of wage labor and modern capital accumulation when they hired workers for the first time. Merchants began to employ workers and pay them to produce directly some of what they sold. Increasingly, people established businesses that did nothing but produce for the market with hired labor. In the process, the capitalist system came into prominence, finally blowing apart the symbiotic relationship of merchant and crown and overthrowing European feudal economies that had survived for more than a thousand years.[2] Adam Smith's *An Inquiry into the Nature and Origins of the Wealth of Nations*, published in England in 1776, was a central text used to explain the practicality and theoretical coherence of this transformation from the point of view of rising capitalist authority.

The great explorations of the sixteenth and seventeenth centuries brought most of the Western Hemisphere under European domination, as well as parts of Africa. By the end of the nineteenth century, European domination extended to nearly all peoples on earth.

Although dominant rulers have established empires and fought wars far back in human history, millennia before capitalism emerged, empire in the capitalist era is qualitatively different from earlier forms. Roman emperors ruled as far north as Scotland, across Europe, North Africa, and the Middle East. The Mongols, led by Genghis Khan and his successors in the thirteenth century, established an enormous contiguous land empire stretching from what is now Korea across Asia, Iran, and Iraq to Eastern Europe. These and other early empires functioned to exact tribute to the conquering army, amassing great wealth and personal power for the dominant ruler.

But the wealth of empire was not turned into capital until more modern times. While Spain treated its holdings in the New World mainly as sources of direct plunder of wealth in gold and silver, England, arriving in the hemisphere more than a hundred years later, came with more advanced economic ideas in mind. By the end of the seventeenth century, the English had already established the basic features of modern capitalist empire. In this form, domination served the purpose of drawing raw materials to the center, where they could be processed into commodities using capitalist methods. It also created markets for these products in the empire's remote holdings. Without these markets, the surplus created by the new and growing working class could not fully be turned into money profit.

The United States emerged from British colonies that had been founded in this process during the seventeenth and eighteenth centuries. Our country's history is intimately bound up with the myriad ways in which the American colonies served and were shaped by English political and economic interests as capitalism took root there. The colonies supplied raw materials for English manufacture—everything from beaver skins to tobacco to cotton. The hats and coats, textiles, and clothing that then came back to the growing colonial market underpinned the development of English manufacture. The slave trade brought enormous wealth to English shipping magnates and merchants in Liverpool and Bristol, while the southern slave economy was the foundation of wealth and early capital accumulation in the American colonies. At the same time, colonial merchants and domestic manufacture were disadvantaged by English rule.* The American War of Independence, running from 1776 to 1783, grew out of the economic relations of emerging capitalist empire.

---

* To secure India as a market for English textiles manufactured with cotton taken from the subcontinent, English rule in India prohibited local production of textiles despite centuries of Indian skills and creative imagination. This history lay behind the power of Mahatma Gandhi's choice of the simple spinning wheel as a symbol of the Indian people's resistance to English rule in the 1930s and 1940s.

Another consequence of the global reach of early capitalist development is the character of many colonial areas as settler states. The economies
of European countries developed on their own soil as new classes came
to power as capitalism emerged locally at the expense of traditional local
feudal elites. But in the US, as in Canada, Australia, New Zealand, South
Africa, and, in modern times, Israel, the newly emerging capitalist system
followed an especially tragic pattern. Settlers coming from abroad imposed
their new system on the Indigenous peoples in totally and immediately
disruptive ways. As part of their strategy to occupy the land, the settlers
displaced and marginalized the Indigenous population, most of whom were
either killed in battle, died from European diseases previously unknown
to them, or were forcibly displaced to remote reservations.

These settlers established themselves as the "relevant population," in
the words of Bill Fletcher Jr.[3] Perhaps the clearest example comes in the
implications of the opening words of the US Declaration of Independence,
where our nation's founders declared it "self-evident" that "all men are
created equal." But the founders clearly meant all *white men*. Our founding
documents were meant to be relevant in this narrow sense, excluding as
irrelevant any claim to "life, liberty, and the pursuit of happiness" by Black,
Asian, or Indigenous peoples, and all women.

To establish their domination, settlers required the application of
military force. They had to overcome the resistance of Indigenous peoples
through violent suppression, as well as fight off the incursions of competing
European powers. In the American colonies, and during the first hundred
years and more after the establishment of the United States, this involved the
slaughter and forced displacement of whole nations of Native Americans.[4]
Their land was taken for railroad rights-of-way and given to the railroads to
sell or develop in alternating square miles along those rights-of-way. Native
land went to tens of thousands of homesteaders in the course of the Indian
Wars that killed or displaced hundreds of thousands of Native Americans
after the Civil War. The roots of American capitalism drew deeply from
this genocidal multigenerational dispossession.

War and military conflict have taken many forms in capitalist history.
They have been fought on various scales, from local battles to worldwide
conflagrations. Starting in the sixteenth century, emerging colonial powers
that were engaged in global exploration fought wars to determine which
countries would dominate new territory for raw materials and markets.
They fought for naval supremacy to control shipping lanes on the high seas.

They fought to defeat local resistance. This happened not only in settler states, but also in countries like China and India. There, where the English ruled through the cooperation of local elites, they still faced widespread popular rebellions that required violent suppression.

These wars of Native suppression and interimperialist rivalry came to a crescendo of destruction in the nineteenth and twentieth centuries. The numbers of dead were so large as to be nearly incomprehensible. In what became the Belgian Congo, a private holding of King Leopold II and the source of enormous wealth taken through the forced labor of native people, the Belgians slaughtered around ten million people.[5] During World War I, at Ypres alone, hundreds of thousands of soldiers died in extended trench warfare that resolved nothing, but continued in the vain attempt to settle the rivalry between the rising German capitalist ruling class and the French and English they hoped to supplant. In the 1930s, German expansionism continued, precipitating World War II. As difficult and heroic as the joint US, British, Canadian, and French invasion of Normandy was in June 1944, at that time "the bulk of the damage inflicted on German forces was in the eastern campaign—80% of their battle casualties—and it was here that the overwhelming weight of the Wehrmacht was concentrated."[6] The Soviet Union suffered more casualties during the war than Germany or the US. Out of a population of about 160 million at the start of the war, nearly twenty-five million people died, about ten million troops and fifteen million civilians, and millions more were wounded.[7]

The organization of capitalism's global reach changed following World War II. Recoiling from the horrors and expense of two world wars, elites in the traditional European imperial countries set about to promote political structures to settle differences. Chief among these is the European Union, which has integrated former rivals into an intricate web of trade and regulatory connections that have systemized capital's dominion across the continent. Europe is now an economic entity competing with the US, China, and Japan, while also cooperating with them in the establishment of common rules of international economic behavior in the World Trade Organization (WTO).

The period after World War II also marked a change in the relations between imperial and colonial powers and the peoples and nations they had oppressed. Beginning during World War II in Asia, and extending throughout Africa in the years following, wars of national liberation and independence exploded. By the mid-1970s every colony in the Dutch,

English, French, Japanese, and Portuguese spheres of domination had won formal political independence. After Alaska and Hawaii became states in 1959, only Puerto Rico has remained a colony of the United States, together with the US Virgin Islands and Guam.

Yet the newly independent nations were not free to develop outside the influence of continuing Great Power rivalries, especially those of the Cold War between the United States and the Soviet Union. Wars of national liberation were anathema to capitalists in power. Directed against capitalist empires, they were typically led by socialist or communist forces, with the support of the Soviet Union. Following World War II, the US emerged as the dominant capitalist power and took the lead in challenging these independence struggles. The result was a series of proxy civil wars between the US and China or the Soviet Union, most notably destructive in Korea, Vietnam, Central America, and Angola. The US also took deadly measures to crush democratically elected leftist (but not communist) governments of long-standing independent countries: Iran (Mohammad Mossadegh,1953); Guatemala (Jacobo Árbenz, 1954); Congo (Patrice Lumumba, 1961); Brazil (João Goulart, 1964); Dominican Republic (Juan Bosch, 1965); Chile (Salvador Allende, 1971); and Honduras (Manuel Zalaya, 2009). Guaranteeing dominance of US economic interests has required the capacity to project overwhelming military power across the planet in defense of those interests.

Most Americans are barely aware of this history. Yet in each of the affected countries, almost everyone knows very well how their people were oppressed, tortured, and killed in large numbers and can tell you the exact years in which the injustices occurred. They hold the United States responsible in significant measure. Think of it in terms of the schoolyard bully. He beats up and robs fellow students of their lunch money. The victims tend to remember what happened for the rest of their lives. But the bully hardly knows whom he has robbed two days later, as he is on to his next victim.

The educational, political, and cultural institutions of the US and other colonial and imperial countries foster amnesia. Except for some academic centers denounced by right-wing media and political personalities as anti-American, these institutions do virtually nothing to recall this history of domination. Yet we cannot understand the world around us if we ignore this history. Our movement needs a strong element of international labor and environmental justice solidarity; not charity, not to apologize or spout self-indulgent mea culpas for past US actions, but to help right those wrongs in current common work across borders that confronts a common enemy. This solidarity, if it is not patronizing charity but genuine solidarity, must be a two-way street, in which we gain knowledge and strength from other peoples' efforts to secure dignity and independence, as they gain insights from us.

During the years of the Cold War, the United States amassed the largest and most technically powerful military in history.* It has matured into the massive core of what Dwight D. Eisenhower warned against in his famous 1961 farewell address as president, when he coined that memorable phrase "military-industrial complex."□

Immediately after World War II, the US and Britain, then preeminent among the capitalist powers, established a set of international economic institutions designed to promote the growth of international trade and create a stable international monetary system to facilitate it. Trade among countries had shrunk by almost 90% during the Great Depression and World War II. The peace that followed the war was designed to reverse that collapse. To that end, negotiators from forty-four Allied countries met at Bretton Woods, New Hampshire, in July 1944 and agreed to create the International Monetary Fund (IMF) to stabilize national currencies and encourage renewed growth. They established the World Bank to provide aid to poor countries for their development and entry into international markets. Seeking further to reverse the collapse of trade, the General Agreement on Tariffs and Trade (GATT)† followed in 1947, designed gradually to reduce the tariffs that had choked off international trade during the Depression, as one country after another raised tariffs to protect domestic industry from foreign competition.

As the US and other capitalist economies developed in subsequent decades, the balance of power shifted among major economic centers. In the process, these institutions needed adjustments to their functions and missions. After the Cold War ended, with the fall of the Soviet Union in 1991, capitalism became the dominant social system worldwide. Within four years the major capitalist powers established the WTO to govern international economic relations. The World Bank and IMF took on new

---

* The technical capacity to wage war has been more or less tightly constrained in its application since World War II by political considerations. These arise both in domestic politics, as people grow weary of the costs and casualties of war, and in limits imposed by international alliances. Most importantly, wars of domination are constrained by the powerful will of colonized people to resist. Here again we see that, as in production, the technical and the social are mutually determined, in this case forming the dialectic that drives and shapes war making.

† A *tariff* is a tax a country imposes on imports to restrict them in favor of domestic production.

responsibilities regarding the people of countries whose governments sought their assistance, translating their original missions into the design and imposition of austerity measures imposed on the general population, such as cutting government subsidies for food and housing and allowing markets to dominate economic activity.

But the trade agreements embodied in the WTO and regional agreements such as the North American Free Trade Association (NAFTA, among the US, Mexico, and Canada) differed from postwar trade concerns in one vital way. The new accords emphasized free flows of capital, opening poor and middle-income countries to the penetration of foreign capital investments and financial activity, while continuing to lower tariff barriers in the trade of goods and services.

With the increasing integration of contemporary capitalism into a world system, important changes have occurred before our eyes. The relatively free flow of capital across national borders means that class structures have taken shape across national boundaries. In the current era of globalization, we can see evidence of an international capitalist class spanning in its operations many countries and continents. Today's capitalists move production from one country to another to escape taxation and regulation, and to take advantage of lowest-wage labor. They have created international supply chains that contribute to the emergence of worldwide class structures. They have homes in several economic hubs simultaneously, traveling easily among New York, London, Paris, Frankfurt, Johannesburg, Singapore, and Sydney; they meet several times a year at international conferences in Davos, Switzerland; Aspen, Colorado; Jackson Hole, Wyoming; and other pleasant environments. While the COVID-19 pandemic has led to some recognition of the fragility of international supply chains, the basic architecture of global capitalism remains.

As these arrangements have come into being, they have intensified the asymmetry of power between the working and capitalist classes. As the capitalist class has become more integrated across national borders, workers, too, have become part of one or another element of a global supply chain. In the process, a more interconnected global working class is coming into existence. They produce automobiles, computers, and other durable consumer goods whose parts are produced in many countries, coming together in yet another country for final assembly.

This international supply chain also sustains the global reach of Goldman Sachs and similar financial corporations. In global terms, the capitalist class has the advantage of international mobility while working class people seeking to move to other countries in search of better wages and working conditions face capitalist-imposed barriers, even when they are in search of asylum to escape terror and death squads. Capitalists are free to organize their production, financial, and commercial networks globally. Workers, on the other hand, are blocked from organizing into common struggle across national boundaries. They have very little capacity to organize resistance even within their own countries. The ability of capitalists to move their activities relatively easily among countries also weakens the power of national governments to regulate them or constrain their power over working people.

The focus on both trade and capital flows has been necessary for capitalists to organize and protect the international supply chains that have come to characterize manufacturing since the early 1990s. These global networks require poorer countries to allow American capital to move money into them to invest in local production, and then to allow the products to ship across the globe as free as possible from tariff and other barriers. Free flows of capital also allow US commercial and investment banks to do business in other countries, competing with, and sometimes owning part or all of local financial institutions. The EU, UK, and China make similar demands.

The demands that financial and commercial capital insist upon for access to international markets, and power in participating in them, go along with the need for these unproductive sectors to attach themselves to the surplus arising from productive businesses in countries where they invest. Only through this connection are financial and commercial businesses able to capture a portion of surplus created elsewhere in the economy, anywhere in the world. This helps to explain US demands in trade negotiations to give global access to US finance and commercial enterprise, and intense US demands for rent-seeking intellectual property rights protection in contentious negotiations with China and other countries.*

When US manufacturers set up shop in less-developed economies, they provide technology equivalent to what is in use in the US but now linked to workers who are paid much less than their US counterparts. The

---

* *Rent* is a payment made possible by scarcity, whether natural in the case of land or artificial as in the case of patents, copyright protections, or other restrictions to competitive production that the US has demanded in the name of intellectual property rights.

result is increasing surplus, drawn from the international working class in production overseas, but either brought back to US shareholders or reinvested by these US firms abroad in similar circumstances. This is what happens when the flow of capital created in poor countries flows out of those countries into the hands of US corporations. Similar flows occur when other advanced countries invest in the developing world. China is doing the same thing in its Belt and Road program, in which Chinese companies undertake industrial projects and build infrastructure in poor countries while pressing large amounts of debt upon those countries to pay China for the projects.

Just as surplus in a capitalist economy, after it is produced socially, is redistributed into private hands, moving it toward relatively more efficient capital-intensive firms, surplus is distributed among national economies. As long as capital flows are relatively free, countries with relatively capital-intensive economies, or highly specialized financial sectors, can grow rich by bringing to themselves surplus that has been produced in relatively low-wage, less-advanced economies. Beyond the traditionally advanced capitalist economies, Taiwan, South Korea, and Singapore are examples of relatively capital-intensive economies; Vietnam, Bangladesh, and El Salvador examples of relatively poor, labor-intensive economies.

US corporate access to world markets requires the projection of US military power on a global scale. American overseas military operations and the requirements of a massive military force deployed worldwide have profound impacts on our domestic society as well. In recent decades we have seen with our own eyes the increasing militarization of domestic police forces. Street protests here in our own country are now met with police in full military tactical gear—body armor, shields, helmets, automatic weapons–using armored personnel carriers and sophisticated military surveillance techniques, supported by helicopters and drones. Far from a presence "to protect and to serve," they instead resemble an occupying army. They are often taken as such by people in rebellion against police violence directed at Black people and by the political leaders who insist on having such police forces ready to deploy.

At the federal level, we have a budget reflecting the dramatically warped set of priorities inherent in militarism that leaves basic human needs unattended. In 2021, the US military budget was more than the military budgets of the next nine countries combined—China, India, the UK, Russia, France, Germany, Saudi Arabia, Japan, and South Korea—seven of which are US allies.[9] In 2019 the US military absorbed well over half (53%) of all federal discretionary spending. Compared with that, 1% went for food and agriculture, 3% each for transportation and international affairs, and 4% for the environment and energy (which includes spending for nuclear weapons).[10] Even small reductions in the military would easily make possible doubling expenditures in other areas more vital to the needs of working people. We see the same distortions of priorities in city budgets across the country, where allocations to police take an outsized amount of money. At both federal and local levels, militarization diverts resources urgently needed to fund diplomacy, as well as the housing, education, health care, roads, bridges, and ports needed for economic development.

Environmental Devastation

In precapitalist cultures, spiritual beliefs often integrated human activity with nature, understanding them to be intimately bound up with one another. Experience taught people how to live as communities connected with the natural environment, even as they altered it locally to sustain agriculture or to conform to their nature-related spiritual practices.[11] In capitalism, where each individual is thought to be a freestanding part of the social order, independent of any other except through arm's-length market exchanges, we think very differently. People are no longer considered part of nature. Nature becomes a "resource" that entrepreneurs should have a right to access to get materials necessary for production and the making of profit. "Nature" and "society" appear to become disconnected, rather than being understood as a unity of opposites whose tension is central to all economies, most dramatically in private capital accumulation.

In the same way that capitalist thinking dismembers society into a collection of distinct and sovereign individual persons, it dismembers nature into a collection of "resources." Capitalist thinking focuses on oil, or fish, or coal, or soil, or water, as if these can be taken or left alone depending only on a narrow calculation of costs and revenues. We learn to think as if they are not part of ecosystems that pull them all into complex networks, with human beings in the mix.

In early stages of capitalist development, the folly of such dualistic thinking was hidden because economic growth had not yet generated a crisis. There was localized environmental damage, but it had not reached the scale required to badly affect nature in its vast expanse. But during the second half of the twentieth century it had already become clear to those who examined the matter closely that human economic activity had reached a scale threatening to destabilize environmental relationships in ways that would cause widespread suffering. Rachel Carson's 1962 book *Silent Spring* was an early warning that shocked the country with its stark report on the effects of pesticides poisoning the environment.[12] By the mid-1960s, the science of greenhouse gases and climate change was already known.[13] It was present in the science fiction writing of Ursula K. Le Guin, who wrote in 1969 that increased concentrations of CO_2 would alter the atmosphere in ways leading to large increases in temperature, making a world where a character sharing this ominous vision of the future says, "I am glad I shall not be present."[14]

What explains this destructive behavior? To begin, the very idea of separating human economic activity from nature, the natural order, is a mistake. It is an example of the dualistic thinking that bedevils so much of the economic and social commentary dominating our culture. People *are* elements of nature, as much as oak trees or zebras.

People, like all other animals, adapt to changing natural environments. But for people, as individuals and as groups, those changes are mediated through social institutions that expose different people in the same changing environment to different stresses. Those institutions also afford different people in the same changing environment different capacities to adapt. We saw this recently with the starkly different impacts COVID-19 had on different racial and economic segments of society. We also saw that people in different segments of society were more, or less, able to rearrange their lives safely to escape the deadly consequences of the virus newly introduced into the environment. We see it in the differential impact of hurricanes and floods on rich and poor communities. Such class and racial disparities are the foundation of movements for environmental justice that seek to protect the most marginalized, who are therefore most vulnerable in the face of environmental hazards of all sorts.

We have seen in chapter four that capital accumulation requires each capitalist to compete with all capitalists to be able to take for themselves some part of the total surplus produced socially by the productive working class. The dominance of this competition leads inexorably to the practical requirement that each business must expand or die. Those who fail to grow in the end submit to the ever-growing market and political power of those who do grow. With no plan to regulate the social consequences of this dynamic, eventually nature itself comes under challenge. At that point, when the logic of capital accumulation brings the world to the point of natural catastrophe, capitalism meets its own limits. No earlier economic system had this effect.

We need to reflect on the fact that, after a while, seemingly unlimited economic expansion runs into constraints imposed by the natural environment. At that point, the demands of continuing capital accumulation begin to degrade the natural environment from the point of view of human needs, which in turn undermines the capacity of capitalism to continue on its historic path. Experience forces us to realize that human activity and nature are not wholly distinct, the latter simply available for the taking by the former. Each informs and shapes the other in another unity of opposites driving economic, social, and natural history.

Capitalist practice leads away from confronting this central reality in several ways: the dominance of short-run thinking; the narrowness of private accounting of costs and benefits; and limits on government regulation. Of these, the last is the key element because government regulation is the only way to impose long-term socially responsible behavior on private actors to protect and advance the public interest. Pursuit of narrow self-interest without regard to its larger social impact becomes dysfunctional and ironically undermines individual success itself. It is only in a well-functioning whole that the individual can flourish. But the sanctity of private property rights that capitalists assert in following their economic interests makes it extremely difficult to impose effective social restraints on private economic decisions.

The imperatives of competition also lead to short-run thinking. Occasional declarations by corporate leaders that recognize the importance of taking social consequences into account in their corporate decision-making soon run up against the logic of competitive pressures that make self-regulation of private behavior ephemeral at best. In 2019, for example, the Business Roundtable, which brings together the CEOs of almost two hundred of the largest US corporations, issued a statement that "redefines the purpose of the corporation to promote 'an economy that serves all Americans,'" the latest in a series of corporate commitments to "stakeholder capitalism."[15] That sounded good, and the statement drew widespread interest in the media and business press because it committed the leaders of the most consequential corporations in the country to take account in their decisions of the interests of all "stakeholders"—their workers, customers, suppliers, and communities, as well as shareholders.

But, a year later, the air was out of the balloon. The stresses of the COVID-19 crisis and the demands for racial justice that arose in 2020 proved a test of the new principles. The crises proved too much for them. A corporate study, funded by the Ford Foundation and reported in the *New York Times* a year after the initial statement, found that "signatories have done no better than other companies in protecting jobs, labor rights and workplace safety during the pandemic, while failing to distinguish themselves in pursuit of racial and gender equality." In one egregious example, Marriott, the hotel company, announced in March 2020 that they were forced by the pandemic to lay off tens of thousands of workers, yet a mere two weeks later announced a $160 million dividend payment to its shareholders.[16] In a follow-up study exploring experience with the pledge on its second anniversary, reported in the *Wall Street Journal*, the authors "found evidence that the signatory CEOs didn't intend to make any significant changes to how they do business."[17]

Champions of free markets have long asserted that if we only allow people enough time to respond to market conditions on their own, any economic imbalances that might appear in the short run will be corrected in the long run. But, as economist John Maynard Keynes trenchantly replied during the years of the Great Depression in the 1930s, "In the long run we are all dead." Keynes developed a theory of capitalist economic instability that justified the corrective intervention of governments to do what markets alone were incapable of doing. In a similar vein, businesses that wait for the long run often die while, in the short run, competitors cut their economic throats. The dynamic promoting short-run focus for corporate decision-making is often blamed for executives' concentration on their corporate quarterly earnings, which influence current stock prices, the basis of bonuses that form a large portion of executive compensation. But the consequences of short-run thinking are far deeper and more difficult to control than their effect on executive compensation.

The legal requirements of private economic calculation also narrow what a business must take into account only to those costs it has to pay itself. The business does not have to take into account the social costs of its activities when calculating its profits. Economists term the social costs unaccounted for in private business calculations "externalities," because they are external to the requirements of private accounting. This explains why businesses do not account for the broader consequences of their private action. Economists have long recognized the presence of externalities in capitalist markets. Air and water pollution caused by manufacturing processes are common examples. The damage from soot falling from power-plant chimneys onto people's clothes and into their lungs causes those people to pay more for laundry and health care. Acid run-off from paper mills going into rivers kills off fish and makes the water undrinkable.

Yet those costs in terms of health, diminished capacity in the fishing industry, and water purification requirements, which are very real in society, are hidden because the economic decision-makers in the power and paper industries do not have to pay for those costs. Unlike the cost of materials, fuel, or labor, which the company does have to pay, they are external to the firm's decision-making. In these circumstances, by encouraging too much output of harmful products, profit-maximizing decisions by individual businesses lead to social dysfunction. The business pushes onto others in society the external costs it imposes but does not have to pay for. Private profit exaggerates the overall net gain of the business in society because it does not take into account the social as well as the private costs.

Economists have long understood such "market failures" and have come up with many ways to force businesses to pay for the social costs resulting from their activities, to internalize these otherwise external costs. When the adverse effects arise from a single company, lawsuits may eventually force the company to pay damages. Regulation and class action lawsuits can sometimes address the effects of whole industries, as happened with cigarette manufacturers. But these methods all involve government regulation or other intervention into private markets, which corporations fiercely resist, using all available political, legal, and public relations methods.

A further challenge to the global environment arises from modern warfare, and military preparations for it. The US military, swollen to imperial proportions, is the greatest single consumer of fossil fuels on the planet.[18] Furthermore, reliance on fossil fuels drives resource wars for access and control of fossil fuel reserves. Meanwhile, military exercises, to say nothing of actual war fighting, destroy natural environments. One example of this reality is highlighted in the long but ultimately successful campaign to end US naval bombardment of the Puerto Rican island of Vieques in 2003, which had wreaked havoc on the island.[19] It is obvious in the wide destruction of the natural and built environments of Iraq, Syria, Libya, Yemen, and other countries devastated by war in recent years. We must understand that resolution of the environmental crisis we face must also involve the demilitarization of US foreign policy and the sharp reduction of military operations worldwide.

Crises in Capitalist Society

Environmental degradation is not the only form of crisis capitalist societies face. The accumulation of capital and its associated economic expansion do not proceed smoothly over time. They are interrupted periodically by economic disruptions unheard of in earlier societies (which of course had problems of their own). They arise from the same underlying problems inherent in the process of capital accumulation that we have seen drive environmental degradation: short-run thinking; adverse social consequences from private decision-making; and the inability to control private economic decisions through social (government) planning.

Since the early nineteenth century, capitalist economies have experienced periods in which production has collapsed and large numbers of businesses have gone broke. These periods have been called crises, panics, recessions, and depressions; they are unlike anything ever experienced before. Enslaved people were not laid off. In the normal course of feudal life, no serf was forcibly removed from access to basic means of survival (land) and left to starve. Freed from the bondage of serfdom and slavery, however, workers experience new forms of degradation and destitution, both on the job and in the desperation of unemployment.

Economic crisis arises in capitalism when the conditions of accumulation interrupt accumulation. Think of it as capitalism tripping over its own feet. In one way or another, economic conditions that lead to expansion create new conditions that undermine the expansion. This can happen in a number of ways that can vary over time from downturn to downturn.

For example, in the upswing capital investment brings more factory buildings and equipment online to meet increasing demand, in an uncoordinated process of individual business decisions. If these physical materials increase at a rate greater than the increase in productive workers hired to use them, there can come a time when the surplus created by the workforce decreases as a fraction of the total capital used to buy the required equipment, materials, and labor power. If this happens in a single company or industry it will not affect the economy as a whole, although it may improve the profitability of one company if it alone is in a better position to compete for a share of the surplus created by all. But if nearly every business invests to get a competitive advantage in this way and it becomes a generalized social phenomenon that physical capital is advanced for production in ever greater proportion to the labor required to use it, then, on a social scale, labor power, the part of capital that creates surplus, becomes a smaller fraction of the total capital. What improves profitability when one company does it can bring about the opposite when all businesses do it. At that point, after a broad unregulated, unplanned growth in business investment and available capacity relative to the workforce, the whole economy can experience a reduction in the growth of available surplus, which, after all, arises only from the now relatively smaller productive work force. When that happens, profits tend to fall in the economy, investment tends to be cut back, business slows, workers are laid off, remaining workers also see their incomes decline, and we go into an economic downturn. The downturn continues until the conditions of profitability return and investment picks up again.

This is an example of what is sometimes called the "fallacy of composition," in which we see that the total is not necessarily the simple sum of its parts. If one firm invests in new capacity, the results for that firm may be quite different, even the opposite, compared with what happens if everyone else does the same. In another example, if one person saves more, their savings increase. If everyone else in society also saves more at the same time, then people overall will tend to buy less as they save more, market demand for products will tend to fall, production will fall, people will get laid off, and wages decline. The consequence could then be that everyone may actually be able to save less because they all tried to save more. Here again, the sum of individual decisions leads to an opposite social outcome.

An economic crisis can also happen if the working class receives "too much" in higher wages during an expansion. When the economy approaches full employment, competition for labor may result in businesses offering wage increases to attract workers from other employers. If workers' wages increase faster than their productivity, profits can fall, again resulting in an economic downturn if the condition extends throughout the economy. In this case, too, the downturn continues until the underlying conditions of profitability return.

Or the reverse can happen when production in the upswing increases rapidly as each business expands to take maximum advantage of the possibility for greater sales. Each business makes decisions on the basis of its own hopes for private profit. In the absence of any plan for the overall output for the industry, it can happen that adding up all the individual business decisions to increase output eventually leads to a dysfunctional social result in which the market as a whole is swamped with output beyond what buyers are prepared to buy. Again, if this is widespread, business in general cuts back, workers are laid off, and a downturn sets in until underlying conditions change and output again expands. This is another example of the fallacy of composition at work—the action of a single person or business has one effect, if taken alone, but the opposite effect if everyone does it.

There are also financial crises, driven by disruptions in the systems of credit that capitalist economies create. The 2008 crisis is, at this writing, the most recent in a centuries-long series of financial meltdowns that have resulted in vast damage and suffering in the US and throughout the world. Their specific causes have varied over time. But they all share a foundation in the fallacy of composition, in which what looks like a money-making strategy if one bank does it turns into social disaster if many do it.

Capitalists do not like depressions or financial crises, although some deep-pocketed capitalists can gain by buying up failing rivals. Capitalists do not want disruptions in their profit-making. Over the history of capitalism, they have promoted many policies and institutions to prevent crises or mitigate their effects. When I was an undergraduate taking my first economics class in 1962, the professor told us that economists had figured out how to smooth out the business cycle and end unemployment. They proposed the application of fiscal policy based on the theories of John Maynard Keynes, adjusting taxes and government spending to compensate for market failures. I was thrilled, having seen the terrible effects of unemployment growing up in Detroit. The promise of Keynesian policy drew me into majoring in economics and becoming an economist.

Since then, however, the "Chicago School" of free-market economists based at the University of Chicago has challenged Keynesian thinking, claiming instead that careful control of the money supply can end capitalist crises. Their reliance on monetary policy and free markets has won many adherents among defenders of corporate power and changed government policy dramatically in recent decades. But, all in all, I am sorry to report that, so far, despite these many fiscal and monetary approaches to the problem, experience shows that crises are inherent in capitalism.

What we have seen as fallacies of composition we can also understand as examples of the contradiction between social production and private appropriation inherent to capitalism. Because there is no way to plan overall economic activity in capitalism, there is no way within the logic of the capitalist economy to address the perverse consequences of social production undertaken for private gain. This unity of opposites is capitalism itself, as are its consequent economic crises. Government intervention may address some aspects of this contradiction and relieve some of the ill effects of crisis, but only by imposing some social discipline on the behavior of individual capitalists. This of course raises capitalists' political hackles.

The idea of "crisis" conveys something acute, a sharp break from what is normal. The crises I have described are like that, turning points from economic growth and capital accumulation to periods of economic decline. But in a society divided by class and race and gender and beset by dramatic and increasing inequality, not everyone moves together through these booms and busts.

In the United States, many tens of millions of people live in what can only be called *chronic* crisis. Upswings barely reach communities where poverty, social marginalization, neighboring environmental pollution, illness, and poor education persist through national good times as well as bad. In thinking about capitalist crises, the chronic kind must not be forgotten as we address the periodic acute crises that afflict us from time to time.

Privatization—Everything Becomes a Commodity

A commodity is anything that is produced for sale in a market, rather than for direct consumption or use by the person or family who produced it. Commodity production existed long before capitalism, as we see in the presence of market squares going back millennia around the world. In earlier societies commodity production was at most a sideline, marginal to the dominant methods of production and distribution of what we now call goods and services. The World Bank reported that in 2022 half the world's population lived on less than $6.85 per person per day, while 8% of the population, 648 million people, lived on less than $2.15.[20] Unimaginable in Western experience, it makes sense when we realize that they buy almost nothing in the market, producing almost everything on a subsistence basis for direct consumption. They are desperately poor, but they can live on so little income because they do not live in capitalist economies. In their relatively remote homelands, their need for money is limited because commodity production is not yet a central and defining characteristic, but still lurks at the outer edges of the traditional social order.

As capitalism gradually emerged from within feudal societies in England, Europe, and more recently in China and other developing economies, more and more goods and services came to be produced as commodities. Because commodities trade for money, this development increasingly allowed surplus to take the form of money, which could be reinvested into greater production, unlike earlier forms of surplus that we have seen took the form of specific objects.

As capitalism developed, more and more people came away from earlier forms of labor and increased the numbers of the working class. In this transition, the laboring population left arrangements in which they mostly grew their own food and made their own clothes and household necessities. Instead, workers came into a world in which they had to buy these necessities because, in the slums of growing cities, they no longer had any regular connection to land and because their working hours were so long that they had no time or energy for much household production. The expansion of markets involved the gradual conversion of what was traditionally household production available for immediate consumption into the product of a business that one sells or buys in the market. In this way the growth of the working class, the spread of commodity production into ever more areas of human consumption, and the rise of capitalism as a dominant economic system all came together.

Commodity production became a powerful engine for the creation of wealth, which capitalist institutions concentrate into the hands of the relatively few who dominate the economy. Ultimately, the rising capitalist class was able to overthrow and replace the feudal economic, political, and cultural institutions within which it originated.

The fact that wealth arises from commodity production gives an urgent incentive to anyone who wants to become rich to find a way to produce one or another commodity and bring it successfully to market. It is in the very logic of capitalism to generalize commodity production. This form of production for the first time contributes to the introduction of the "social division of labor," in which people or small local communities no longer have to produce everything they need. Instead, people can specialize in making one item as a commodity, sell it in a market, and use the money to buy what they need from other producers who have also specialized to produce different products.

Later the production of each of these products is further refined into the "detail division of labor," in which the work making a specific product is itself divided into many steps, each done by a different worker, with still other workers taking the parts into the process of final assembly. This specialization allowed for the mass production that arose in the early twentieth century—Henry Ford invented the assembly line only in 1915—and the increases in productivity that underlay the explosion of wealth in capitalist societies.

But commodification reaches far beyond the advantages of the division of labor. As market competition intensifies in the making and selling of one product, entrepreneurs seize upon some other product they can supply where there is less competition, meeting some need others had not yet recognized, thought how to satisfy, or to create. This fuels often-frantic efforts to convince people that they must buy what they never had before, had never heard of, had never thought they needed, now conveniently available for a price in the market. Advertising and marketing campaigns were unknown before capitalism because there was no need to bolster commodity production. But because the process of commodification of everything is inherent to capitalism the result has been an explosion of resources devoted to marketing and advertising through the twentieth century into the twenty-first.

Commodification extends into the internal working of corporations as well. The advantages that specialization brings to efficient operations often results in firms contracting out functions once performed internally, sometimes called outsourcing. This can range from simple examples, such as a business taking care of payroll and related tax payments for other businesses, to the complete hollowing out of the corporation through subcontracting almost everything about the product except its branding. Nike is an example of such a hollowed-out corporation; beyond product design, Apple is another.

Political demands to privatize government functions are another form that the economic imperative for commodification takes.[21] Such traditional public functions as schools, the postal service, prisons and detention facilities, and military operations are increasingly under pressure to leave the realm of government provision. Sometimes these arrangements take the form of private companies taking over the activity altogether, as when public bus routes are sold off to private companies. At other times, private companies are brought in as contractors to perform the function, paid for with public funds, but now undertaken for private profit. The process is usually driven by free-market ideology, with results that very often fail to provide the efficiencies proponents claim.[22]

The operations of private military contractors came under public scrutiny when heavily armed Blackwater employees escorting US State

Department personnel in Baghdad killed seventeen people in Nisour Square in 2007.[23] A Congressional Research Service study reported that, while the US Marine Corps has traditionally had responsibility for protecting State Department facilities, now about 90% of personnel deployed to protect US embassies and diplomatic facilities around the world work for private security contractors.[24] A 2017 academic study addressed the effects:

> In sum, the privatization of diplomatic security is an increasingly widespread practice. Yet the use of armed guards to provide diplomatic protection has frequently proved problematic. Fraud, overbilling and the insufficient staffing, vetting and training of private security guards have not only resulted in wasteful spending, but have also jeopardized the security of diplomatic posts. Moreover, insufficient monitoring, unclear accountability mechanisms and permissive rules for the use of firearms have sometimes translated into abuses and human rights violations. In such cases, the armed protection of embassies and foreign service personnel has undermined the effectiveness of the diplomatic activities that it is intended to enable.[25]

Protecting private markets from government encroachment is a central demand of corporate leaders and lobbyists. When President Barack Obama began the process of formulating what became the Affordable Care Act, for example, the first thing his office did was invite representatives of the big insurance, hospital, and pharmaceutical corporations to set out their needs and demands, what they required to not oppose whatever would emerge in the legislation. They made it plain that there could be no "public option," let alone a Medicare for All or other single-payer system in the reform. And there was none.[26]

As capitalism functions in the United States, health care remains a commodity, provided for the profit of private insurance and pharmaceutical companies and large hospital consortia that operate to the detriment of public health and the health of many tens of millions of people.

We have seen that the focal point of some of the most vital movements of the early twenty-first century arose in consequence of the workings of the capitalist system. The profound influence of this system extends far beyond the workplace. Knowing this context gives activists and organizers a better grounding for cooperation across what are now too often isolated issue-based campaigns. That in turn will contribute to building the broad movement required to turn our country in a radically different direction.

Notes

1   Marco Polo, *The Travels of Marco Polo* (New York: Penguin Classics, 2016).
2   See, for example, Maurice Dobb, *Studies in the Development of Capitalism* (New York: International Publishers, 1963 [1946]).
3   Bill Fletcher Jr., "How Race Enters Class in the United States," in *What's Class Got to Do with It? American Society in the Twenty-First Century*, ed. Michael Zweig (Ithaca, NY: Cornell University ILR Press, 2004).
4   Roxanne Dunbar-Ortiz, *An Indigenous Peoples' History of the United States* (Boston: Beacon Press, 2014); Rick Sapp, *Native Americans, State by State* (New York: Chartwell Books, 2018).
5   Adam Hochschild, *King Leopold's Ghost* (New York: Houghton Mifflin Harcourt, 1998), 233.
6   Richard Overy, *Russia's War* (New York: Penguin Books, 1999), 327–28.
7   National World War II Museum, "Worldwide Deaths in World War II," accessed August 28, 2021, https://www.nationalww2museum.org/students-teachers/student-resources/research-starters/research-starters-worldwide-deaths-world-war.
8   Dwight D. Eisenhower, "Farewell Address," January 17, 1961, Lillian Goodman Law Library, Yale Law School, accessed August 28, 2021, https://avalon.law.yale.edu/20th_century/eisenhower001.asp.
9   Stockholm International Peace Research Institute, "Military Expenditures by Country, 1949–2021," accessed March 23, 2023, https://www.sipri.org/databases/milex.
10 National Priorities Project, "The Militarized Budget 2020," June 22, 2020, https://www.nationalpriorities.org/analysis/2020/militarized-budget-2020.
11 William Cronon, *Changes in the Land: Indians, Colonists, and the Ecology of New England* (New York: Hill and Wang, 2003).
12 Rachel Carson, *Silent Spring* (New York: Houghton Mifflin Harcourt, 2002 [1962]).
13 President's Science Advisory Committee, *Restoring the Quality of Our Environment*, Report of the Environmental Pollution Panel (November 1965), accessed August 28, 2021, https://carnegiedge.s3.amazonaws.com/downloads/caldeira/PSAC,%201965,%20Restoring%20the%20Quality%20of%20Our%20Environment.pdf.
14 Ursula K. Le Guin, *The Left Hand of Darkness* (New York: Walker and Company, 1969), 225.
15 Business Roundtable, "Business Roundtable Redefines the Purpose of a Corporation to Promote 'An Economy That Serves All Americans,'" August 19, 2019, https://www.businessroundtable.org/business-roundtable-redefines-the-purpose-of-a-corporation-to-promote-an-economy-that-serves-all-americans.
16 Peter Goodman, "Stakeholder Capitalism Gets a Report Card: It's Not Good," *New York Times*, September 22, 2020, updated December 2, 2020, https://www.nytimes.com/2020/09/22/business/business-roudtable-stakeholder-capitalism.html.
17 Lucian A. Bebchuk and Roberto Tallarita, "'Stakeholder' Talk Proves Empty Again," *Wall Street Journal*, August 19, 2021.
18 Union of Concerned Scientists, "US Military and Oil," June 30, 2014, https://www.ucsusa.org/clean_vehicles/smart-transportation-solutions/us-military-oil-use.html.
19 Nathalie Schils, "Puerto Ricans Force United States Navy Out of Vieques Island, 1999–2003," Global Non-Violent Data Base, July 7, 2011, https://nvdatabase.swarthmore.edu/content/puerto-ricans-force-united-states-navy-out-vieques-island-1999-2003.
20 Marta Schoch, Samuel Kofi Tetteh Baah, Christof Lakner, and Jed Friedman, "Half of the Global Population Lives on Less Than US$6.85 Per Person Per Day," World Bank, December 8, 2022, accessed July 12, 2023, https://blogs.worldbank.org/developmenttalk/half-global-population-lives-less-us685-person-day.
21 Donald Cohen and Allen Mikaelian, *The Privatization of Everything: How the Plunder of Public Goods Transformed America and How We Can Fight Back* (New York: New Press, 2021).
22 Elliott D. Sklar, *You Don't Always Get What You Pay For: The Economics of Privatization* (Ithaca, NY: Cornell University Press, 2000).

23   Kevin Peraino, "Blackwater: The Confidential Iraqi Incident Report," *Newsweek*, September 29, 2007, https://www.newsweek.com/blackwater-confidential-iraqi-incident-report-100777.

24   Alex Tiersky and Susan B. Epstein, *Securing U.S. Diplomatic Facilities and Personnel Abroad: Background and Policy Issues* (Washington, DC: Congressional Research Service, July 30, 2014), 5, https://fas.org/sgp/crs/row/R42834.pdf.

25   Eugenio Cusumano, "Diplomatic Security for Hire: The Causes and Implications of Outsourcing," *Hague Journal of Diplomacy* 12, no. 1 (December 23, 2017), https://doi.org/10.1163/1871191X-12341345.

26   Michael Kirk, "Obama's Deal," PBS *Frontline*, April 13, 2010, https://www.pbs.org/wgbh/pages/frontline/obamasdeal/etc/script.html.

CHAPTER SEVEN

Religion, Values, and Interests

"Every major religious tradition places challenging oppression and criticizing systems of injustice at the center of its moral considerations.... This moment requires us to push into the national consciousness a deep moral analysis as the foundation for an agenda to combat systemic poverty and racism, war mongering, economic injustice, voter suppression, and other attacks on the most vulnerable."
—Rev. William J. Barber II and Rev. Liz Theoharis

With the above words, Rev. William J. Barber II and Rev. Liz Theoharis introduced the Poor People's Campaign: A National Call for Moral Revival.[1] This movement, successor to the Poor People's Campaign initiated by Rev. Martin Luther King Jr. shortly before his death in 1968, embodies the close connection between religious interpretation and class interests. While the clergy engaged in the Poor People's Campaign take to heart the first sentence in the epigraph and seek a social practice that accords with it, many evangelical Christian clergy and other religious leaders promote an interpretation of gospel that puts the accumulation of wealth and opposition to homosexuality and abortion at the center of their beliefs and practice. They champion a political agenda at odds with its counterpart in the Poor People's Campaign. In this chapter we will investigate ways in which religious expression, and values and ethics more generally, influence and are influenced by social conditions and class divisions.

Religion and ethics take on lives of their own, at any moment only loosely related to economic dynamics. But they remain connected dialectically rather than being completely independent. The same is true for cultural norms and political institutions. Tensions between economic fundamentals and their political, cultural, and ethical contexts arise as class dynamics alter social conditions. These in turn come to outgrow and challenge the traditional beliefs and institutions that were better suited to earlier socioeconomic arrangements. We will see an example of this shortly in modern historical developments in Catholic social teaching.

Progressive movements need to be alert to such changing dynamics and include and encourage religious activists as they confront opposition within their faiths. Class differences percolate through religious, cultural, and educational institutions and beliefs, as we will see with race and gender in the next chapter.

Religion

Perhaps the most famous single critical assessment of religious belief is Karl Marx's observation that religion is "the opium of the people." On this basis, for generations many leftists have opposed religious training, practice, and institutional power. They have dismissed them as delusional distractions from reality that poison working people's minds and prevent them from dealing with the exploitation and oppression they face. They have looked with skepticism at the religious motivations of progressive faith leaders.

But we should read the whole passage. It suggests that Marx's view was far more nuanced and sympathetic. He wrote: "Religious suffering is, at one and the same time, the expression of real suffering and a protest against real suffering. Religion is the sigh of the oppressed creature, the heart of a heartless world, and the soul of soulless conditions. It is the opium of the people."[2]

Here Marx makes two important observations. Religion is "the sigh of the oppressed," and it offers relief from pain. In that way religion supplies "heart in a heartless world." Those who condemn religion as delusion should consider the importance of the comfort that religion gives to suffering people. Secular-minded progressives don't have to be religious themselves to treat those needs with respect.

This cultural and political statement must, however, be taken in the context of the other insight Marx contributes: that religion is both an expression of, and protest against, actual suffering. Religion reflects the social conflicts and material contradictions in society, and is shaped by them.[3] For many people, religious institutions play guiding roles in directing personal behavior. The content of religious guidance is, therefore, of great importance to those who rule, and to those who would challenge that rule. In other words, religious institutions and beliefs are also arenas for the assertion of class power and venues for class conflict.

This is not unique to capitalist society. The Catholic Church played a central role for centuries in justifying and maintaining feudal rule in Europe, far beyond the "divine right of kings." The rise of capitalism in Europe included challenges to Catholic hegemony with the rise of Protestant faiths more consistent with attitudes required for the practical tasks of capital accumulation.[4] Catholic doctrine also eventually changed to accommodate more effectively the new social circumstances.

As capitalism has developed, the injustices of its class, race, and gender divides have called for religious response and reinterpretation. The resulting differences in religious views, which create tensions within denominations, correspond to the material conflicts they address. Some Christian churches defended racial slavery and continued to preach white supremacy well into the late twentieth century.[5] Other Christian churches preached abolitionism and advocated racial equality. Some Christian teachings counsel worker submission to capitalist discipline.[6] Others assist strikers and admonish corporate executives to honor their workers.[7]

The development of modern Catholic social teaching exemplifies the dynamic links between religious doctrine and secular class conflict. As socialist influence spread throughout the working classes in Europe in the last half of the nineteenth century, Pope Leo XIII in 1891 issued the first encyclical to address the relationship between labor and capital, *Rerum Novarum*, a fascinating document.[8] He wasted no time getting straight to the point.

After noting the rise of class conflict in the encyclical's first paragraph, the Pope immediately warned against "crafty agitators [who will] pervert men's judgments ... to stir up the people to revolt." In the fourth paragraph, we find sympathy for the fear every capitalist feels when confronted by a rising working class: "To remedy these wrongs the socialists, working on the poor man's envy of the rich, are striving to do away with private property." *Rerum Novarum* presents what Leo XIII saw as the church's urgent response to socialism. To blunt the influence of socialist organizers, the church—for the first time—had to present itself and its teachings as legitimate alternatives. The church required its own enumeration of the rights and responsibilities of labor and capital.

Pope Leo XIII put it this way:

Now, in preventing such strife as this, and in uprooting it, the efficacy of Christian institutions is marvellous and manifold. First of all, there is no intermediary more powerful than religion (whereof the Church is the interpreter and guardian) in drawing the rich and the working class together, by reminding each of its duties to the other, and especially of the obligations of justice.

Of these duties, the following bind the proletarian and the worker: fully and faithfully to perform the work which has been freely and equitably agreed upon; never to injure the property, nor to outrage the person, of an employer; never to resort to violence in defending their own cause, nor to engage in riot or disorder; and to have nothing to do with men of evil principles, who work upon the people with artful promises of great results, and excite foolish hopes which usually end in useless regrets and grievous loss.

The following duties bind the wealthy owner and the employer: not to look upon their work people as their bondsmen, but to respect in every man his dignity as a person ennobled by Christian character. They are reminded that, according to natural reason and Christian philosophy, working for gain is creditable, not shameful, to a man, since it enables him to earn an honorable livelihood; but to misuse men as though they were things in the pursuit of gain, or to value them solely for their physical powers—that is truly shameful and inhuman. Again justice demands that, in dealing with the working man, religion and the good of his soul must be kept in mind. Hence, the employer is bound to see that the worker has time for his religious duties; that he be not exposed to corrupting influences and dangerous occasions; and that he be not led away to neglect his home and family, or to squander his earnings.[9]

Following this encyclical, the church began its organized resistance to socialist thought and practice. It established Catholic trade unions that sought faithful collaboration between labor and capital, condemning the militant efforts of socialist unions. The church established Christian Democratic political parties in Europe to challenge the class-conscious leadership of socialist and communist parties. Even when European socialism split into radical communist organizations and reformist socialist ones during and after World War I, the church, in a 1931 encyclical by Pope Pius XI, to mark the fortieth anniversary of the publication of *Rerum*

Novarum, was clear: "no one can be at the same time a good Catholic and a true socialist."[10] Unfortunately, this continuing attitude of antisocialist, anticommunist, anti-Marxist teaching led the church to close collaboration with fascism in Spain, Germany, and Italy before and during World War II, and in parts of Latin America, and East and Southeast Asia, after World War II.

But this reactionary view was not the only thread of Catholic social doctrine after the war. Following the reforms of Vatican Council II (1962–65), organized by Popes Paul VI and John XXIII, which called on the church to address the changing demands of the modern world, a dynamic new theology emerged as a result: liberation theology.

Two important characteristics of liberation theology, which first took hold in Latin America, brought its adherents into sympathetic alignment with socialist movements: the "preferential option for the poor"; and the belief that social structures, not just individual behavior, can be sinful. As Brazilian Catholic priest Leonardo Boff explained, "There are structural evils that transcend individual ones. The church is, whether it likes it or not, involved in a context that transcends it. What shall be its function? Shall it be oil or sand within the social mechanism? ... It ought to participate, *critically*, in the global upsurge of liberation."[11]

This was a call to the church in clear response to the "upsurge of liberation" that had recently been sweeping through many countries in Africa, Asia, and Latin America, most led by socialists or communists of one stripe or another. These movements shook their societies to the core and demanded the attention of anyone concerned for the poor. Leonardo Boff and other liberation theologians engaged "critically," but they engaged sympathetically. They saw the church as an institutional base for mobilizing the poor and working people as active agents in their own liberation, a process they said must involve challenging the church itself insofar as it is an institution that supports and mirrors these sinful structures.[12]

Salvation, in liberation theology, is not a result of individual piety; it requires constructive individual participation in the collective social movements to banish sinful structures and bring liberation to ordinary people. Gustavo Gutiérrez, one of the most important Protestant voices of Latin American liberation theology, put it this way: "It is also necessary to avoid the pitfalls of individualistic charity.... The term ["liberation theology"] refers also to [people] considered in the fabric of social relationships.... It means the transformation of a society of structures to benefit a few who appropriate to themselves the value of the work of others. The transformation ought to be directed toward a radical change in the foundation of society."[13]

James H. Cone, one of the earliest voices of liberation theology in the United States, defined Black liberation theology, independently of Latin American developments, in a similar way: "The language of theology challenges the societal structures because it is inseparable from the suffering community."[14] Cone explained: "The task of Black Theology is to make sure that Black faith *remains critical of itself* so that Black religion can continue to function as a creative revolutionary challenge to structures of injustice."[15] Here Cone is pointing to the struggle required inside the Black church to bring the thought and power of liberation theology to the forefront in the church, to make it an instrument of liberation for its people. The same requirement is present in every faith.

Gayraud S. Wilmore added that "Black [Liberation] Theology ... makes room in its formulations for an understanding of liberation that includes the contributions of Native American, Hispanic, Asian, and White brothers and sisters in struggle for the humanity made possible for all by the cross of Christ."[16] And Cone, adding the dimension of class into his analysis in 1986, wrote, "Anyone who claims to be fighting against the problem of oppression and does not analyze the exploitive role of capitalism is either naïve or an agent of the enemies of freedom."[17] We find this outlook in the call that Rev. William Barber and Rev. Liz Theoharis have put at the center of the Poor People's Campaign: A National Call for Moral Revival, quoted at the start of this chapter.

These tenets reflect working class values of mutual aid, based on theological principles that oppose the extreme individualism of capitalist society. In practice, they challenge the power relations central to the capitalist system and those within religious hierarchies that apologize for them. To make these tenets operational, political education among poor and working people, and within religious (and secular) institutions, progressives must make explicit the values involved and expose the structural issues we all must engage.

This difference in class orientation within theology also underlies different approaches people take to poverty. The approach consistent with capitalist power proposes to treat poor people as separate individuals who for one reason or another lack the means to escape poverty. Their suffering is then addressed with individual attention, either through acts of charity or with the provision of education, social skills, or other requirements that individuals need to succeed in the labor market.

A systemic approach, on the other hand, starts from the understanding that poverty happens to the working class, that the poor are best understood as workers in hard straits.[18] This opens the door to seeing that the disproportionate incidence of poverty in Black and Hispanic communities is not a matter of personal failures, but rests in the history of white supremacy, coupled with the common condition they share with white workers who are also poor. White workers with this understanding can more easily escape the grip of racist stereotypes used to characterize poor people in the US and find common cause with Black people who are in the same boat.

The radical class content of liberation theology caught the attention of Cardinal Joseph Ratzinger before he was elevated to be Pope Benedict XVI in 2005. Writing a sharp critique of liberation theology in his role as leader of the church's Congregation for the Doctrine of the Faith in 1984, Cardinal Ratzinger said: "It must be criticized not just on the basis of this or that affirmation, but on the basis of its classist viewpoint ... which has come to function in it as a determining principle.... Moreover in setting aside the authoritative interpretation of the Church, denounced as classist, one is at the same time departing from tradition.... one returns to the opposition of the 'Jesus of history' versus the 'Jesus of faith.'"[19]

This last comment refers to the interpretation of Jesus in liberation theology that emphasizes the example of his historical outrage at social injustice and his radical overturning of the moneychangers in the temple. Cardinal Ratzinger criticized this "historical" approach, seeking instead to give prominence to the traditional interpretation Christian theology assigns to Christ as mystical savior. In their challenge to liberation theology, Cardinal Ratzinger and other critics, Protestant as well as Catholic, reject the "classist" assertion that structural change is the essence of salvation. Despite their ready appeals to charity on behalf of the poor, in leaving the matter there they take their place among apologists for capitalist power and continuation of the capitalist structural conditions that generate human suffering.

The influence of liberation theology rippled through US Catholic teaching into the 1980s. In 1986, the US Conference of Bishops issued a letter on the economy that supported workers' rights to unions, full employment, and other progressive goals.[20] This was a good example of the kind of problems that Lewis Powell, in his 1971 memo to the US Chamber of Commerce, had identified as progressive targets that had to be reversed.* And, indeed, from the mid-1980s, there followed, in the US and throughout the Catholic world, a shift in Catholic social teaching firmly away from liberation theology. This rightward shift coincided with the increasing power of neoliberal capitalism as it asserted ever-greater economic, cultural, and political dominance from the 1980s onward.

A similar dynamic had transformed Buddhism in Japan as the country modernized and embraced capitalism. As Indian writer Pankaj Mishra put it, Buddhist leaders there "became ideologues of the new nationalism.... Zen Buddhism became by the twentieth century the mascot of a progressive, rational, and politically unified Japan, a sign of its cultural superiority over the rest of Asia.... Many Buddhist leaders had little trouble endorsing Japanese imperialism."[21] This is a surprising role for a tradition associated with peace and spiritual contemplation. But it is not surprising as an example of the plasticity of belief under the pressures of social change.

We know from experience that progressive politics can connect with all religious communities.[22] This is possible because religious instruction and practice inevitably become bound up with the social conflicts of the times. Just as secular politics reflect class differences, these differences show up as internal divisions in religious communities as they confront the issues of the day. Martin Luther King Jr. brought theological understanding to the side of the Vietnamese in his opposition to the US war there, in 1967 calling on the US to get "on the right side of history" worldwide, as the civil rights movement was making progressive history at home.[23] But that anti-imperialist view drew immediate and sharp criticism, and even condemnation, from many leaders of King's Baptist denomination, as well as other religious leaders and secular moderates in the civil rights movement of the day.

As religiously based social movements confront suffering and oppression and assert the unity of all people in the image of God, leaders in religious communities will speak to the conflict in ways, sometimes open and sometimes implied, that reflect class interests. Clergy will oppose or support these movements, often speaking in religious terms. Working people and their allies need to be guided by a working class understanding of the religious texts of their faith.

Progressive action in the secular world emboldens its counterparts among the religious; and the reinforcement also goes the other way. But

---

* See the introduction for the details of the Powell memorandum.

history suggests that, as we saw in the example of Catholic social teaching, conflict in the material world, manifest through secular action, ultimately is the dominant force and context for shaping the development of religious doctrine.

I was reminded of this point in a workshop on the social role of tribalism and religion that I attended at a conference of civil society organizations in Baghdad in February 2019. I asked the standard Western question of the Muslim participants: "Where are the moderate imams to counteract the fundamentalist imams?"

They answered with this story: A short time earlier, an influential imam issued a fatwa, a religious ruling and instruction, interpreting Islamic law to prohibit any Muslim person from participating with Christian friends in any celebration, party, or social gathering related to Christmas. The effective response, my workshop mates explained, came not from another imam's contrary teaching on the subject but from thousands of Muslims, mostly young and many devoutly religious, openly celebrating Christmas in Baghdad long into the night with their Christian friends. The religious Muslims who participated were answering the fatwa with action that expressed in practice their own more open, tolerant understanding of their faith, not with some contrary fatwa. It is social practice, not in the first instance dispute over religious doctrine in the abstract, these Iraqis explained, that carries the power to shape the role of religion in society and exert the social pressure required ultimately to adjust a dominant religious teaching.

In her book *Black Wave*, journalist Kim Ghattas explains how this dynamic process has played out across the Middle East and South Asia, from Egypt to Pakistan, since the mid-1970s.[24] There, the struggle within the faith for the meaning of Islam has been brought to a head and profoundly shaped by nonreligious considerations, as "a religious war had been invented by men hungry for power, land, and guns."[25] In the course of these social upheavals, interpretations of Islam changed dramatically. Many Islamic beliefs and practices are not fixed and permanent across time. The same is true of Christian and Jewish beliefs and practices. We should understand that all religions have been deeply transformed in the context of broader social conflicts.

Ghattas points to Nasr Abu Zaid, an Egyptian writer and Qur'anic scholar who died in Cairo in 2010, just before the Arab Spring uprisings, as an example of recent stirrings among Muslims toward reconciliation with secular modernity. "He disagreed virulently with the idea that Muslim society was intrinsically retrograde. He saw the way forward very differently [from those who sought a Western triumph over Islam through culture wars fought out in the clash of civilizations]: salvation did not have to come from the West. Islam's transition to modernity would come from within.... He was walking in the footsteps of nineteenth-century Salafist thinkers like Muhammad Abduh, those who took inspiration from the wisdom of the prophet's companions to forge a way forward in the modern world."[26]

Many assume that the expression and transmission of basic values requires a religious framework. But there are value systems—guides to right behavior—that have no religious root. Confucianism and Buddhism are examples, although some forms of Buddhism suggest religious beliefs. As with activists in faith traditions, the values secular activists hold are intertwined with the material interests they pursue. Secular as well as religious activists espouse and cherish progressive values because these values nourish and secure people in their lived experience. We then seek the expression of these values and interests in the specific interpretations of ethical and faith traditions that enshrine them.

In a movement that embraces all faith traditions, we need to be careful not to give pride of place to the language and imagery of any one tradition. That specificity belongs to each tradition, but when it comes to a progressive movement that unites people across all traditions, the terms of its unifying language must express concepts that are common to all and unique to none. These are the terms of progressive values, those that embrace caring and mutual aid, limits to individualism, and respect for the dignity of all people.

Crossing all faith and secular traditions, the human need to recognize and embrace spiritual experience is profound. "Spiritual" connotes a state that is not narrowly rational, but more a feeling that transcends understanding, an approach to existence that goes beyond materialism. People sometimes think that one must be religious to be spiritual, or that a Marxist could not be spiritual. Progressive politics sometimes disdains the spiritual, just as it sometimes holds religion at arm's length.

But religion and spirituality are not the same. Although I am not a religious person, I have sometimes had spiritual experiences of awe and wonder when contemplating the magnificence of nature, or when thinking of the enormous complexity of society and variety of humanity. I have had spiritual experiences—moments of intense emotional feeling—watching a child at play, or asleep. Ugliness and pain can induce awe and wonder, too. The experience of an epiphany is not a rational act. It is a sudden deeply moving realization of some truth or relationship; it is a spiritual matter. But it does not require religious belief, although for many people the experience calls to mind the mystical power that they believe manifests God.

Religious faith can justify wars and great cruelty, or it can foster peace and human dignity. The same is true for secular systems of values. Appeals to reason alone have led us to vast improvements in medical sciences that greatly advance humanitarian practice. But they also led to the Terror following the French Revolution and the human devastation of Stalinist-era "scientific socialism." It may help to think of reason paired with spirituality as a unity of opposites in the practice of compassion.

Values and Interests

Individualism is one of the central values in capitalist culture. The sanctity of the individual arose as early capitalist development disrupted the feudal order whose ruling class relied on a very different set of principles to justify its power. When rising capitalists sought to break free from the oppressive bonds of feudalism, they turned to philosophers John Locke, Edmund Burke, and others who justified the new order of private property and economic entrepreneurship with a new set of moral principles consistent with that order. Historian Eric Hobsbawm put it clearly: "The armies of the rising middle class* needed the discipline and organization of a strong single-minded morality for their duties."[27]

The dominant values championed in capitalist society reflect and justify the material interests of the capitalist class. These are the sanctity of all forms of private property and the right of individuals to use their property in their own interests. The philosophical writings of John Locke and others who systematized the principles required to accept capitalist practices came to prominence exactly because they wrote just as rising capitalism was challenging feudal Europe. As the saying goes, "There's nothing more powerful than an idea whose time has come." These new economic interests were reflected also in the norms of political democracy, which were at first very limited, applying only to white men with property.

The working class has a different set of values, corresponding to their different material circumstances. These are the values of hard work, coupled with mutual caring and mutual aid. Over time, the working class

---

* "Middle class" here refers to the newly rising merchants and business owners in a middle position between feudal aristocracy and peasants, precursors to the modern capitalist class.

has won participation in political democracy, first for white men with-out property, then for African American men, at least formally, after the Civil War, and finally for women. Champions of the working class have also extended concepts of political democracy to demands for economic democracy, in which workers help shape management practices and busi-ness decisions that affect them.

From FDR's New Deal in the Depression to Lyndon Johnson's 1960s Great Society, progressive politics were explicitly rooted in the values of mutual caring, mutual aid, and economic democracy. These values are grounded in life experience, especially among working people. During the ordinary hardships and stresses of working class life, people tend to look after their neighbors, as they would have their neighbors look after them. These are working class values—values intertwined with particular material experiences and interests.

Progressive values extend from mutual aid to the importance and legit-imacy of collective action. No one can go it alone. Experience again has shown that for working people individual dignity and personal power come from and are protected by collective action. They are not merely a matter of individual will. They are not automatically conferred on working people by ruling authorities who believe in dignity and personal empowerment as abstract values, to be cherished and lived by as a matter of principle. They arise from workers exerting collective power over corporations and other economic institutions through unions and other channels of economic democracy to go along with political democracy. Freedom, democracy, justice, goodness, liberty, and dignity; all these categories are abstractions. They acquire different specific meanings in lived experience at different times, depending upon the class interests and balance of class forces at play.

One of the great ironies of American politics is the way that the Republican Party has, from the 1970s, established itself as the "values party," calling themselves "pro-life" and "pro-family" while undercutting every support for a better and longer life for working people and their children. As part of the long campaign to reassert capitalist power, envisioned by Lewis Powell in his memo to the Chamber of Commerce, the Republican Party and its allied religious leaders have changed the content of morality in the public's mind, shifting it from the mutual aid and economic democracy of the New Deal to the "culture wars" focused on the issues like abortion and who-do-you-sleep-with. This shift created wedge issues that have been effective in dividing workers from each other and their common purpose.

The Democratic Party has failed to confront this narrative effectively. In recent decades, its politicians have failed to champion traditional working class values. They have tended to stress policies instead, addressing what the party presents as workers' interests. They have treated values as secondary, or more often ignored the subject. In doing so, they have ceded the territory to the individualistic values that correspond to capitalist interests.

The labor movement has contributed to this confusion. The AFL-CIO proclaims that labor rights are human rights, grounding their legitimacy in the 1948 United Nations Charter of Human Rights. This framework can be powerful, but if left in this one-sided way it is actually damaging to working people because it turns away from the assertion of mutual aid and economic democracy that built unions in the first place. It promotes in a one-sided way the human rights of the individual without grounding those rights in the power of collective action and concern for the needs of mutual aid.[28]

Ironically, "individual rights" is exactly what anti-union politicians use to justify "right to work" laws that protect the individual right of workers to choose *not* to be in a union, or their right *not* to support their union coworkers through the payment of dues or agency fees, even though they keep the benefits of the contracts the union negotiates with their employer. The same influences have led to the substitution of individual arbitration to resolve contract disputes, replacing in practice and eroding in their principles the power of collective action through union bargaining or class action lawsuits.

The difficulty here is in the belief that human rights can be understood and defended as individual rights without acknowledging that individual rights for workers are meaningless unless they are exercised collectively. The rallying cry of striking sanitation workers in Memphis in 1968, "I am a man," asserted fundamental individual humanity. It won respect and support across the country and appears on signs at labor and civil rights demonstrations to this day. But the workers expressed their human right in the context of collective action, a strike.

It is a human right to live in dignity, have adequate food, shelter, health, and well-being. It is a human right to develop a life of meaning according one's own curiosities. But these rights, thought by many proponents to be inherent in each individual, cannot be realized by individuals simply left to act alone. In a class-conflicted society, formal equality afforded to all can quickly become gross inequality in practice. As the French writer Anatole France sarcastically observed: "In its majestic equality, the law forbids rich and poor alike to sleep under bridges, beg in the streets and steal loaves of bread."[29] When workers and the poor cannot engage in the collective action necessary to achieve these rights, the promise of them is an empty offer.

Ironically, the 1960s cultural rebellions, often expressed in the call for "drugs, sex, and rock n' roll," contributed to the neglect of social solidarity. Although countercultural creativity shared in the rebellion against war and racism then shaking the country, its foundation was individual expression, individual self-fulfillment, individual freedom. It was a "do your own thing" sentiment that challenged the consumer conformity of the 1950s (we smirked appreciatively when Pete Seeger sang Melvina Reynolds's takedown song of houses in suburbia "all made out of ticky-tacky and they all look just the same"), and rightfully opposed the narrow bounds of Cold War politics and racist thinking that dominated our politics and culture. This tradition lives on in the socially permissive attitudes of most Baby Boomers, often easily combined with the individualism inherent in libertarian politics and free-market economics. David Brooks captured something important in this regard in his 1999 book *Bobos in Paradise*, in which he characterized the newly emerging upper class at the turn of this century as "bourgeois bohemians" who live out a combination of counterculture hippie sensibility with a relentless capitalist business ethic.[30]

As in so many aspects of social life, class dynamics underlie differences in our understanding of values; our choice of values carries with it the empowerment of one class or another. Progressive politics cannot simply be a fight over policies. As Rev. Barber and Rev. Theoharis have put it: "The Poor People's Campaign: A National Call for Moral Revival aims to shift the distorted moral narrative, often promoted by religious extremists, from a focus on narrow issues like prayer in school, abortion, and gun rights to a focus on how our society treats the poor, those on the margins, the least of these, LGBTQ folks, workers, immigrants, the disabled and the sick; to how we institutionalize equality and equal representation under the law; and how we realize the desire for peace, love and harmony within and among nations."[31]

A moral revival cannot happen in the abstract. The content of moral revival has force, gains traction, during times that provide the material circumstances in which they make sense, in which they serve some class interest in action. The COVID-19 pandemic shockingly exposed deadly differences in social conditions depending on class, race, and ethnicity. While millions of workers lost their jobs, wealth data from Forbes showed that in the first six months of the pandemic of 2020, the wealth of 643 US billionaires grew by 29%, up by $845 billion, from $2.95 to $3.8 trillion dollars![32] Perhaps *that* will propel a new public understanding of morality more consistent with the experiences and interests of working people. It is a task our movements must make explicit.

Values and interests are different but not wholly distinct. They are best understood as a unity of opposites expressed in dynamic political practice. As politics bring changes to social circumstances, our understanding of interests and values change. They do not embody "permanent truths." Interests and values are rooted ultimately in people's material circumstances. If these circumstances are sharply different according to class, interests and values will also be different for different classes. As the working class vies for power, it has to challenge the capitalists' values framework, starting with its central feature, individualism. We turn to this set of issues in the following chapter.

Notes

1   The epigraph is from the introduction to *The Souls of Poor Folk: Auditing America 50 Years After the Poor People's Campaign Challenged Racism, Poverty, the War Economy/Militarism, and Our National Morality*, pp. 18–19, accessed August 29, 2021, https://www.poorpeoplescampaign. org/wp-content/uploads/2019/12/PPC-Audit-Full-410835a.pdf. For more on the principles, policies, and activist program of the Poor People's Campaign: A National Call for Moral Revival, see https://www.poorpeoplescampaign.org.

2   Karl Marx, *Critique of Hegel's Philosophy of Right*, in *The Marx-Engels Reader*, ed. Robert C. Tucker, 2nd ed. (New York: W.W. Norton, 1978), 54.

3   Karl Marx, "Theses on Feuerbach," in *The Marx-Engels Reader*, ed. Robert C. Tucker, 2nd ed. (W.W. Norton, 1978), 143–45.

4   Max Weber, *The Protestant Ethic and the Spirit of Capitalism* (New York: W.W. Norton, 2008 [1904]).

5   Robert P. Jones, *White Too Long: The Legacy of White Supremacy in American Christianity* (New York: Simon and Schuster, 2020).

6   Ken Estey, *A New Protestant Labor Ethic at Work* (Eugene, OR: Wipf and Stock, 2011).

7   Jeorg Rieger and Rosemarie Henkel-Rieger, *Unified We Are a Force: How Faith and Labor Can Overcome America's Inequalities* (St. Louis, MO: Chalice Press, 2019).

8   Pope Leo XIII, *Rerum Novarum*, accessed August 29, 2021, http://www.vatican.va/content/ leo-xiii/en/encyclicals/documents/hf_l-xiii_enc_15051891_rerum-novarum.html.

9   Pope Leo XIII, paras. 19–20.

10   Pope Pius XI, *Quadragesimo Anno* (1931) paragraph 120, accessed August 29, 2021, http:// www.vatican.va/content/pius-xi/en/encyclicals/documents/hf_p-xi_enc_19310515_ quadragesimo-anno.html.

11   Leonardo Boff, *Jesus Christ Liberator* (Maryknoll, NY: Orbis Books, 1978), 46; emphasis in original.

12   Leonardo Boff, *Church: Charism and Power—Liberation Theology and the Institutional Church* (New York: Crossroad, 1985).

13   Gustavo Gutiérrez, *A Theology of Liberation* (Maryknoll, NY: Orbis Books, 1973), 67.

14   James H. Cone, *A Black Theology of Liberation*, 40th anniv. ed. (Maryknoll, NY; Orbis Books, 2010), 4.

15   James H. Cone, epilogue to *Black Theology: A Documentary History, 1966–1979*, ed. James H. Cone and Gayraud S. Wilmore (Maryknoll, NY: Orbis Books, 1979), 622; emphasis added.

16   Gayraud S. Wilmore, "The New Context for Black Theology," in *Black Theology: A Documentary History, 1966–1979*, ed. James H. Cone and Gayraud S. Wilmore (Maryknoll, NY: Orbis Books, 1979), 605.

17   James H. Cone, preface to the 1986 edition of *A Black Theology of Liberation*, 40th anniv. ed. (Maryknoll, NY: Orbis Books, 2010), xxii.

18   Michael Zweig, "Class and Poverty in the U.S. Economy," in *Religion and Economic Justice*, ed. Michael Zweig (Philadelphia: Temple University Press, 1990).

19   Joseph Ratzinger, "Instruction on Certain Aspects of the 'Theology of Liberation,'" (Rome: Congregation of the Doctrine of the Faith, August 6, 1984), x.3 and x.8, accessed August 29, 2021, http://www.vatican.va/roman_curia/congregations/cfaith/documents/rc_con_cfaith_doc_19840806_theology-liberation_en.html.

20   National Conference of Catholic Bishops, *Economic Justice for All: A Pastoral Letter on Catholic Social Teaching and the U.S. Economy*, November 1986, accessed August 29, 2021, http://www.usccb.org/upload/economic_justice_for_all.pdf.

21   Pankaj Mishra, *An End to Suffering: The Buddha in the World* (New York: Picador, 2004), 306.

22   Michael Zweig, "Economics and Liberation Theology," in *Religion and Economic Justice*, ed. Michael Zweig (Philadelphia: Temple University Press, 1990), 3–49.

23   Martin Luther King Jr., "Beyond Vietnam: A Time to Break Silence," address at Riverside Church, New York City, April 4, 1967, accessed August 29, 2021, https://www.crmvet.org/info/mlk_viet.pdf.

24   Kim Ghattas, *Black Wave* (New York: Henry Holt, 2020).

25   Ghattas, *Black Wave*, 287.

26   Ghattas, *Black Wave*, 265.

27   Eric Hobsbawm, *The Age of Revolution* (New York: Vintage, 1996), 219.

28   Joseph A. McCartin, "Beyond Human Rights: Understanding and Addressing the Attack on Public Sector Unions," *Human Rights Review* 12, no.4 (December 2011); Joseph A. McCartin, "Democratizing the Demand for Workers' Rights: Towards a Reframing of Labor's Argument," *Dissent* 52, no. 1 (Winter 2005): 61–66.

29   Anatole France, *Le Lys Rouge (The Red Lily)*, 1894, 118.

30   David Brooks, *Bobos in Paradise: The New Upper Class and How They Got There* (New York: Simon and Schuster, 1999).

31   Barber and Theoharis, *The Souls of Poor Folk*, 17.

32   Saloni Sardana, "U.S. Billionaires' Wealth Grew by $845 Billion During the First Six Months of the Pandemic," *Business Insider India*, September 17, 2020, accessed August 29, 2021, https://www.businessinsider.in/stock-market/news/us-billionaires-wealth-grew-by-845-billion-during-the-first-six-months-of-the-pandemic/articleshow/78173140.cms.

CHAPTER EIGHT

Cultures of Capitalism

Individualism and Its Limits

During the Cultural Revolution in China in the late 1960s and early 1970s, people described their politics through a series of opposing arguments known as "two-line struggles": The revolutionary line that led down the "socialist road" challenged the reactionary line of the "capitalist road." One such struggle presented this burning question: Which attitude is correct: "public first, self second"; or "public first, self not at all"?

For a time, the correct answer asserted by the Chinese Communist Party leadership was the second formulation. "Self not at all" was the path to the bright communist future; "self second" showed a continuing commitment to a lingering holdover from capitalist individualism that, left unchecked, would lead the country back to the old order.

At the time I favored the first formulation despite its bad odor in the Maoist circles I was part of. It gave some opening to self-interest, but put the needs of society foremost. Its clear message was that the individual should be subordinate to the needs of social development, but at least there was *some* recognition of a legitimate claim to self-concern, denied in the call for "self not at all."

I have since come to believe that both expressions are wrong. I think we should understand the all-important relationship between the individual and society as "self first, in the public interest."

Two examples embody this general maxim. Before a plane takes off, flight attendants instruct the passengers that in case of an emergency when the oxygen masks come down, first put on your own mask and then help the person next to you who may be having trouble. The same principle governs an early part of the training of firefighters and emergency medical technicians. When responding to an emergency, one's first responsibility has to be to oneself, to one's own safety. Once that is secure, the rescue worker can proceed to help others. If you are down because you hurried too quickly to respond to an emergency and forgot to protect yourself, you cannot help anyone; you will even make matters worse because rescue resources will have to be diverted to help you instead of those whose needs called you out in the first place. Similarly, if you don't put that oxygen mask on first, you could pass out before being able to help the person in the next seat.

In these cases, and in general, the principle is to secure oneself and then go on to help or be of service to others. Here we need to avoid an easy dualism that suggests "oneself" as independent of "others," that sees us all as a collection of separate individuals. Taking this view to a ridiculous extreme, British prime minister Margaret Thatcher famously asserted that "there is no such thing as society."

Charles Dickens's biographer Jane Smiley captured the dialectical unity of opposites that connect the individual and society in explaining why that nineteenth-century novelist remains a towering literary figure to this day. "Dickens is still with us, reminding us always that the individual and the group are both present simultaneously, never to be dissolved into each other, but never to be separate, either."[1] We should respect the dialectical unity of self and society. We cannot secure ourselves alone, cannot exist alone, but only in our relationships of mutual aid with others. Nor should society be lifted as an abstraction above the people who compose it.

This principle is not the individualism of capitalist values, which can be expressed as "self first—full stop." We don't say to our airplane seatmate "I got my oxygen mask on, what's the matter with you?" The attitude of "self first—full stop" would keep volunteer firefighters and EMTs from volunteering at all. Individualism of this sort underlies and justifies capitalist practice. It recognizes no needs beyond one's own. It forms the basis of capitalist values. "Self first—full stop" is an individualism that has turned into selfishness and greed.

Capitalists' claims to personal responsibility for their own business successes, and their common assertion that workers, too, are individually responsible for their own life experiences, do not correspond to the actual social character of capitalist production. They reflect a type of individualism that does not correspond to the economic and social realities of our interconnections. The falseness of this idea means that "self first—full stop," generates a dysfunctional society, full stop.

Reflecting again on the problem posed in China's struggle over the relationship between the individual and society, we begin to see that socialist society is not simply capitalism with a minus sign in front of it. People building socialism need not throw out everything that exists in capitalism.

Capitalism develops useful technologies. It creates enormous productive capacity. It creates realms of personal freedom unheard of in earlier societies. None of these creations should be considered in the abstract; they can all be defined as practical matters in specific social contexts. All of these creations must be carried forward into the future, but in ways that put them to the advantage of all people, not just those few who dominate capitalist society.

From the point of view of working people, there is nothing wrong with demanding personal dignity and agency. No successful movement in the advanced capitalist world can challenge this demand. The question is: agency for what purpose? As Bob Dylan put it so succinctly in one of his gospel songs: "You gotta serve somebody."[2] That's where class comes in.

Self-service as greed serves capital. Self-service in the form of responsible citizenship, in which the individual accepts the need to pull their own weight to the degree reasonably possible, but in service to the community, is constructive and can serve working people. Self-service doesn't have to turn into dysfunctional personal greed, any more than technological advances have to destroy workers' livelihoods.

Some people challenge the idea of class consciousness as a violation of their individuality. "I'm me, an individual, not some cog in a class." Of course we are each of us an individual. But there are two problems with this complaint. First, it ignores the reality that each individual is also a social being. Being in the working class, or in the capitalist class, or being a middle class professional or small-business owner, definitely contributes to shaping who we are as individuals. It can only help to guide us in life's journey if, along with our various other identities, we understand and are conscious of our class circumstance.

By stripping each person of their social relationships, the individualism of capitalism has destroyed the individual's integration into the social networks of meaning that in earlier societies were provided by belonging to a tribe or local community, religion, or guild. In modern society, the nation and its state have become the overarching identity that has rooted and activated or constrained the individual. We have seen megachurches rise to provide identity in community, often in the context of religious nationalism. Social movements can also provide community, such as "the beloved community" cherished in the civil rights movement of the 1960s in which a sense of comradeship and mutual caring in a common struggle for justice gave meaning and personal identity in something larger than oneself.

It's telling that people often strongly assert their individuality when it comes to challenging the idea that they belong to a class (especially the working class), but not in relation to other important identities. No one complains that being an American, or a Catholic, or white violates their sense of individuality or sense of identity. Those categories are accepted as more or less natural foundations of identity.

Only when it comes to class identity have so many people learned to withdraw into the sanctity of individuality. Yet children raised within the capitalist class learn from childhood that they are part of an exalted class with properly deserved privileges. Class consciousness at the top is accepted; in fact it's a requirement of class rule.[3] Class consciousness among workers, however, is a threat to capitalist class rule, which is why it is often ridiculed in the media and popular culture as a threat to individuality and democracy. It isn't class consciousness that's the problem. It's which class is conscious.

Creative work in science and the arts requires special consideration. It unfolds in individual imaginations and speculative thinking. One cannot know where these human efforts will lead. One cannot know in advance what scientific inquiry will be translated into useful technology, or not. One cannot know in advance what work of art will inspire or comfort or give pleasure to those who engage with it. Subjecting artists and scientists to demands for direct and immediate social usefulness mistakes their nature. One cannot expect creative imagination to respond to anything beyond the individual energy and creative power of the artist or scientist doing the work, not necessarily with any thought of its social purpose.

If scientists and artists are to contribute to a better world, they must be allowed to flourish on their own, for their own sake. What will be useful, what will be enjoyable, what will be uplifting, what will be challenging or illuminating, will emerge over time out of the broadest pool of creative efforts. Such work cannot thrive in a context of political or ideological censorship. Constructive critique and peer review are essential to the development of science and the arts. Censorship and suppression are poisonous.

Individualism and Education

The terrible burden of student-loan debt is a direct consequence of the application of individualism to higher education. It has its origins in the economic analysis of economist Gary Becker who proposed that we think of spending for education as an investment with a measurable rate of return arising from the higher lifetime earnings that education brings.[4] In this way of thinking, education creates "human capital," much as business investment creates physical capital. Students going to college, according to this view, should think of themselves as capitalists investing in their future, laying out tuition and fees, giving up income they might earn instead of going to school, all to reap the return of greater earnings in the future. This approach replaced the earlier understanding that going to college was a search for personal satisfaction in acquiring knowledge or finding a compatible marriage partner, or to gain the knowledge and wisdom that responsible citizenship requires.

Becker and others found that money spent on tuition and other college fees pays very high rates of return, far higher than what the student or the family could make by investing the money in the stock market while going directly into the labor force from high school. The logic of capital investment then suggests that students who can't afford the cost of college should borrow the money, as long as the interest rate is lower than the rate of return on the investment in human capital, the cost of going to college. In this way of thinking, the student is the equivalent of the corporation, which borrows to finance new factories and office buildings as long as the added revenues from the project will more than pay back the loan and interest.

Leaders of colleges and universities did the math, too. They soon understood that they could raise tuition far beyond what students and their families could pay out of pocket, as long as students could borrow what they couldn't afford. And so here we are as of this writing with student debt at the end of the first quarter of 2023 totaling $1.6 trillion, more than the value of all outstanding auto loans and 60% more than total revolving credit card debt at that time.[5]

Lenders understood their vulnerability holding such large amounts of debt if the economy would go into deep recession. Many former students would lose their jobs and perhaps have to declare personal bankruptcy, making outstanding student debt worth fractions of its face amount. To protect themselves, financial institutions lobbied Congress to change the bankruptcy law, which Congress did in the 2005 Bankruptcy Abuse

Prevention and Consumer Protection Act, just three years before the economy sank into the deep financial crisis of 2008–9.[6] To make sure students couldn't "abuse bankruptcy," the law provided that no student loan—federal or private—could be discharged in bankruptcy unless the borrower could prove repaying the loan would cause "undue hardship," a condition that is incredibly difficult to demonstrate unless the person has a severe disability. It essentially lumps student loan debt in with child support and criminal fines—other types of debt that can't be discharged through personal bankruptcy.[7]

Application of the capitalist concept of individualism to higher education has also come with significant reductions in state budget support for public colleges and universities. These shortfalls have contributed to the pressure to increase tuition, as budget cuts have been excused, even justified, by the apparent ability of public higher education institutions to raise tuitions financed by student debt. Deep reductions in state support for what are now only nominally public colleges and universities have effectively privatized them. This has been done by forcing their finances to come increasingly from tuition, fees, and corporate and private foundation sponsorship of academic and research programs.

But the fast-increasing privatization of higher education is more than a budgetary matter. Privatization corresponds to the abdication of social responsibility for higher education, as though it had value only in the returns to individual students, who should then be responsible for its costs. Gone is the idea that public education at all levels is necessary for an educated citizenry to be able to play a constructive role in the broad responsibilities of democracy. Education, like health care, is an investment for the public good. Treating it mainly as a private matter, a terrible consequence of capitalist individualism, is a direct threat to democracy.

Applying capitalist individualism to education also diminishes the value of learning that doesn't contribute to creating salable skills the student will need in the labor market. Literature, history, philosophy, sociology, cultural anthropology, languages, art, and theater all have lost college majors; they can't generate the incomes needed to pay back student loans and are experiencing cutbacks at many colleges and universities. Instead, STEM (science, technology, engineering, and math) programs receive more funding. While elite high schools in wealthy neighborhoods continue to offer students a wide and challenging curriculum, in public schools that serve mostly working class communities the emphasis is on basic language and math skills. Civics, history, and the arts have been pushed to the margins of required curricula.

Another thread in the education story runs back to slavery days. Doris Kearns Goodwin, in her book *Team of Rivals*, chronicling the political dynamics of the Civil War period, quotes New Yorker William H. Seward in 1848 comparing the different attitudes toward education in free and slave societies. "Free labor, [Seward] said, demands universal suffrage and the widespread 'diffusion of knowledge.' The slave-based system, by contrast, 'cherishes ignorance because it is the only security for oppression.'"[8] Also reflecting on post–Civil War times of Reconstruction, W.E.B. Du Bois ironically observed: "Unfortunately, there was one thing that the white South feared more than the Negro dishonesty, ignorance, and incompetency, and that was Negro honesty, knowledge, and efficiency."[9] Ruling elites have long been aware that too much education for laboring people can be dangerous.

Our primary and secondary education for working class kids is largely restricted to the vocational skills of reading, arithmetic, and basic mathematics. Higher education for working people is typically limited to training in technical skills to support employment. These are important capacities to acquire. But for the working class to be in a position to exercise full democratic control over the direction of society, working people, no matter what their job, need to develop the capacity for critical and strategic thinking.

Capitalists and their political leaders are trained to think strategically. That's what they do: give strategic direction to their businesses and to the larger economic and political system, as well as its general culture. The exclusion of the arts, philosophy, history, and social sciences from the core of working class knowledge is another form of "cherish[ing] ignorance." It is an even more effective means of securing their oppression than police power mobilized to crush a strike or street protest.

Culture

In a letter to her friend Jane Welsh Carlyle written in the 1840s, Victorian novelist Geraldine Jewsbury reflected on the difficulties facing creative women: "We are indications of a development of womanhood which as yet is not recognized. It has, so far, no ready-made channels to run in, but still we have looked, and tried, and found that the present rules for women will not hold us—that something better and stronger is needed."[10] Novelist George Eliot put it similarly when describing the title character in her novel *Silas Marner*: "Culture had not defined any channels for his sense of mystery."[11]

Painting, sculpture, film, dance, theater, photography, music, literature, design—all these elements of culture are channels for human expression. The thoughts and feelings conveyed in these forms rarely have anything explicitly to do with the economy or class. Yet culture does channel our sense of mystery, our imagination, into forms that exist in and influence society. Once again, a dialectical approach helps us get a better understanding of culture when we see it as a process of molding and shaping, rather than as a collection of fixed works or forms.

When considering culture in this way, it makes sense to ask whether its channels, its processes, its molding power, its available forms play some role in class dynamics. They do.

Culture is a process. The processes that shape creative activity sometimes reinforce dominant class dynamics, sometimes challenge them, sometimes remain neutral. But culture, religion, and politics are realms in their own right, with practitioners and intellectual participants who may or may not have any knowledge of, or interest in, the economic arrangements around them. Yet culture shapes, and is simultaneously shaped by, the social circumstances in which it finds expression. As we come to address and seek to change economic structures that contribute to human suffering, we confront the ways in which economic dynamics are reflected in all aspects of society, including culture.

Biographer Claire Tomalin placed personal cultural expression in a social context when she described one of her greatest discoveries in writing her memoir *A Life of My Own*: "Through the process of examining my life, I thought I might understand myself better. One thing I have learned is that, while I used to think I was making individual choices, now, looking back, I see clearly that I was following trends and general patterns of behavior which I was about as powerless to resist as a migrating bird or salmon swimming upstream."[12] What feel like very personal decisions are often far more influenced by social trends and conditions than we realize at the time.

I first experienced in a deeply affecting way the connection between individual stories and social events in 1965, when I was in the audience watching a performance of Bertolt Brecht's play *The Rifles of Señora Carrar* in a Black church in Indianola, Mississippi. The local voter registration project brought the Free Southern Theater troupe, created by SNCC to aid in their organizing efforts, to town to perform for the people as part of the mobilization they were building, in the face of a fierce white terror campaign.[13]

Brecht wrote the play in 1937 to capture some of the anguish of the Spanish Civil War, which had begun the previous year. The question the play addresses is the meaning of neutrality in the context of class struggle. Señora Carrar is a peasant woman with two sons, whose husband has been murdered by the fascist forces of Generalissimo Francisco Franco. The sons want to take the guns in the house to join the antifascist forces fighting to restore the Spanish republic after Franco's military coup. Señora Carrar, fearing for their safety, wants them to stay out of the conflict. They insist it would be wrong to allow fascism to take hold without resistance and, at the end of the one-act play, they convince Señora Carrar to give them the guns.

The play had a powerful effect on the audience in Indianola. In the discussion afterward, the audience delved into the two subjects of the play—is it right to be neutral when a deeply moral fight is raging around you; and what about nonviolence? These were the exact issues the Black people of Indianola were facing in their own lives at that moment. But the play allowed them to explore these questions, so raw and fraught if confronted directly, by treating them at a distance, at the remove the play afforded. The play also connected Mississippi Blacks with Spanish peasants in their common condition in ways that could never happen from a lecture covering the same questions. It showed them the deep human context of their condition. The play and the audience discussion afterward motivated at least some to dare to register to vote.

Culture is of course not simply a direct expression of class dynamics. It has a life of its own in its many forms, where issues of aesthetics and tradition play fundamental shaping roles. But culture is a complicating element of the economic system. Culture has the power to bring out or hide, represent or muddle, focus or blur the economic dynamics of its surrounding society. In doing so in one way or another, culture impacts, and is impacted by, class dynamics in profound ways.

The novels of Ayn Rand from the 1940s and 1950s, for example, reflected and came to exalt the extreme individualism and power of capitalist aspirations. *The Fountainhead* and *Atlas Shrugged* became cultural beacons for corporate resistance to the New Deal and energized those who held more radically conservative sentiments that were rising at around the same time. Such cultural works played their part in advancing the political agenda of the Powell memorandum of 1971, that blueprint for reasserting capitalist domination across all social realms, pushing back against the widespread criticisms that social movements of the time were directing at capitalism.

Cultural work can also demean the working class, as in the megahit TV series *All in the Family*, which aired originally from 1971 to 1979. The central character, Archie Bunker, is a working class, middle-aged, white loudmouth bigot. And that's the whole point, wrapped as it was in funny sketches and sharp exchanges in which Archie gets as good as he gives from his daughter, son-in-law, and long-suffering but occasionally feisty wife Edith.

The show was written by Norman Lear and starred Carroll O'Connor, both stalwarts of the liberal Hollywood establishment. Tellingly, in *All In the Family,* Archie is the worker, while his liberal working class daughter, son-in-law, and wife are not presented as part of the working class, but as students and women. At a time when the civil rights and women's movements were powerful social forces for change, and the LGBTQ movement was gaining visibility and legitimacy, the demonization of the working class, strikingly represented by a white man, became permissible beyond the narrow circles of corporate power.* This cultural ridicule directed at working class men in the person of a white worker, and the erasure of class identity from women and Black people in the name of the progressive values of feminism and racial tolerance, contributed to the social climate in which unions lost power and the working class, now mostly—erroneously—seen as white men, faded in the popular imagination into a reactionary, unpleasant force unworthy of sympathy and political support.

Sociologist Penny Lewis has convincingly shown the errors in the dominant representation of anti–Vietnam War activists simply as middle class students and elites. Corresponding to this mistake is the dominant representation of workers at that time as patriotic stalwarts of American values, represented in the iconic image of construction workers beating up antiwar protesters in lower Manhattan in 1970. In fact, antiwar sentiment in the working class grew dramatically as the war went on, especially among vets, their families and friends, and others subject to the draft. Among wealthy elites and their political representatives, support for the war was widespread. Lewis shows how false representations of these realities have generated substantial damage to our culture and politics.[14]

---

* Some unions, especially in the building trades, were notorious for their exclusion of women and Blacks from their ranks. This gave weight to what became wholesale attacks on the working class (wrongly represented in the culture as "white men") in the late 1960s and 1970s.

There are also powerful works of literature, film, song, and photography that illuminate the lives of working people with sympathy and understanding. Among the vast number of examples, consider starting with the novels of Charles Dickens, who presented the poor in ways that pricked the conscience of Victorian England. Upton Sinclair's novel *The Jungle* exposed the terrible conditions of work in Chicago slaughterhouses at the turn of the twentieth century, spurring enough public outrage to get Congress to create the Food and Drug Administration to force improvements in working conditions and product safety. In *The Grapes of Wrath*, John Steinbeck captured the desperate lives of Dust Bowl refugees and their humanity in the face of heartless and vicious treatment by Oklahoma banks and California growers. The writings concerning the working class and the poor by Amiri Baraka, Audre Lorde, Naomi Replansky, Elizabeth Strout, and August Wilson; the films of Barbara Kopple and Ken Loach; the photography of David Bacon, Margaret Bourke-White, and Gordon Parks; the scholarship of Michael Denning, Roxanne Dunbar-Ortiz, Juan Gonzalez, Robin D.G. Kelley, Paul Lauter, Tillie Olsen, Raymond Williams, and Janet Zandy—and so many others—all contribute to the culture of working class pride and assertion in the face of hardship.

Music, too, has been central to working class culture. Billy Bragg in England and Hazel Dickens, Leadbelly, Pete Seeger, and Bruce Springsteen in the US have reflected working class life and sustained people in action. These and many other artists have given expression and strength to working people in ways that provide channels for their feelings and experiences.

But working class culture is not just the product of established artists. The Bread and Roses project of SEIU Local 1199 in New York City brought the voices of ordinary working class people to the fore, most notably in its Unseen America project under the direction of Esther Cohen. I was involved in its first undertaking, in 2001, that gave cameras and film to Central American day laborers working on Long Island. Fifteen workers recruited through the Workplace Project, a worker center at the heart of the Latinx community on Long Island, took those cameras to document their lives in any way they saw fit. Each week they would meet together with a professional photographer in the photo lab at SUNY Stony Brook to examine their images, describe what they were trying to capture, analyze the images to learn about such technical aspects as capturing light and shadow, composition, and ways an image might better convey what they wanted it to. After months of repeating this process toward ever-greater effectiveness in thousands of images, the workers sat together to curate an exhibition of a few dozen of their photographs that were framed and mounted for public viewing.

I vividly recall how moved I was to see the intent look on the faces of two young Salvadoran day laborers as they watched their week's images appear in the chemical bath of their film (in the days before digital cameras were standard), how engrossed they were in the project of learning self-expression in this medium. Later, their exhibit was mounted in the library of the high school whose students had included two young men who had recently lured two day laborers into their truck one morning only to take them to a deserted site and beat them nearly to death, a hate crime that had become notorious in the area. The humanity of the photo exhibit provided a superb backdrop for discussions with the students and teachers in that school.

Eventually over one thousand Unseen America photo projects across the country gave workers the chance to document their own lives, leading to public exhibits, often with captions written by those who had taken the pictures.[15] One garment worker who had labored in New York City's Chinatown sweatshops for over thirty years said at the opening of the show she and her coworkers created: "I feel like a frog who's jumped out of a well."

Cultural expression can be a liberatory force. Representations of working class life are all too rare in mainstream culture and too infrequently cultivated among ordinary workers. Thankfully, the Labor Arts website displays a multiform collection that celebrates and documents many examples of the artistic and cultural heritage of working people.[16]

But there is another, more personal, sense in which to consider culture: variations in the ways individuals in different classes learn and live within different norms of what's considered appropriate and desirable behavior. Working class studies scholar Jack Metzgar explains just this point in an article titled "There is a Genuine Working-Class Culture."[17] Metzgar echoes community psychologist Barbara Jensen's distinction between a working class culture of *belonging* and a middle class culture of *becoming*.[18] The aspiration of becoming—like upward mobility in career—emphasizes individual accomplishment and the effective distinctions a person can make favoring themselves over others who are at once colleagues yet also competitors for promotion and grants. A person in a *becoming* culture, at work and frequently outside of work, is very often thinking about how to advance, how to stand out.

The culture of most working class jobs is different. The job is not the focus of aspiration. Rather, it provides the foundation for identity in belonging to one's family and circle of friends. One's identity is expressed in skill on the job, but in large part also in hobbies, volunteer work, fixing up the house, and preparing and enjoying family gatherings. It is a different way of being compared with a typical professional life.

I recall walking a strike picket line with a health aide at a nursing home on Long Island in the year 2000. I asked her about her job, and if she'd like to train to be a nurse, or even a doctor. "No," she said, "I love helping people in my job as an aide. That's what I want to do and then I want to go home to my family. I don't want the responsibilities of a nurse or a doctor. But I want to be treated with respect as an aide, which this place doesn't do. That's why I'm on strike. They don't treat me with respect."

Metzgar asks: "How could having a job rather than a career not result in and require a different kind of culture, a different set of predispositions, and expectations, norms and values, and ways of living a life? ... The presumption that careers are always and everywhere better than jobs blinds [professionals] to the preservation of self and the choice of simple integrity that often lies at the core of working-class young people's rejection of middle-class ways."[19]

These particular class differences have political consequences. Blindness to them can prevent middle class activists from understanding how their behaviors and attitudes can contribute to the attraction some working class people find in right-wing attacks on "elites." As Metzgar puts it:

> If middle-class professionals [i.e., media pundits, politicians, and academics] go on treating working-class people as if they are just underdeveloped versions of ourselves, it will continue to piss them off, often mixed with dangerous levels of ethnic, racial, and nativist resentments [which these elites warn against] as economic conditions get worse. But if we realize how much we depend on them and how much they depend on cultural dispositions different from ours, we might just recognize how much a job culture of being and belonging might offer us.... We might also come to political accommodations that would enable us, together, to mount the kind of strong countervailing force to our ruling class that would provide the economic base for both class cultures to flourish once again.[20]

Navigating these personal differences in class attitudes is essential when organizers and activists from middle class backgrounds work closely with organizers and activists from the working class. Sociologist Betsy Leondar-Wright has been at the forefront of investigating the resulting dynamics of cross-class interactions in meetings, organizational leadership, and the process of doing movement work.[21] For example, she has found that middle class organizers tend to emphasize commitments to abstractions like "democracy" and "transparency" while those from the working class tend to focus on concrete programmatic objectives. In meetings, organizers from middle class backgrounds also tend to speak more frequently and at greater length than their working class counterparts.

These and related differences are rooted in different class cultures that can lead to frustrations and alienation among people on both sides of the class divide when they attempt to work together. Through the organization Class Matters, Leondar-Wright and others have developed a number of exercises to exemplify the differences and guide people through them. Increased awareness of these cultural questions opens the way to bridge class differences among progressives constructively.[22]

It is essential to bridge this chasm. It will take the combined efforts of middle class and working class activists and organizers to develop the progressive politics necessary to move society toward implementing the interests of working people and marginalized communities. We cannot reach that goal without simultaneously addressing white supremacy, patriarchy, and cultural domination in the class dynamics that give context and urgency to them all. It's a tall order! To make progress, it will help to remember that class is a question of power, as are race and gender. With this understanding, uniting across racial, ethnic, gender, and class lines becomes more possible to imagine and bring into reality.

Notes

1   Jane Smiley, *Charles Dickens* (New York: Penguin, 2002), 209.
2   Bob Dylan, "Gotta Serve Somebody," track 1 on *Slow Train Comin'*, Columbia, 1979.
3   G. William Dohmoff, *Who Rules America?* 7th ed. (New York: McGraw Hill, 2013), esp. chaps. 2 and 3.
4   Gary Becker, *Human Capital* (New York: Columbia University Press, 1964).
5   "Total Debt Balance and Its Composition, 1Q 2023," *Quarterly Report on Household Debt and Credit,* p.2, Federal Reserve Bank of New York, accessed July 12, 2023, https://www.newyorkfed.org/medialibrary/Interactives/householdcredit/data/pdf/HHDC_2023Q1.pdf?sc_lang=en .
6   Julia Kagan, "Bankruptcy Abuse Prevention and Consumer Protection Act (BAPCPA)," *Investopedia*, April 26, 2023, https://www.investopedia.com/terms/b/bapcpa.asp.

7   Kayla Webley, "Why Can't You Discharge Student Loans in Bankruptcy," *Time*, February 9, 2012, https://business.time.com/2012/02/09/why-cant-you-discharge-student-loans-in-bankruptcy.

8   Doris Kearns Goodwin, *Team of Rivals: The Political Genius of Abraham Lincoln* (New York: Simon and Schuster, 2005), 133.

9   W.E.B. Du Bois, "Reconstruction and Its Benefits," in *W.E.B. Du Bois: A Reader*, ed. David Levering Lewis (New York: Henry Holt, 1995), 187.

10 Geraldine Jewsbury to Jane Welsh Carlyle, *Selections from the Letters of Geraldine Endsor Jewsbury to Jane Welsh Carlyle*, ed. Mrs. Alexander Ireland (London: Longmans, Green and Co., 1892), 348.

11 George Eliot, *Silas Marner* (New York: Penguin, 1996 [1861]), 10.

12 Claire Tomalin, *A Life of My Own* (New York: Penguin Books, 2018), xi–xii.

13 Hilton Battle, Dorothy Marcic, and Kimberley LaMarque Orman, "Theatre without Walls: Free Southern Theater and New Heritage Theatre Group," *American Theater*, July 5, 2021, https://www.americantheatre.org/2021/07/05/theatre-without-walls-free-southern-theater-and-new-heritage-theatre-group.

14 Penny Lewis, *Hardhats, Hippies, and Hawks: The Vietnam Anti-War Movement as Myth and Memory* (Ithaca, NY: Cornell University Press, 2013).

15 Esther Cohen, ed., *Unseen America: Photos and Stories by Workers* (New York: Regan Books, 2006).

16 Labor Arts is a web-based resource. See https://www.laborarts.org (accessed August 29, 2021).

17 Jack Metzgar, "There Is a Genuine Working-Class Culture," in *Routledge International Handbook of Working Class Studies*, ed. Michele Fazio, Christie Launius, and Tim Strangleman (London: Routledge, 2021).

18 Barbara Jensen, *Reading Classes: On Culture and Classism in America* (Ithaca, NY: Cornell University Press, 2012), 54.

19 Metzgar, "Genuine Working-Class Culture," 237.

20 Metzgar, "Genuine Working-Class Culture," 239.

21 Betsy Leondar-Wright, *Missing Class: Strengthening Social Movements by Seeing Class Cultures* (Ithaca, NY: Cornell University Press, 2014).

22 Activities and resources are available at https://class-matters.org.

CHAPTER NINE

Race and Gender in Class Society

Although economic activity is the bedrock foundation of all societies, people are also profoundly engaged with and affected by race and gender dynamics. Each of these aspects of society has a life of its own. People devote themselves to work in these areas, often without much thought of economics. Even so, each is intimately bound up with the class dynamics central to the economy. In this chapter we will look at some of the ways economic relations extend into these aspects of society. We will see how a dialectical understanding of these features, not as isolated aspects of life but in their relations to each other and to class dynamics, helps to ground the work we need to do to address economic, racial, and gender injustice.

Race

Race is not just a demographic reflected in the tables of chapter five and other descriptions of US society. It is not just a census taker's checkbox, or some pollster's focus of interest. Race is an instrument of social control, directed at white working people as well as Blacks. As political scientist Adolph Reed Jr. has put it, "Class—as an expression of location within the political economy—is the framework in which race attains meaning."[1]

Race is not an inherent part of some supposed biological hierarchy. In the United States, race has developed in ways that are deeply enmeshed with society's class dynamics. Race and class are separate and different of course, but they constitute a unity of opposites. Neither exists in the US without the other entwined in it. The tensions in this contradiction within US society help drive its path of change.

From the beginning of colonial settlement up to the present time, the mutual determination of race and class has been operating in our country. In our settler state, as in all such societies, Native peoples were the first to be excluded from what Bill Fletcher Jr. has dubbed "the relevant population," as the settlers came to think of themselves. But as early settlements grew throughout the seventeenth century, especially in the all-important colony of Virginia, "white" and "Black" went beyond skin color to take on profound social meaning. By the early part of the eighteenth century the "relevant population" had become white only.

The English began to consolidate systematic racial slavery in the Colonies after Bacon's Rebellion in 1676, a united uprising of African and English bond laborers that had burned Jamestown, Virginia's capital at the time, to the ground.* In putting down the rebellion, the English ruling authorities decided to implement the age-old technique of "divide and conquer." As historian Ted Allen has shown, by extending Africans' limited-term bond labor to lifetime slavery, converting them (but not their English counterparts) and their children into outright property with no rights, the rebellious population was divided and turned against itself in the newly constructed guise of white and Black people.[2]

To this day we live with the consequences of this historic exclusion of people of African descent from the "relevant population," a status still invoked to exclude them from being "true Americans." Donald Trump's championing of the false "birther" claim that Barack Obama was born in Africa is one recent example of this, as is the epidemic of police shootings of Black people in communities across the country. So long-established and still so devastatingly present: white supremacy and the racism that justifies it are, for now at least, integral to American society.

Understanding that racism is an instrument of social control designed to divide workers from one another helps us to understand that racism also harms white workers, in addition to the far greater harm done to African American workers and the Black population in general. The degradation of Black people into slavery did practically nothing to elevate the actual living conditions of white workers, tenant farmers, and sharecroppers. Their conditions *appeared* to have become better, not absolutely but only

---

* Ironically, the united demand of English and African bond laborers urged the further marginalization of Native peoples, whose land the rebels wanted the British to seize more aggressively so that, upon release from their required period of bonded labor, the rebels could have access to it.

in comparison with those of their Black counterparts consigned to chattel slavery. Whites were allowed to keep rights that became prohibited to Black people: the right to own property, to bear arms, to use the court system, and much more. Even so, beginning in slavery days, white small farmers in the South were relegated to marginal land in the hills and mountains, while the wealthy white slaveholders took the most fertile land for themselves.

The only "improvement" white workers gained from white supremacy was what African American scholar W.E.B. Du Bois identified as the "psychological wage," his term for the subjective reward white workers got from the feelings of superiority they found in their higher status *compared with Black people*, and their apparent common bond with the white elites who ran society. In 1836, John C. Calhoun, the South's principal proponent of states' rights and slavery, explained this forthrightly: "With us, the two great divisions of society are not rich and poor, but white and black; and all the former, the poor as well as the rich, belong to the upper class and are respected and treated as equals, if honest and industrious, and hence have a position and pride of character of which neither poverty nor misfortune can deprive them."[3]

With the growth of the US industrial economy in the last half of the nineteenth century, however, the situation regarding white workers grew more complex. The opportunities for economic advancement that opened up in the process accrued almost exclusively to workers of European heritage. These workers experienced real material gains denied to their Black working class counterparts—now freed from their former enslavement—whether in the form of access to credit to start a business, or access to industrial jobs that offered more than they could hope for as a sharecropper or tenant farmer. In factories and mills across the country, whites got the best jobs. Brutal as these working conditions often were, Black workers were channeled into the dirtiest, most dangerous, most unhealthy jobs, or excluded altogether.

In the twentieth century, the reforms of the Depression-era New Deal, although expressed in universal terms, nevertheless benefited white workers far more than Blacks. The Social Security program, for example, was drafted with compromises that excluded household and agricultural workers from its benefits. Senators and congressmen from southern states had demanded these exclusions because over 90% of African American workers held those jobs. The Social Security Act also excluded public sector workers from the program, including teachers, postal workers, and other reasonably stable positions where Black people had been finding relatively better incomes and working conditions.

Southern leaders would not accept New Deal reform without compromises that protected their class power, particularly over Black labor. That's why it was unacceptable to them to give Black workers access to Social Security and other New Deal protections that would have strengthened their social standing and individual capacities: it threatened white supremacy. Racist policies excluded farm workers from New Deal benefits, but because two-thirds of all US sharecroppers at the time were white, they, too, were denied those benefits.[4]

We find similar compromises in the 1935 National Labor Relations Act (Wagner Act). Without explicit reference to race, the act protected workers as they organized unions, contributing to their rapid growth in the late 1930s. But, as with Social Security, the Wagner Act excluded agricultural, household, and government workers from protection, effectively leaving almost all Black workers out of the new advantages ruling elites had extended to white workers. The same restrictions continued into the reforms of Second New Deal laws in 1938. Minimum wage legislation and other fair labor standards protections such as the standard forty-hour week, with overtime beyond, once again exempted agricultural, household, and public sector workers.

This racist pattern extended to the GI Bill that followed World War II. The bill was a powerful reform that allowed millions of returning soldiers to get an education, finance new homes, and establish a new high in the standard of living for working class families. But, once again, it was undercut by the compromise with Jim Crow power in the ruling class. Administration of these federal programs was given to state officials, who usually contrived to apply racist restrictions that kept GI Bill benefits away from Black veterans.

This history establishes the material basis of what is sometimes called "white privilege." Historian Ira Katznelson put it another way in the title of his book describing these policies, *When Affirmative Action Was White*.[5] Throughout the nineteenth- and twentieth-century development of industrial capitalism in the United States, corporate practices and government programs deliberately offered opportunities and advantages to workers of European descent, while at the same time keeping them out of the reach of Native Americans and Americans of African, Asian, and Latin American descent.

To say white privilege exists is not to say that all white people are guilty of racist oppression applied to Black people. The privileges are integral and deeply rooted parts of US society and come to white people automatically,

RACE AND GENDER IN CLASS SOCIETY

without their action or intent. That is why recognizing white skin privilege is neither a condemnation of all white people nor a matter of personal guilt. It is simply a fact of life that, once acknowledged, should act as a spur to determination among white people to dismantle the social structures that perpetuate it. There are many targets for this struggle.

As Ira Katznelson shows, affirmative action is nothing new. White people who now oppose affirmative action to benefit Black people, calling it a violation of a "level playing field," ignore—or are literally ignorant of—the long operation of a greatly tilted playing field that deliberately and affirmatively bolstered white advantage and privilege for generations, as evidenced by the way the laws we've just looked at were written, and by racist hiring practices and myriad private sector means to exclude Black people from access to education, credit, jobs, and other avenues of opportunity available to whites.

These material differences in racial experience complement and reinforce the "psychological wage" that Du Bois identified. But just as bond laborers from England did not create racial slavery, white workers did not create white privilege. Such privileges were the creations of white ruling elites, whether slave owners or captains of industry, and their political agents. Once these patterns were institutionalized and made to seem normal, it was easy to lose track of their origins.

White privilege is built into the social structures in which we grow up. It is reinforced in the cultural and political norms that guide our social experiences. Within the working class, the need to escape the pressure of competition that workers face in capitalist labor markets has led many workers of European heritage to latch onto being "white." They seek advantage by allowing, if not actively demanding, the exclusion of "others" from their competitive search for jobs, housing, education, and other benefits made possible by capitalist development. But in the long run these advantages come back to undercut the ability of white workers to advance their own position. What they gain in immediate privilege they lose in long-term weakness grounded in a divided working class unable to muster its full strength to push back against the power of capital.[6] Not least in its consequences was the use of Black workers to break the strikes of white workers.*

---

* Of course this strikebreaking offered no real gains for the Black workers, who were pushed aside once the strike was broken. This mirrors the experience of Black troops who fought for the US in World War I, World War II, Korea, and Vietnam, only to face racist exclusion on their return from war.

We find continuing evidence of the ill effects of racism on white work-ers. To this day, states in the old slave South, where racism was most virulent and its traditions most valued, as evidenced by the continuing affection for the Confederate battle flag as a marker of proud southern heritage, tend to have the lowest levels of union membership, education, income, and wealth for white workers as well as Black; as well as the lowest life expectancy and the highest poverty rates for white workers as well as Black workers. Throughout the country, whenever white workers deflect their frustrations and anger onto Black people, the white workers also lose.

In the end, white economic elites have been the only real winners from the imposition of racial slavery, white supremacy, and racism. They have won and maintained their status and power through control over the lives of all working people by keeping them divided.

White supremacy has had a terrible and destructive impact on Black people, still seen almost every day in news about racial inequalities in income and wealth, police violence, disproportional deaths from COVID-19, and, more generally, unequal access to basic health care. What is less well known and less easily seen, but vital to understand and communicate, are the ways in which white workers, too, have been held back and disad-vantaged materially. We will return in the next chapter to consider more carefully how to navigate issues of race among white people.

White economic elites have broken the united power of working people when whites in the working class followed the lead of John C. Calhoun and his modern followers, tending to see themselves aligned with the inter-ests of white elites rather than with fellow workers who were Black. This cross-class alliance of whiteness refocused the anger white workers felt over the conditions of their lives, mistakenly directing it at Blacks, Hispanics, Asians, Muslims, and Jews, instead of the real sources of power shaping their conditions. Donald Trump rose to the presidency in 2016 in part on this racist foundation.

Structural Racism

Racism is more than the personal opinion of an individual racist whose mind needs to be changed or enlightened. Racism is structural, rooted and reinforced in the operations of social structures that guide us through life. We need to understand how racism and white supremacy are deeply rooted instruments carried forward within institutions that shape people's opinions and life outcomes. We need to challenge those structural channels and their institutional reinforcements.

We see this process in the educational system that still provides significantly fewer and inferior resources to schools with mostly Black students. We see it in "redlining" and other forms of financial discrimination that prevent Black families, farmers, and business owners from getting fair access to credit. We see it in the ways that Black people are systematically segregated in housing markets across the country.[7] We see it in voter suppression measures designed to reduce the political power of Black citizens. Despite gains stemming from the civil rights movement of the 1950s and 1960s and the election of a Black president, we continue to see it in demeaning media representations of Black people in cultural and media institutions, and their relative absence from positions of authority.

A particularly dramatic example of this appeared when viewers of a 2020 Facebook video that featured Black men were offered follow-on options for "more videos about primates." In the same vein, Google's algorithms in 2015 labeled pictures of Black men as gorillas.[8] These openly racist references didn't arise from conscious racism at Facebook and Google. They arose from unconscious and pervasive racism in society, from which the algorithms learn. There is so much racist vitriol on the internet that directly and consciously makes those disgusting connections that an AI algorithm "learns" to pair them automatically and presents it as a natural thing. Far from natural, racism is baked into the cake of US society. Contrary to the old saying that you can't unscramble an egg, and mixing the metaphor, we can unscramble racism from the cake.

The significantly more harmful impact of the COVID-19 pandemic in Black communities is another clear reflection of structural or systemic racism. July 2021 data from the US Centers for Disease Control and Prevention (CDC) show that the rate of deaths from COVID-19 were twice as high for Black people as they were for whites, while the rate of Black hospitalizations was nearly three times that of whites. Hispanic and Native American people had even worse outcomes compared with whites.[9]

In their report, the CDC looked into contributing factors that help to explain these racial disparities. They found, "Inequities in the social determinants of health, such as poverty and healthcare access, affecting these groups are interrelated and influence a wide range of health and quality-of-life outcomes and risks.... These factors and others are associated with more

COVID-19 cases, hospitalizations, and deaths in areas where racial and ethnic minority groups live, learn, work, play, and worship."

The CDC identified structural differences in life circumstances that are important to understanding the relatively high rates of COVID-19 infection and death among Blacks, Hispanics, and Native Americans.[10] They were more likely to be working in occupations that exposed them to risks of contagion, for example in health care, food processing and grocery store work, driving buses and trucks, and other jobs delivering "essential services." This was coupled with transportation difficulties in getting to doctors and health care facilities. Further, because a disproportionate number of people of color lost jobs that carried insurance, more lost access to health care during the pandemic, while most of those who remained at work in low-paying jobs had no health coverage to start with. Some lived in crowded urban spaces; some were homeless. All of these circumstances were exacerbated by poverty and the stress of continuing racial and ethnic discrimination. Taken together, these structural conditions contributed to a greater presence of harmful preexisting medical conditions like hypertension and diabetes that make COVID-19 more deadly.

Structural racism also affected the lives of Black business owners. The legacy of redlining that limited Black access to credit in recent decades has meant that their businesses typically have relatively weak connections to the banks that managed the Paycheck Protection Plan, which allocated over a trillion dollars to small businesses trying to survive the economic collapse after March 2020. This redlining history limited African American access to government loans to small businesses during the 2020 COVID-19 crisis.[11] The US Small Business Administration also found that the Paycheck Protection Plan failed to prioritize "underserved and rural markets," putting businesses owned by Blacks, women, Native peoples, and rural whites all at a disadvantage, contrary to the purpose of the program.[12] Note that, again, rural and poor whites also suffer from being "underserved."

The police and vigilante killings of Black people, which have galvanized a new set of protests since the murder of Trayvon Martin, add up to more than a series of individual racist acts. They reflect systemic racism, continuing the shameful history of terror that was a central feature of US race relations following the Civil War. The Economic Justice Institute has documented 4,075 racial lynchings in the US between 1877 and 1950, mostly but by no means exclusively in the old slave states.[13] An average of fifty-six Black people were lynched in each of these seventy-three years. That's more than one person hanged from a tree, burned to death, or thrown into a river to drown in an extrajudicial murder *every week for seventy-three years*. It is undeniably a horrific legacy of domestic terror inherited by our twenty-first-century society, deeply embedded in the consciousness of Black people across the country.

The impetus to lynching reinforced a narrative of racial difference and a legacy of racial inequality that is readily apparent in our criminal justice system today. Mass incarceration, racially biased capital punishment, excessive sentencing, disproportionate sentencing of racial minorities, and police abuse of people of color all reveal structural problems in American society that were shaped by the existence of racial slavery for nearly two hundred years before formal Emancipation following the Civil War, and the reign of terror directed at the Black community after the betrayal of Reconstruction.

Yet we know from history that institutions of white supremacy can be challenged and defeated. The Civil War destroyed slavery. The long legal battle challenging racial segregation ultimately undid the racist legal fantasy of "separate but equal" in the 1954 *Brown v. Board of Education* Supreme Court decision, in law if not in practice. The civil rights movement of the 1950s and 1960s put an end to Jim Crow legal segregation, and in a Second Reconstruction it secured federal legal protection for basic civil and voting rights for Black people.

Gains rising from the modern civil rights movement are visible across the country. Substantial numbers of African Americans now pursue careers in law, as doctors, business owners, professors, politicians, and other professional positions far beyond what was possible under Jim Crow. There has also been a successful entry of a small number of Blacks into the ruling class. Barack Obama became US president. Archconservative Clarence Thomas is on the Supreme Court, ironically having replaced Thurgood Marshall, the architect of the legal assault on Jim Crow whom Lyndon Johnson placed on the court in 1967. Colin Powell and Condoleezza Rice were Republican-appointed secretaries of state, Eric Holder and Loretta Lynch Democratic-appointed US attorneys general. In 2020 there were five CEOs among the Fortune 500 companies[14]—not many, but beyond the situation in 1957 when E. Franklin Frazier considered the Black bourgeoisie to be mainly composed of morticians, store-owners, and people with stable jobs in the postal service.[15]

Yet the continuing poverty and racial exclusion faced by millions of African Americans suggests that very different experiences within the Black community over the past fifty years have produced and exposed a greater class divide within it. This bring to mind the words of Angela Davis who said: "The challenge of the 21st century is not to demand equal opportunity in the machinery of oppression, but rather to identify and dismantle those structures in which racism continues to be embedded."[16]

We get a sense of the tenacity with which those structures and white supremacy operate in American society when we consider how every advance against them has called forth a reactionary backlash. Newly designed institutions arose to accomplish the same oppressive purposes. The defeat of slavery and the power of Reconstruction gave way to Black Codes and Jim Crow. The defeat of Jim Crow in the Second Reconstruction in the 1950s and 1960s gave way to mass incarceration, greater racial segregation of neighborhoods and schools, and new forms of voter suppression.

This tenacity is not based on personal preferences or the deranged mental states of wild white supremacists—though they exist and are a serious danger to society. The driving force of reaction is based in the continuing need some people have to find ways to divide working people and weaken their power to limit the power of capital. Who are these people? They are the representatives of capitalist authority, urgent defenders of the basic arrangement of class power in society. They often appeal to "the good old days" when overt racism was acceptable and their class authority was largely unchallenged. They are, for example, the people who support and legislate voter suppression techniques while also doing what they can to suppress union organizing drives, whether in North Carolina or Wisconsin or the many other places where similar toxic politics are at play. This combination of racist and antiworker rule extends, as we have seen, all the way back to the founding of our country. White workers have every interest in opposing these racist policies. No progressive working class movement can succeed without confronting this history and fighting to set it right.

White Supremacy in Other Forms

White supremacy has always had a broader target than people of African descent. But the creation of the social category "white" in the first place has its foundation in the establishment of African racial slavery and the forced imposition of its racial categories on workers of European as well as African origins. Becoming white has required being "not Black."

This dynamic enters into the way the US Census keeps track of racial counts. While interracial marriages and mixed-race children have increased in number, and since 2000 have been recognized in census data, leading to a long-term assimilation of minorities into the mainstream, New York University sociologist Ann Morning observes that Black people have been a notable exception to this assimilation. This is "not surprising," she says, "because of the history we have. Because for the longest time blackness was kind of the symbol of what it was not to be part of society."[17]

In US census data, ethnicity is separate from race, and both are distinct from religion. Hispanics, for example, can be of any race. A person of any race or nationality can be Muslim or Jewish. In political life, these distinctions are often blurred. Hostility toward Hispanics, Muslims, or Jews is often called racism in movements that oppose the marginalization and denigration of these groups, or defend them from immigration restrictions.

These various forms of marginalization share with anti-Black racism the exclusion of groups from the "relevant population," exclusion that originated in the destruction of Native peoples and the enslavement of African labor. The dynamic of each specific ethnic history seeks to raise "white" people, the "true Americans" (which for centuries also meant Protestant), to superior social and economic status. This is what was behind the chants of "Jews will not replace us" in the white nationalist rally in Charlottesville, Virginia, in 2018, and the continuing stream of antisemitic sentiment prominent in white nationalist circles.

In another example, the marginalization of people from Mexico and Puerto Rico originated when their countries were taken in war, their people subjected to the disdain and contempt that conquerors reserve for the conquered. The Mexican War of 1848 brought 55% of Mexico under US control, accounting for what came to be California, Nevada, Arizona, New Mexico, and parts of Utah and Colorado. But the population of Mexican heritage in those states in many cases dates back over four hundred years. They rightly say: "We didn't cross the border; the border crossed us."

Puerto Rico came under US domination in the Spanish-American War of 1898, along with Cuba, the Philippines, and other Pacific islands. The domination of those countries by large US corporations throughout the twentieth century, extending also to El Salvador, Guatemala, Panama, and other countries of Central and South America, created widespread urban poverty and empowered corrupt right-wing regimes that would enable and share in US corporate plunder. These conditions go a long way to explain the flow of large numbers of people from those countries to the US in recent decades, in what writer Juan Gonzalez has aptly called the "harvest of empire."[18]

The marginalization of Spanish-speaking people in the US has extended most visibly in recent years to people from Central and South America, especially if they have some African or Indigenous heritage. They are the most recent targets of immigration hysteria. While it has different specific origins from African slavery, the exclusion of people of Hispanic origin from the "relevant population" is also rooted in colonial history and serves to divide and weaken the US working class.*

US history offers repeated examples of new groups of immigrants being excluded from the American standard. When they were not barred altogether from entry, as with the Chinese Exclusion Act of 1882, many workers were marginalized for decades after their arrival: the Irish in the mid-nineteenth century; Jews, Hungarians, Italians, and others from central, eastern, and southern Europe in the late nineteenth and early twentieth centuries; later immigrants from East and South Asia; and, most recently, people from Central and South America. These exclusions often played out at work, where the labor force was divided and set against itself. In a rare example of working class unity across ethnic lines, the class-conscious Industrial Workers of the World (IWW) in 1912 organized workers from over forty countries in a successful three-month textile strike in Lawrence, Massachusetts, a strike that gave us the feminist anthem "Bread and Roses" to reflect demands for fair wages and dignity on the job.

However, over time and across generations, people of these ethnic and religious origins have largely been absorbed into the mainstream of American life, although antisemitism still assaults Jews, with increasing deadliness during the Trump era. Those from European countries have become "relevant," which is essentially to say "white," although people of South Asian and East Asian descent still face discrimination. In the "Americanization" process, each group has come to define itself as "not Black," which remains the bedrock of racial differentiation as a social

---

* All racial and ethnic categories are actually complex amalgams of people with very different histories. The terms "Hispanic" or "Latinx" are constructs that combine people from many countries with a great variety of cultures and languages, sometimes with antagonistic relations among them. The same is true for the terms "white" and "Black," which also encompass varieties of sometimes historically hostile ethnic and religious populations from Europe and Africa.

matter. In Detroit auto factories in the 1920s and 1930s, for example, immigrant Polish workers lived as neighbors to Black workers and saw them as equals in the plant. But many of their children and grandchildren, as they acculturated to American life, adopted racist attitudes and became "white."[19]

Italians coming to the US in the nineteenth century faced exclusions that brought them into close working and social contact with African Americans. Their close connections were often revealed with deadly force, for example in 1890 when eleven Italians falsely accused of murder in New Orleans were dragged together from jail and lynched. The resultant outcry from the Italian government caused President Benjamin Harrison to establish Columbus Day to honor Italian contributions to the United States.[20]* After decades of further discrimination and negative stereotyping, Italians have gradually become "white" in the United States.

Gender

Patriarchy and the oppression of women have been central to many societies in human history, although there are also examples of matriarchal societies in which women held real power. Patriarchy has taken on particular forms in different times and places. In capitalist economies, these traditions operate in ways that constitute another dynamic unity of opposites, gender and class. While each of these elements is distinct from the other, there can be no deep understanding of gender in our society unless it is connected with an understanding of class. And a thorough investigation of class dynamics inevitably leads us to consider how they shape, and are shaped by, gender experiences. These relationships are further complicated by racial dynamics in gender as well as class.

From the earliest days of capital accumulation, women have played a central role in the labor force. At first, women worked for money in the home, weaving or doing other piecework they delivered to some of the newly emerging capitalists whose businesses were taking root in growing towns and cities. The earliest wage labor from which capital accumulation began was the labor of such women.

As the manufacturing world developed more fully, young single women left their homes to work in early factories and mills. Black women

---

* Ironically, Christopher Columbus, a sailor from Genoa, had been enlisted and financed by King Ferdinand and Queen Isabella of Spain, so his voyages brought Spanish, not Italian, influence to the New World. Columbus never set foot on any land that eventually became part of the United States.

in the US mainly worked in the fields and as maids and cooks and nannies. But the demands of patriarchy drove most working women, especially those who were white, back into the home when they married.

Since capital accumulation occurs through activity undertaken in markets, it is easy to forget the unpaid household labor that is so central to our economy and the accumulation of capital. While men are increasingly staying home to look after the children as the women in the household work in paid jobs, it is still overwhelmingly the case that women do the bulk of household labor, whether they have outside employment or not. In their household functions, women are not paid, even though their work is central to the creation of one of the most important commodities in the capitalist system: labor power, the mental and physical ability of workers to work.

This nurturing work, vital as it is, is carried on outside the market. Because it is unpaid it is uncounted in capitalist measures of production. For the first time in history, we have an economic system that excludes much of women's work from the core economic activities it values. This exclusion gives patriarchy a new mechanism to trivialize and demean women. Economists have estimated that in 2018 the market value of women's unpaid household labor in the United States was $1.5 trillion, if valued at the national hourly minimum wage. Taking the entire world into account, unpaid women's labor that year reached $10.9 trillion dollars.[21]

Patriarchy subordinated women in the home by asserting the uniquely capitalist norm that the man would earn enough for the entire family. This supposedly relieved the woman from the need to go out of the home, but also made her entirely dependent financially on her husband.* While middle and upper class men might make enough to support the new expectation of the housebound wife, working class men often didn't make enough for the family to survive. Women took paid work into the home in the way of laundry or childcare and tended the household vegetable garden. Millions of women also worked as servants in the homes of others, or in jobs open to them in the textile industry.

Women have always been active in the paid labor force, although until recent decades not nearly in proportion to their numbers in society. Since the 1970s, when men's wages, which had risen steadily after World War II, stopped going up, the strains on family finances pushed many women into

---

* The US temperance movement that culminated in Prohibition was led by women who wanted to end their husbands' drinking up the paycheck at the local bar on payday.

the workforce. Now two people needed to work to maintain a standard of living that has hardly risen for working families since then. The extra output from the family went to capital as surplus, not to workers in the form of better living conditions. This greater degree of worker exploitation has contributed to the well-known, ever-greater inequalities of income and wealth in the United States, and throughout the capitalist world.

Women's wages have been vital in providing basic needs for their families. But the central role of women's work in the history of capitalist development has long been overlooked or denigrated, as in a male chauvinist story, common at the time, that I heard in a 1960s labor economics class. Our male professor "explained" that women worked only for "pin money" to tuck in their bras on dates in case they didn't end up liking the guy and had to get home on their own. This (supposedly) marginal attachment to work was thought to explain why women were (wrongly) supposed to be very hard to organize into unions.

In fact, throughout the twentieth century women have been central to organizing the US labor movement.[22] The 1909 "Uprising of 20,000,"[23] a months-long strike of women garment workers in New York City, was sparked and led by twenty-one-year-old Russian Jewish immigrant Clara Lemlich, who went on to transform the International Ladies' Garment Workers Union. She and other women workers, mostly young immigrants, set the stage for the union's substantial growth following the Triangle Shirtwaist Factory fire. On March 25, 1911, the fire killed 146 workers, mostly young immigrant Jewish and Italian women.[24]

International Women's Day (IWD), celebrated in the US and around the world every year on March 8, grew as a memorial for the Triangle deaths. It has since become a commemoration and tribute to the dignity and strength of women workers everywhere. In the United States, IWD expanded into Women's History Month, also in March, during which forums, films, and rallies illuminate all aspects of women's experience.

Women's central role in working class organizing has continued in many forms, often militant. The 1937 autoworkers' forty-four-day sit-down strike against General Motors in Flint could not have been won without hundreds of women engaged in street actions around the plant during the length of the strike. The film *Salt of the Earth* depicts the decisive role of women joining with miners on strike in the Southwest after World War II. After mine owners got a court injunction prohibiting the miners themselves from picketing, the women took over the picket line and confronted the police. In portraying this class battle, the film also conveys the complicated gender issues raised as the women's active organizing challenges traditional male authority within the family and provides the basis for the women's growth in confidence and stature.

The film *Norma Rae* brought to wide public attention the role of women in organizing textile workers. Thousands of domestic workers, almost all immigrant women, undertook years of painstaking work to organize Domestic Workers United, which was able to press the New York state legislature to pass a "Domestic Workers Bill of Rights" in 2010.[25] In 2018, teachers struck successfully statewide for higher pay and better classroom conditions in Arizona, Oklahoma, and West Virginia, bringing thousands of women into the streets and into leadership. In 2012, Karen Lewis led the Chicago Teachers Union in a strike that established the union as a powerful force in alliance with parents and community organizations, winning improved education for Chicago's public school students.

Yet women have traditionally had to fight for leadership roles within their unions. And they have had to fight to win priority status for their particular needs in collective bargaining negotiations, everything from paid family leave to the provision of women's bathrooms and menstrual supplies in them, to shift schedules that allow for attentive child care, to equal inclusion in apprenticeship programs and other training opportunities.

This working class history is rarely the focus of attention. As labor historian Dorothy Sue Cobble has pointed out, middle class professional women who tend to overlook working class experience typically dominate academic women's studies programs. Meanwhile, men who too easily overlook women's experiences have dominated the study of labor history.[26]

Second-wave feminism, the feminist movement that exploded in the 1960s and 1970s (the first wave having been the movement begun in the nineteenth century to secure for women the right to vote), demanded that labor markets open up to the full and equal participation of women. Some women gained entry into the building trades and got work as firefighters, as well as breaking into other working class occupations long dominated by men. But the biggest social consequence came in opening up the professions to women, where they had rarely been allowed before. Educated women who had previously been limited to work as teachers and nurses eagerly became doctors, lawyers, business managers and executives, television news anchors, state governors, US senators, and Supreme Court justices. There has now been a credible major-party candidate for president and a woman elected US vice president. But the lives of women nursing home attendants, call center workers, beauticians, and working class jobs in the food and hospitality industries where millions of women labor, have been little affected.

Second-wave feminism also brought forth a fierce backlash beginning in the 1970s. Most notably led by Phyllis Schlafly, a Florida attorney, this reactionary pushback focused most intently on overturning the 1973 Supreme Court decision, *Roe v. Wade,* that guaranteed women the right to an abortion. Opposition to abortion rights, the refusal to allow women to control their own bodies, was tied to a reactionary view of women in general, seeking to keep them in their traditional place according to the rules of patriarchy.[27]

Not incidentally, this assertion of patriarchal privilege found a welcome home in the Republican Party in the late 1970s as it adopted cultural issues for a supposed moral high ground in its political campaigns. Susan Faludi analyzed this reactionary response to second-wave feminism in her iconic book *Backlash.*[28] Unsurprisingly, she found that the oppression of women played a supporting role in the assertion of capitalist power, which is the heart of Republican Party economic policy. We see this in the focus Republican politicians place on "culture issues" such as ending reproductive rights for women and passing laws that prohibit the teaching of racial justice issues in US history. Republicans have come to present themselves as the party for the working class, relying on these positions to hide their policies of corporate tax cuts, rollbacks of business regulation, and stripping back "entitlement programs" essential for the well-being of all working people. A key challenge to that assertion of capitalist power involves all working people fighting for women's access to the complete array of health services, as well as engaging in honest discussions of US racial history.

While all women benefit from reproductive freedom, it remains true that the impact of abortion restrictions is qualitatively different for women in the working class, compared with professional women. For example, women with few resources cannot travel easily to access health care prohibited where they live, nor can they as easily afford to take time off from work. Women of all classes suffer from the power of patriarchy. But those experiences are not always the same in their particulars across class lines.[29]

Race crosscuts gender experiences, as it does in the case of class. Until the 1970s, white women after marriage typically worked only at home, whereas Black women typically worked as field hands, or in domestic work for white women, or factory work when it was available, in addition to nurturing their families at home. In 1969, Frances Beal introduced the idea of "triple jeopardy," using it as the title of a Third World Women's Alliance publication. Beal came out of the male chauvinist environment of the Student Nonviolent Coordinating Committee (SNCC) office and its civil rights organizing in the South, but male chauvinism was prevalent throughout the student, antiwar, and civil rights movements of the time, north, south, east, and west.

Beal expressed and explored the complicated existence of poor and working class Black women, who experienced simultaneously the triple oppressions of class, race, and gender. More recently, triple jeopardy was apparent in the shooting deaths of eight women, mostly of Asian origin, in three massage parlors in Atlanta. As writer and journalist May Jeong expressed it: "The victims lived at the nexus of race, gender, and class."[30]

We see this complicated pattern playing out again in the greater impact of COVID-19 on Black women in the US. Their adverse health outcomes have been exacerbated not only by the stress of systemic racism but also by the occupations Black women disproportionately hold in frontline industries like hospitality, retail, and health care. Many of these positions are low-paid and do not usually offer paid sick leave. As Kellie McElhaney, professor at the University of California at Berkeley Haas School of Business, put it: "It's layer upon layer of inequity."[31] These layers of oppression extend into the trans community as well, among whom at least thirty-one people were violently killed during the first nine months of 2020, the majority transgender women of color.[32]

From slavery days, the experiences of Black and white women have been different. Differences continued through the era of Reconstruction and also in the suffragist movement, where African American women played important roles and built distinct forms of feminist engagement. The Nineteenth Amendment to the US Constitution, passed in 1920, gave all women the right to vote, but in those places where Jim Crow voting laws and racial intimidation succeeded in preventing Black people from voting the gain was effectively limited to white women.

In the early days of second-wave feminism, dominated by middle class white women, Gloria Steinem, for instance, made a practice of working closely with African American women,[33] but such individual efforts did not ultimately bridge the two communities. Angela Davis has illuminated this complex history in her book *Women, Race and Class*.[34] Kyla Schuller has documented many ways in which white suffragists and second-wave feminists have marginalized and sometimes even opposed the efforts of Black feminists to address the power of patriarchy.[35] These different, parallel, sometimes-conflicting movements continue to demand attention in progressive movements today.

The chasm appeared again in a 2019 controversy over the construction of a monument in New York City's Central Park to honor women suffragists on the 100th anniversary of the passage of the Nineteenth Amendment. The monument featured only two women: Elizabeth Cady Stanton and Susan B. Anthony, both white, both justifiably identified with the suffrage movement. But, as historian Liette Gidlow has shown, Black women's struggle for the franchise was powerful and followed a parallel track to white efforts.[36] She documents how the suffrage movement that led to the passage of the Nineteenth Amendment had also drawn vision and strength from such African American women leaders as Sojourner Truth, Ida B. Wells, and Mary Church Terrell. They are as well known among Black feminists as Stanton and Anthony are known among white feminists, and should be known by all. African American women protested the absence from the Central Park memorial of leaders from their history. The organizers of the memorial replied that the statue only had room for two people![37] That's where the matter stood until protests intensified. The result was a redesign that included Sojourner Truth with Stanton and Anthony in the final monument placed in Central Park in summer 2020.[38]

We can see something more of the operation of structural racism and its relation to gender and class in data reflecting infant mortality rates. Class differences play out within racial groups. In a detailed study of nearly two million births in California between 2007 and 2016, researchers found that infant deaths among babies born to white mothers in the lowest 10% of the income distribution were twice as frequent as those born into the top 10%. Black infant mortality differed by income as well but was not as dramatic as for whites; death rates for those in the bottom 10% of income were one and a half times higher than the death rate among the top 10%.[39]

We see the operation of structural racism when we look at the data more deeply. They show that in California, one of the most progressive states in the country, controlling for the age of the mother, "infant and maternal health in Black families at the top of the income distribution is markedly worse than that of white families at the bottom of the income distribution." In the years of the study, there were 437 infant deaths per

100,000 births in the top 10% of Black income while there were 350 deaths per 100,000 births in the bottom 10% of white income. The study found that taking account of income differences "does not appear to meaning-fully close the gap between racial and ethnic groups."[40] It's not just income that explains the differences we see. It's race as such. It's also class as such. Both operate and together drive the varied experiences of white and Black women and children in the United States.

Race, gender, and class are aspects of lived experience that form dialec-tical unities of opposites. They energize complex social dynamics. At any time and place, conditions will bring one or another of these contradictions to the fore. Questions of race may take center stage, as they did after the murder of George Floyd. Or the fight for gender equality may become the main event, as evidenced by the #MeToo movement. Or class issues like the Fight for $15 campaign to raise the minimum wage may require the movement's immediate attention.

Building a vibrant, united movement requires recognizing the mutu-ality of the concerns arising in different constituencies. It also requires widespread attention to particular forms of suffering as movements grow to address them. This calls for keeping class, race, and gender in mind simul-taneously while respecting their different effects.

This is quite difficult to do and requires conscious effort. Patient and respectful analysis of conditions in each time and place, undertaken jointly by leaders, organizers, and grassroots activists, have to determine how the movement sets its priorities, how it deals with multiple issues simultane-ously (sometimes known as "walking across the street and chewing gum at the same time"). Each focal point, whether class, race, or gender, will be the main event for a time, then give way to other priorities as conditions change. But as we move from one to another principal focus, we need to avoid pitting the one against the others, claiming for it some permanent priority status. What is a priority will change over time and place, and then change again. How we address each of these dimensions of life must be shaped by its mutual relationships with the others in order to move all progressive interests forward over time.

Notes

1   Adolph Reed, "Race and Class, Class and Race," *The Nation*, March 6/13, 2023, https://www.thenation.com/article/society/race-class-intersectionality-atlanta.

2   The most thorough presentation of this history is contained in Theodore W. Allen, *The Invention of the White Race*, 2 vols. (London: Verso, 1996).

3   Calhoun quoted in Robert Elder, *Calhoun: American Heretic* (New York: Basic Books, 2021), 496.

4   "Sharecropping," in *Slavery by Another Name*, directed by Sam Pollard, premiered on PBS February 13, 2012, https://www.pbs.org/tpt/slavery-by-another-name/themes/sharecropping.

5   Ira Katznelson, *When Affirmative Action Was White: An Untold History of Racial Inequality in Twentieth-Century America* (New York: W.W. Norton, 2005).

6   Bill Fletcher Jr. and Fernando Gapasin, *Solidarity Divided* (Berkeley: University of California Press, 2008); Michael Goldfield, *The Southern Key: Class, Race, and Radicalism in the 1930s and 1940s* (Oxford: Oxford University Press, 2020).

7   Richard Rothstein, *The Color of Law: A Forgotten History of How Our Government Segregated America* (New York, Liveright, 2017).

8   Ryan Mac, "Facebook Apologizes After A.I. Puts 'Primates' Label on Video of Black Men," *New York Times*, November 3, 2021, https://www.nytimes.com/2021/09/03/technology/facebook-ai-race-primates.html.

9   US Centers for Disease Control and Prevention, "COVID-19 Hospitalization and Death by Race/Ethnicity," July 16, 2021, https://www.cdc.gov/coronavirus/2019-ncov/covid-data/investigations-discovery/hospitalization-death-by-race-ethnicity.html.

10   US Centers for Disease Control and Prevention, "Health Equity Considerations and Racial and Ethnic Minority Groups, " July 24, 2020, https://www.cdc.gov/coronavirus/2019-ncov/community/health-equity/race-ethnicity.html.

11   Emily Flitter, "Minorities May Struggle to Obtain Relief Loans," *New York Times*, April 11, 2020, https://www.nytimes.com/2020/04/10/business/minority-business-coronavirus-loans.html?searchResultPosition=11.

12   Office of the Inspector General, US Small Business Administration, "Flash Report: Small Business Administration's Implementation of the Paycheck Protection Program Requirements," May 2020, accessed August 29, 2021, https://www.sba.gov/document/report-20-14-flash-report-small-business-administrations-implementation-paycheck-protection-program-requirements.

13   Equal Justice Initiative, *Lynching in America: Confronting the Legacy of Racial Terror*, 3rd ed. (Montgomery, AL: Equal Justice Initiative, 2017), https://eji.org/reports/lynching-in-america.

14   Phil Wahba, "The Number of Black CEOs in the Fortune 500 Remains Very Low," *Fortune*, June 1, 2020, https://fortune.com/2020/06/01/black-ceos-fortune-500-2020-african-american-business-leaders.

15   E. Franklin Frazier, *Black Bourgeoisie* (Glencoe, IL: Free Press, 1957).

16   Davis quoted on *Black Mail Blog*, accessed August 29, 2021, https://blackmail4u.com/tag/angela-davis-quotes.

17   Morning quoted in Janet Adamy and Paul Overberg, "The Census Predicament: Counting Americans by Race," *Wall Street Journal*, November 17, 2020.

18   Juan Gonzalez, *Harvest of Empire: A History of Latinos in America*, 2nd. rev. ed. (New York: Penguin Books, 2011).

19   August Meier and Elliot Rudwick, *Black Detroit and the UAW* (Oxford: Oxford University Press, 1979), 178.

20   Brent Staples, "How Italians Became 'White,'" *New York Times*, October 12, 2019, https://www.nytimes.com/interactive/2019/10/12/opinion/columbus-day-italian-american-racism.html.

21   Gus Wezerek and Kristen R. Ghodsee, "Women's Unpaid Labor is Worth $10,900,000,000,000," *New York Times*, March 5, 2020 (written to mark International Women's Day), https://www.nytimes.com/interactive/2020/03/04/opinion/women-unpaid-labor.html.

22   Dorothy Sue Cobble, *The Other Women's Movement: Workplace Justice and Social Rights in Modern America* (Princeton: Princeton University Press, 2005).

23 Tony Michels, "Uprising of 20,000 (1909)," Jewish Women's Archive, *The Shalvi/Hyman Encyclopedia of Jewish Women,* accessed August 29, 2021, https://jwa.org/encyclopedia/article/uprising-of-20000-1909.

24 Editors, *history.com,* "Triangle Shirtwaist Factory Fire," accessed August 29, 2021, https://www.history.com/topics/early-20th-century-us/triangle-shirtwaist-fire.

25 Tiffany Ten Eyck, "Domestic Workers in New York Win First-Ever Job Protections," *Labor Notes,* July 2, 2010, https://labornotes.org/2010/07/domestic-workers-new-york-win-first-ever-job-protections.

26 Dorothy Sue Cobble, "When Feminism Had Class," in *What's Class Got To Do with It? American Society in the Twenty-First Century,* ed. Michael Zweig (Ithaca, NY: Cornell University Press, 2004), 25.

27 Kristin Luker, *Abortion and the Politics of Motherhood* (Oakland: University of California Press, 1985).

28 Susan Faludi, *Backlash: The Undeclared War against American Women* (New York: Crown, 1991).

29 See, for example, Kathleen Geier and Curve contributors, "Does Feminism Have a Class Problem?" review of *Lean In: Women, Work, and the Will to Lead* by Sheryl Sandberg, *The Nation,* June 11, 2014, https://www.thenation.com/article/archive/does-feminism-have-class-problem.

30 May Jeong, "The Deep American Roots of the Atlanta Shootings," *New York Times,* March 19, 2021, https://www.nytimes.com/2021/03/19/opinion/atlanta-shooting-massage-sex-work.html?action=click&module=Opinion&pgtype=Homepage.

31 McElhaney quoted in Bethany Garner, "Why Black Women in the U.S. Are Being Hit Hardest by Coronavirus," *BusinessBecause,* August 7, 2020, https://www.businessbecause.com/news/in-the-news/7138/black-women-in-us-hit-hardest-by-coronavirus.

32 Elizabeth Bibi, "Human Rights Campaign President Alphonso David on the Unprecedented Fatal Violence Against the Transgender and Gender Non-Conforming Community in 2020," October 6, 2020, https://www.hrc.org/press-releases/human-rights-campaign-president-alphonso-david-on-the-unprecedented-fatal-violence-against-the-transgender-and-gender-non-conforming-community-in-2020.

33 Carolyn G. Heilbrun, *The Education of a Woman: The Life of Gloria Steinem* (New York: Dial Press, 1995).

34 Angela Y. Davis, *Women, Race, and Class* (New York: Vintage, 1981).

35 Kyla Schuller, *The Trouble with White Women: A Counterhistory of Feminism* (New York: Bold Type Books, 2021).

36 Liette Gidlow, "The Sequel: The Fifteenth Amendment, the Nineteenth Amendment, and Southern Black Women's Struggle to Vote," *Journal of the Gilded Age and Progressive Era* 17 (2018): 433–49.

37 Ginia Bellafante, "A Suffrage Monument Fails Black Women" *New York Times,* January 20, 2019, https://www.nytimes.com/2019/01/17/nyregion/is-a-planned-monument-to-womens-rights-racist.html.

38 Alisha Haridasani Gupta, "For 3 Suffragists, an Honor Long Past Due," *New York Times,* August 7, 2020, https://www.nytimes.com/2020/08/06/arts/design/suffragist-19th-amendment-central-park.html.

39 Claire Cain Miller, Sarah Kliff, and Shannon Lin, "Childbirth Is Deadlier for Black Families Even When They're Rich, Expansive Study Finds," The Upshot, *New York Times,* February 12, 2023, https://www.nytimes.com/interactive/2023/02/12/upshot/child-maternal-mortality-rich-poor.html.

40 Kate Kennedy-Moulton, Sarah Miller, Petra Perrson, Maya Rossin-Slater, Laura Wherry, and Gloria Aldana, "Maternal and Infant Health Inequality: New Evidence from Linked Administrative Data," National Bureau of Economic Research, Working Paper 30693, November 2022, accessed April 1, 2023, http://www.nber.org/papers/w30693.

CHAPTER TEN

Navigating Race and Class

Perhaps the most important consequence of the last chapter's analysis is that as progressive politics unfold in the United States, chief among the difficulties we have to navigate are the relationships among the justice demands of class on one hand and of race, gender, ethnic, and environmental justice on the other. Conflicts arise because class and race are mutually determined, yet at the same time distinct, with ethnic issues drawn into the dynamics as well. Class and gender are also mutually determined, yet again distinct. Our experiences of class, race, gender, and ethnicity reflect this complicated mosaic. They operate as social forces but also within each of us as individuals.

In this chapter, we'll look at the complexity of navigating the whirling currents of working class politics and movements of oppressed and marginalized people in such a way as to have them reinforce one another as much as possible, rather than pitting any one against the others. It's hard. There are no easy answers. Unfortunately, history has shown us time and time again how class, race, and gender movements have clashed countless times to the detriment of all. We need to do better.

There is no way to avoid conflicting interests. But conflicts within the overall movement must be negotiated on the basis of mutual respect and understanding with regard to priorities at any given moment. One-sided responses to oppression that ignore the reality of these mutual determinations too easily lead to counterproductive, often hostile, fractures among progressive forces. To minimize these negative consequences, we need to work with a nuanced understanding of the experiences of different constituencies, and the common ultimate source of their suffering in this society that stems from its domination by capitalism.

Navigating Race and Class

In the immediate aftermath of Donald Trump's election in 2016, there was a notable absence of nuance in progressive commentary on the role that class and race had played in the election.[1] Progressive political analysts broke into two broad camps. One group blamed "the white working class," driven by racism to disregard their economic interests to vote for Trump. These analysts usually ignored the white managers and executives, middle class professionals, and white small-business owners without a college degree who provided the majority of Trump's votes. The other group blamed the Democratic Party for abandoning the working class (usually meaning white workers) to champion "identity politics" in the interests of women and minority groups.

Looking ahead to the next elections, the first group urged progressive movements to double down on the demographic future when the United States would become a "majority minority country." White people would then be the minority and could be outvoted by the incoming majority. The second group urged the abandonment of identity politics and a return to the Democratic Party's historical status as "the working man's party," hoping to regain the loyalty of white voters, especially white men.

Each path is a dead end for progressive politics. Each is one-sided, breaking the dialectic of class with race and gender that we must find a way to respect. No partial working class movement can challenge capital in the long run while leaving any of its sections to the side. That means working class movements have to champion the specific demands and needs of all its racial, gender, and ethnic sections as they face social marginalization. Coming at the problem from the other direction, no racial or gender justice movement can fully emancipate its constituency by leaving its working class members outside its conscious boundaries and ignoring the role of capitalist power in shaping all our lives.

Sorting through this complicated situation will not be easy. In fact, there's hardly a successful example that has taken root for any length of time in US history. Playwright and labor organizer Gene Bruskin has captured the frustration of near misses in his play *The Moment Was Now*.[2] Set in 1869, his drama brings us the words of formerly enslaved abolitionist leader Frederick Douglass; Black labor leader Isaac Myers; and white and Black suffragists Susan B. Anthony and Frances Harper. They argue with and debate each other on stage as their words trace the failed historical attempt to forge unity among their different movements during the post–Civil War Reconstruction period. What they say will be all too famil-iar to us as they foretell current conflicts among our own movements.

Let's consider two of the most significant continuing obstacles to over-coming this history of division: the continuing power of white supremacy, and the difficulties of political education in working class communities.

The deep roots of racism and white supremacy that go to the heart of our society will be extremely difficult to reduce in strength, let alone eliminate altogether. This battle must start by acknowledging that white supremacy is first and foremost a problem that white people must address. White supremacy will loosen its grip only when white people loosen it. Black, Hispanic, Native, and Asian social movements will continue to challenge white supremacy, but they cannot end it until white people give it up. How can that happen?

We can get some insight into what might be involved by looking at different motivations that have led a number of white people historically to dedicate their lives to racial equality.[3] Some have been motivated by religious conviction: "We're all equal as children of God." Some have been motivated by patriotism: our founding national document proclaims that "all men [people] are created equal," and the Fourteenth Amendment to the US Constitution guarantees equality for all under the law. Others have been motivated politically by an awakened class consciousness that underscores the common interests of all workers.

As powerful as each of these arenas of concern may be in getting white people to move away from white supremacy, each arena also lends itself to opposite interpretations that can reinforce it. Historically, there have been white church leaders who used their interpretations of the Bible to legitimize white supremacy and "explain" the inferiority of Black people. We've seen "patriots" waving the flag while in its name upholding states' rights to strip Black people of the vote. And some interpretations of class dynamics use class analysis to undercut the demands and movements of Black people for equality, claiming they will only divide and weaken the working class.

In other words, each of these arenas—religion, patriotism, class poli-tics—is conflicted in its treatment of white supremacy. Each is an arena in which white people must confront and consciously turn away from white supremacy. But each of these arenas is also conflicted along class lines, as is class analysis itself. As antiracist thinking and action arise among white people, especially in connection with Black movements demanding equality, we soon see backlash reactions mount, stoked and funded by capitalist intervention wherever necessary to reinforce the traditions and habits of mind of white supremacy, often inflamed by right-wing media.

That's what happened when big-dollar donations flowed to the Trump campaign and presidency as it gave open permission to neo-Nazis and other white supremacists to influence white workers. Movements can bring about the long-term weakening of white supremacy only insofar as they can weaken the grip of capitalist interests, thinking, and values.

Here it is essential to keep in mind the crucial fact that white supremacy, historically, is the creation of the ruling class, solidly white from the colonial era on until its very recent inclusion of small numbers of Black and other nonwhite people. White supremacy did not originate in the white sections of the working class. But the history of white supremacy and capitalist dominance are such long-term and "natural" parts of our culture that their origins are invisible to most white people. Every white person has racist images presented to them from their earliest days in our culture, in the media, schools, and everyday life. They don't ask for them; the images and ideas are thrust upon them. This is not innate. As the lyric from the musical *South Pacific* goes:

> You've got to be taught
> To hate and fear,
> You've got to be taught
> From year to year,
> It's got to be drummed
> In your dear little ear
> You've got to be carefully taught.[4]

Let's be clear that the people who set the terms for what is carefully taught to our children and reinforced through adulthood, those with ultimate authority, are the ruling class and those who do their work. The frenzied efforts in the early 2020s by state legislatures across the US to banish critical race theory and demonize "wokeness" in schools and universities is an example of this process. Their funds and political leadership provide openings for local mobilizations by right-wing people raising their voices in local school board meetings. Some in the ruling class who do not want to directly challenge the powerful movement for racial justice that arose after George Floyd's murder try with these methods to push discussion of US racial history into private spaces. It will take effort among white people to make these forces visible and see how these conflicts manifest aspects of class dynamics.

But the unlearning has to address racism itself, not just class issues. It will take dedicated education to get white people to unlearn the automatic and internalized apparent naturalness of white supremacy. This process must include personal engagement of some white people with others searching together for the roots of their attitudes about race. Inducing guilt is not the point or the goal. On the contrary, it is to clarify the ways in which racist messages came to be inscribed in white people. The idea is to excavate as much as possible the memories of how it happened, *that* it happened, the better to release their influence.

The unlearning process needs also to involve an educational program that includes the history of white supremacy as an instrument of social control, including control of white workers. It must also convey a solid understanding of capitalist class structure and dynamics. Success in making these points stick will be more likely if the education is part of navigating concrete real-life struggles in which the questions have arisen. Real-life experience is where "aha moments" are most likely to occur.

An example of this process comes from Showing Up for Racial Justice (SURJ), an organization working to mobilize white working class people across the South. Beth Howard, a SURJ leader, explained how white working class rural voters in Georgia came into the 2020 electoral campaign to support the Black senatorial candidate Raphael Warnock, the Jewish senatorial candidate Jon Ossoff, and Joe Biden against Donald Trump:

> What we really try to do is organize around mutual interests, talking to our folks about what white people have to gain from breaking with white solidarity and joining a multiracial movement.... We do that by creating the kind of welcoming space that is centered in working class community.
>
> We have really embraced bold, progressive reforms and candidates, including candidates of color, because we really believe that poor and working-class white people will turn out and vote for candidates who will bring meaningful, progressive change. We embrace talking explicitly about race ... because they [the right] talk about race all the time.[5]

Howard's experience in Georgia contradicts the stereotype that white working class people were inevitably central to Trump's base. "The most angry, volatile Trump-supporting people I talked to were white people with money, mostly white men with money.... I think we need to not continue to scapegoat poor white people and count them out. They are bearing the brunt of these harmful policies and we are taking that fury and that righteous anger and directing it where it belongs, not at other poor and working class people, Black and Brown people, Indigenous people, people of color." Looking beyond any single election cycle, Howard stresses the need for a "strong, deep bench of poor and working-class anti-racist white organizers," calling for a "long-haul investment ... [for] deeper work in more conservative parts of our states."[6]

Clear and straightforward discussions about the intersections of class with race are best undertaken in the course of organizing campaigns for economic and social justice. This is the context in which people of European descent can give up an identity as "white," setting that social category aside. In education related to movement building in each arena—religion, patriotism, and class struggle—we need to dig down into ways in which capitalist interests shape the content of these practices, and how white supremacy thrives in their context.

Exploring these ideas requires a degree of abstract thinking, a concept I'd like to pause on for a moment. As real as their consequences are for each of us, class, race, gender, and power are, after all, abstractions. Yet when most people consider abstractions, such as being white or Black, being an American or a Mexican, a man or a woman, they tend to think in stereotypes. Most people are not trained to think of abstract ideas as analytic categories that embody complicated social and personal dynamics. Looking more deeply into and unpacking stereotypes destroys their power and opens the door to a more realistic understanding of forces shaping our lives.

Grasping the dynamics of social history also requires strategic thinking, looking at a given situation and finding in it the possibilities of paths that can lead to a desired social change. Yet working class children of all races and ethnicities rarely receive in their schools the critical skills required to think strategically and work with abstractions. Their schooling stresses the specific skills in reading and basic mathematics, enough to sustain their training to perform work, even skilled work, on the job under supervision, but rarely includes training in critical thinking.[7]

Capitalist executives, on the other hand, and their senior managers do understand that they themselves require facility in strategic thinking and abstraction. After all, that's what they do on the job: provide strategic guidance to their firms and to public policy. Children drawn into this class as they grow to be adults learn these skills, which are central to the education they receive at public schools in some affluent suburbs, elite private high schools and universities, and at home for those who grow up in families of the elite.

Applying strategic thinking and working with abstractions while confronting white supremacy among white workers is complicated by the fact that white workers accumulated some real benefits when, in Ira Katznelson's phrase, "affirmative action was white." Most people are loathe to surrender these benefits, for themselves or their children. But as capital has become ever-more powerful in the last fifty years, the lives of white workers have steadily worsened with job losses, stagnant and lower wages, as well as hollowed out communities in rural areas and also in major cities. It is a history that has seen the fraying of white privilege and a marked increase of "deaths of despair" spreading among working class whites throughout the country in the forms of increasing suicide and fatal drug overdoses.[8]

The betrayal white workers have felt as part of this history can provide an opening to discussions about who and what is responsible for these developments. That can lead to white workers following the racist and neofascist leadership of Donald Trump and politicians like him, struggling to restore earlier privileges by doubling down on racist and anti-immigrant beliefs. Or it can lead to white workers participating in social movements that confront the people who control the levers of power in the economic and political world. This is an urgent challenge for progressive people.

As we grapple with this political challenge, it will help to recall James Baldwin's observation: "I imagine one of the reasons people cling to their hates so stubbornly is because they sense that once hate is gone, they will be forced to deal with their own pain."[9] This tells us why the proper tone and approach of progressive political education among white workers cannot be a guilt trip. It has to be grounded in a clear explanation of power, a concept workers have no problem appreciating as a critical part of life that they need to understand. Who has the power to inflict the pain that working people experience? Where does the power come from to overcome that infliction? These are questions for political education in movement building. In dealing with anyone driven by wrongheadedness, it is best to approach the work guided by the old religious maxim: "Hate the sin, but love the sinner."

While many white workers have much to learn, they are not the only ones in progressive orbits in that condition. Too often, constituency politics, while focused on the righteous demands arising from communities of oppressed people, disregard questions of class, asserting a one-sided "identity" interest that lets the capitalist class entirely off the hook. Yet Black leaders from Isaac Myers to W.E.B. DuBois to Rev. Martin Luther King Jr., Jesse Jackson, and Rev. William J. Barber II have recognized the vital connections between race and class, and organized accordingly. But their message is often understandably resisted among Black people because of the bitter legacy of centuries of white supremacy and the history of unreliable participation of whites in alliance against it. Many people in marginalized communities find it difficult—if not impossible—to trust in the solidity of white support.

Let's look at one of the most difficult, divisive issues that gripped the labor movement in the recent past: the question of seniority. Seniority rights are essential to protect workers from arbitrary firings by employers, who use the threat of firing as a weapon to discipline the workforce. When unions representing workers who were overwhelmingly white negotiated seniority clauses in their contracts with employers, they established a procedure that governed layoffs, requiring them to fall first upon the most recently hired, and working back through time from there. This insulated workers from arbitrary inclusion in layoffs to satisfy the boss's ability to punish individual troublemakers or to reward toadies and scabs.

The problem emerged when Black workers broke through historic hiring barriers to join white workers on the job. Those Black workers were the most recent hires, which made them most vulnerable to layoffs and firings when the seniority rule "last hired, first fired" was in effect. So any economic downturn for the company would undo the recent hires and reestablish a segregated work force. When Black workers demanded the same seniority protections as white workers, they met fierce resistance. Many white workers couldn't accept weakening their own job security. Standard seniority provisions became part of the structures of racism and white supremacy.

As long as the issue was posed in a way that presented Black job security as a direct threat to white workers' security, the conflict was bound to be bitter, pitting white against Black in traditional racial dynamics. One possible solution to the dilemma would be to ground progressive policy in the purpose of seniority—protecting workers from arbitrary treatment by the employer. If the layoffs were assigned by lottery, with Black and white workers in the same pool, employer favoritism would still be eliminated.

Such an approach would have all workers face the same threat, encouraging them to oppose all layoffs in greater strength together, across race and age differences. The point here is to strategize and see if a path to unity can be found.

The interplay of class, race, and gender does not create or involve a hierarchy of interests. We cannot rightly say that one is central and the others subordinate or peripheral. As community organizer Maria Poblet reported from her experiences, "In Virginia, leaders across constituencies work to avoid having one community's needs pitted against another's, with leaders agreeing to advance different parts of their shared agenda by sequencing their focus—one set of issues now, and another set later."[10]

Racism and male supremacy existed before capitalism. They do not require capitalism for their perpetuation. We cannot assume that weakening or destroying capitalist power and bringing the working class to the fore will automatically resolve such forms of oppression.

We can see evidence of this in the Cuban experience following their 1958 revolution. Historian Elizabeth Dore explored the history of the Cuban Revolution in part through a series of oral histories. She found that after Fidel Castro's 1962 speech in which he declared that racism had been eradicated in Cuba when the revolution abolished capitalism there, "Racism was hushed up and hidden away like a dirty family secret. The official narrative was that the problem of racism had been solved, and measures to combat it were not only unnecessary but dangerous, as they would undermine national unity, and provide ammunition to the enemy."

Yet Dore found that although "disparities between white and Black Cubans declined dramatically ... refusal to talk about race—the traits Cuban society attributes to skin color—and to address racism, operated insidiously to keep Black Cubans out of important sectors." She found that after economic reforms opened up limited private enterprise in the 2000s, "Afro-Cubans lost out relatively to white Cubans ... largely because remittances sent by affluent white Cuban-Americans are behind many of the new businesses.... The regeneration of historic privilege combined with everyday racism is recreating the pre-revolutionary racial divide."[11]

Because oppression calls forth resistance, women will always be in motion, Black people will always be in motion, workers will always be in motion, LGBTQ people, Native American, Asian, and Hispanic people will always be in motion. Each of these movements demands its autonomy, as does the labor movement. The task for leaders of all of them is to navigate the conflicts among them, each showing respect for the others, each working in coalition across constituencies to confront the common core of capitalist rule they all share. At any one time and place, one or another of these oppressions and resistances will be most central to the long-term growth of overall movement power. We all have to analyze the situation and negotiate relations among the various parts of the movement and the timing and sequence of the movement's focus to maintain coherence.

This is no easy matter. There is no formula or rule that can properly take the place of a concrete analysis of time, place, and conditions. The closest recent example might be the Rainbow Coalition that the Rev. Jesse Jackson led in the 1980s, which brought together labor, civil and women's rights organizations, and community groups working for economic justice, with an agenda of international peace and social solidarity.[12] But this promising vehicle for uniting many social movements faltered after Jackson's second run for president in the 1988 Democratic Party primaries, in which he won more votes than any other unsuccessful Democratic Party presidential candidate up to that time. According to the analysis of Bill Fletcher Jr. and Danny Glover, "[It] unraveled ... because of Jackson's move to turn the coalition—the core of his movement—into a personal political operation" to increase his influence within the Democratic Party, thinking he could do that without continuing the movement that put him in that position.[13] In its early stages in 2023, the Poor People's Campaign: A National Call for Moral Revival is the most promising successor to the Rainbow and the promise it held.

We must not base our politics on the old idea that "a rising tide lifts all boats." It will not. As long as white supremacy, patriarchy, and homophobia exert force in society, they must be challenged in their own right. Independent working class politics requires specific attention to all forms of exploitation, oppression, and marginalization, because they are wrong in principle and because they are building blocks in the foundation of capitalist power.

It is no accident that the political forces most dedicated to corporate interests seek to suppress Black, Native American, and Hispanic votes while also opposing unions. They also seek to degrade women by denying them the most basic element of human dignity, control over their own bodies. Securing the rights of all women becomes easier if the women's movement has as its ally a strong labor movement. Securing the rights of working people becomes easier if men go into battle next to the women who demand

their full equality with men. The labor movement and the women's movement will each be greatly strengthened through their support of voter rights,
opposition to militarized policing and cruelty at our borders, and standing
with people of color in deliberate opposition to the techniques of the New
Jim Crow. The recent increasing prominence of women in leadership roles
in labor and racial justice movements is an important positive development.

A Note to White Readers

Every time racial tensions sweep the country we hear calls for "dialogue"
with hope that heartfelt conversations across racial lines will promote
understanding and mutual respect, even racial reconciliation. The uprisings
across the country following the murder of George Floyd sparked hopes for
these conversations on a wider scale than any in recent decades. To make
more progress than we've made until now, I think white people need to
enter into these efforts with some lessons from the past.

I am a white man. I do not presume to speak for Black or other people
of color or their movements, or to give direction for their approaches to
racial dialogue. But as a white person who's been involved in progressive
social movements for over half a century, I've been part of many such
conversations. I've read a lot of history in the course of them, and have
accumulated some experience that I offer to white people coming into these
dialogues now.

In the late 1960s and into the 1970s, Frantz Fanon's book *The Wretched
of the Earth* was an important source of understanding, important because he
told the story of colonialism from the point of view of the people oppressed
by the colonial powers, especially France in Algeria.[14] Fanon, a psychiatrist
from Martinique living in Algeria during the war for independence there,
forced us in Western countries, which were dominating the world against
the resistance of colonized people, to wrestle with the fact that we were *not*
the center of the world. He forced us to hear the voices of the people whom
our leaders and culture had taught us to think of as children, or even to view
as savages in desperate need of our saving presence in their lives. Instead,
he insisted that we hear those voices as belonging to fellow human beings,
demanding the agency and autonomy we took for granted for ourselves,
expressing the righteous anger arising from their oppression. It made for
uncomfortable yet essential reading.

One profound lesson from Fanon is that the oppressor knows very
little about the life of the oppressed, but the oppressed know a great deal

CLASS, RACE, AND GENDER

about their oppressors. This asymmetry of knowledge follows the asymmetry of power. The oppressor dominates with the application of power, brute force when necessary, without feeling the need for particular knowledge or concern for the people they rule, except as an abstract mass that must be controlled. The oppressed, on the other hand, must navigate their oppression by careful attention to what brings harsh responses from those in power. They learn how to hide, and yet maintain, and organize relying on what their oppressors would find displeasing thoughts and actions. They learn how to flatter and cajole them. This understanding is intensely personal, arising from their interactions as personal and political servants and subjects of those in power.

In the course of political education as the oppressed organize among themselves, this understanding takes strategic shape to guide liberation struggles. What made Fanon such a shocking teacher at the time rested exactly in his demand that we in colonial heartlands see ourselves as we are seen by those we oppress, challenging us to accept their knowledge and come to see ourselves as we are, and to give up any imagined moral superiority.

As we white people in the US enter into dialogue on race, we must, if we are serious, enter into those discussions with the commitment to surrender any claim to the moral superiority white people have taken for granted since the invention of racial slavery 350 years ago. That is not easy or automatic. It can be a painful challenge. We would do well to include in our reflections on race the many Black writers who have analyzed the United States as Fanon did for France.

Malcolm X was such a voice in the same era as Fanon. James Baldwin also wrote powerfully at the time about white people in the United States. We can learn a lot about ourselves by quoting Baldwin at some length, beginning with his wise words in a 1963 letter to his fifteen-year-old nephew:

> Please try to remember that what they believe, as well as what they do and cause you to endure, does not testify to your inferiority, but to their inhumanity and fear. Please try to be clear, dear James, through the storm that rages about your youthful head today, about the reality that lies behind the words *acceptance* and *integration*. There is no reason for you to try to become like white people and there is no basis for their impertinent assumption that *they* must accept *you*.... They are, in effect, still trapped in a history which they do not understand;

and until they understand it, they cannot be released from it. They have had to believe for many years, and for innumerable reasons, that black men are inferior to white men. Many of them, indeed, know better, but, as you will discover, people find it very difficult to act on what they know. To act is to be committed, and to be committed is to be in danger. In this case, the danger, in the minds of most white Americans, is the loss of their identity.... Well, the black man has functioned in the white man's world as a fixed star, as an immovable pillar: and as he moves out of his place, heaven and earth are shaken to their foundations.[15]

In another essay, "Down on the Cross," written about the same time, Baldwin goes more deeply into these themes:

White Americans find it as difficult as white people everywhere do to divest themselves of the notion that they are in possession of some intrinsic value that black people need, or want. And this assumption—which, for example, makes the solution to the Negro problem depend on the speed with which Negroes accept and adopt white standards—is revealed in all kinds of striking ways, from Bobby Kennedy's assurance that a Negro can become President in forty years to the unfortunate tone of warm congratulation with which so many liberals address their Negro equals. It is the Negro, of course, who is presumed to have become equal—an achievement that not only proves the comforting fact that perseverance has no color but also overwhelmingly corroborates the white man's sense of his own value. Alas, this value can scarcely be corroborated in any other way; there is certainly little enough in the white man's public or private life that one should desire to imitate. White men, at the bottom of their hearts, know this. Therefore, a vast amount of energy that goes into what we call the Negro problem is produced by the white man's profound desire not to be judged by those who are not white, not to be seen as he is.... I submit, then, that the racial tensions that menace Americans today have little to do with real antipathy—on the contrary, indeed—and are involved only symbolically with color.[16]

It may seem harsh to say that white people's claim to value rests almost entirely on their assertion of superiority over Black people, value "that can scarcely be corroborated in any other way." Because, as Fanon and Malcolm and hundreds of other writers and historians have documented in appalling detail, white European and North American actions around the world have brought about brutal oppression, murder, rape, pillage, torture, and a host of other terrible scourges upon people they have subjugated across the planet, including widespread and long-lasting suffering of working people within those countries. On a personal note, the people who murdered my grandparents and others of my family, and millions of other Jews and homosexuals and Roma and disabled people and communists during World War II, were white also, and arose in a country that had claimed to be one of the most civilized in human history.

As we enter into racial dialogue, it will also help to keep in mind advice from journalist Jess Rohan, who wrote on the subject as it relates to the dynamics of Israeli-Palestinian dialogues that have long been sponsored by the organization Seeds of Peace. Summing up those experiences critically, Rohan warns that to be serious we need to avoid "a dialogue model built to address conflicts without discussing power."[17] In our context, it is not possible to achieve "understanding" of Black or white racial experience without an explicit openness to a deep investigation of power.

I have had students ask me: Why don't we celebrate white history month in the US? After all, February is Black History Month; October is Hispanic Heritage Month; March is Women's History Month. Why do we have these celebrations, but nothing like them for white people? I respond that if we see ourselves through the eyes of those with whom we enter into dialogue, in the US and in countries around the world, as Fanon and Baldwin call upon us to do, we must recoil from the historical meaning of "white." There is nothing to celebrate about being "white" in that historical sense.

We might imagine a white heritage month that brought forward the works of Shakespeare, Mary Shelley, Goethe, Dickens, Madame Curie, Mazzini, Beethoven, Austen, and other intellectual and cultural giants. All had pale skin, but none of them were *white* in the sense of possessing the social power that that identity holds in the United States. Given our current political climate, who would champion a white heritage month? We can guess that it would be used to toast the legacy of Confederate president Jefferson Davis, South Carolina senator John C. Calhoun, Ku Klux Klan leader David Duke, and Supreme Court justice Roger Taney, famous for his 1857 Dred Scott decision that declared that the Black man has no rights that the white man is obligated to respect. Today's white supremacists take these people, and many like them, as the leading lights of their white heritage.

Turning away from a celebration of this heritage as such doesn't mean turning away from the heritage that people of European descent proudly identify with in the accomplishments of people from their countries of origin, either "over there" or after coming to the United States. People rightly deserve to be proud of their Irish heritage, or the accomplishments of the Jewish or Persian or Russian or Italian people through history. The specificity of these subjects of pride actually gains in clarity when they are removed from any association with "whiteness," as people of varied heritages escape from a homogenous racial category.

Millions of white people voted for Trump. Few were out and out militant racists, proclaiming white supremacy as a principle. The majority of white Trump voters resent being lumped in with neo-Nazis. They proclaim their innocence of racist feelings and most probably don't use overt racial or ethnic slurs in conversation. They may work easily and on friendly terms with Black coworkers in offices, factories, and shops. But, whatever their personal behavior, even if they didn't think of it that way, their vote for Trump was a racist act. Their willingness to accept Trump's blatant racism reflects a tolerance of racism as long as they believe there is some payoff for them like lower taxes, better job opportunities, or fewer regulations limiting their business practices. We can think of this as "soft racism": a tolerance of racist policies in exchange for one's own interests. As long as this bargain is unspoken and unexamined, people can accept privilege while denying that privilege exists.

As white people enter into dialogue on racial conflicts in the US, we have to be prepared to give up our identification with "whiteness" in the social and historical sense. We cannot escape having a European heritage, nor, for now, avoid the privileges that accrue to it in the United States, whether we are conscious of them or not. Even though in the 1940s and 1950s I was raised not to think of myself as white in the social sense, I could not escape the advantage I got from the photo I and all other students were required to submit with our college applications, so the admissions office could identify more easily the applications from Black students to set them aside or question them more thoroughly. I cannot escape the fact that when I get pulled over in a traffic stop, my life is not in danger. Without a thought on my part, security guards in stores where I shop do not follow me around the store. I don't have to think about anyone calling the police on me as I walk through Central Park carrying binoculars, looking at birds. I cannot avoid having had the advantage of getting a tenured faculty line at a time when there were very few Black economists, and the economics department that hired me had not the slightest interest in the research or teaching perspectives that a Black scholar interested in Black studies would bring. But, taking a note from Baldwin, I do have the power to "cease fleeing from reality and change it."

Every year in January the Rev. Martin Luther King Jr. is the focus of celebrations of his life and work for racial justice. Invariably, we hear him speak in stirring words about his dream of a society in which people are judged by the "content of their character," not the color of their skin. Until I sat down to think carefully about writing this section, I hadn't realized that I had always taken that to be an aspiration for the treatment of Black people. But, as King surely meant and Baldwin demanded, the same must also hold true for white people. The fact that this came as such an epiphany for me, that the words we celebrate mean that *I* should be judged by the content of *my* character and not the color of *my* skin, brought a sharp emotional charge that had me literally shaking for fifteen minutes before I could force myself to calm down. I saw in my reaction the extent to which I had absorbed and still harbored racist attitudes, however much I had thought myself to be free of them.

If white people are going to engage in productive dialogues on race, among ourselves or with others, we should be prepared to face what Baldwin called the "upheavals in the universe" that result from accepting that we enter these dialogues with nothing more than the content of our character.

Notes

1   Michael Zweig, "White Working-Class Voters and the Future of Progressive Politics," *New Labor Forum* 26, no. 2 (May 2017): 28–36.

2   For more on the play (now a film), see *The Moment Was Now*, accessed August 31, 2021, https://www.themomentwasnow.com.

3   A fuller discussion is in Michael Zweig, "The Mutual Determination of Race and Class: History and Current Implications," in *Routledge International Handbook of Working-Class Studies*, ed. Michele Fazio, Christie Launius, and Tim Strangleman (New York: Routledge, 2021).

4   Richard Rodgers and Oscar Hammerstein II, "You've Got to Be Carefully Taught," accessed June 29, 2023, https://rodgersandhammerstein.com/song/south-pacific/youve-got-to-be-carefully-taught.

5   Beth Howard quoted in Linda Burnham, "Change a State and Shock a Nation: Georgia in the 2020 Elections," in *Power Concedes Nothing: How Grassroots Organizing Wins Elections*, ed. Linda Burnham, Max Elbaum, and Maria Poblet (New York: OR Books, 2022), 15–25.

6   Burnham, "Change a State," 13–32.

7   Samuel Bowles and Herbert Gintis, *Schooling in Capitalist America: Educational Reform and the Contradictions of Economic Life* (New York: Haymarket, 2011 [1979]); Annette Lareau,

Unequal Childhoods: Class, Race, and Family Life, 2nd ed. (Berkeley: University of California Press, 2011).

8   Anne Case and Angus Deaton, *Deaths of Despair and the Future of Capitalism* (Princeton: Princeton University Press, 2020).

9   James Baldwin quoted in Jack Kornfield, *After the Ecstasy, the Laundry: How the Heart Grows Wise on the Spiritual Path* (New York: Bantam Books, 2001), 196.

10   Maria Poblet, "States of Solidarity: How State Alignment Builds Multiracial Working-Class Power," in *Power Concedes Nothing: How Grassroots Organizing Wins Elections*, ed. Linda Burnham, Max Elbaum, and Maria Poblet (New York: OR Books, 2022), 122.

11   Elizabeth Dore, *How Things Fall Apart: What Happened to the Cuban Revolution* (London: Head of Zeus, Bloomsbury Press, 2022), 55–56.

12   Sheila D. Collins, *The Rainbow Challenge: The Jackson Campaign and the Future of U.S. Politics* (New York: Monthly Review Press, 1986).

13   Bill Fletcher Jr. and Danny Glover, "Visualizing a Neo-Rainbow," *The Nation*, February 14, 2005, https://www.thenation.com/article/archive/visualizing-neo-rainbow

14   Frantz Fanon, *The Wretched of the Earth*, trans. Constance Farrington (New York: Grove Press, 1968).

15   James Baldwin, "My Dungeon Shook: Letter to My Nephew on the Hundredth Anniversary of the Emancipation," in *The Fire Next Time* (New York: Vintage, 1993), 8–10.

16   James Baldwin, "Down at the Cross: Letter from a Region in My Mind," in *The Fire Next Time* (New York: Vintage, 1993), 94–95.

17   Jess Rohan, "All Talk," *Jewish Currents* (Spring 2021), accessed November 21, 2021, https://jewishcurrents.org/all-talk.

CHAPTER ELEVEN

Socialism

Socialism finds resonance among people facing lives of unstable employment at low wages, crushing student debt, racial and ethnic marginalization, endless war, and environmental catastrophe. We have seen that each of these conditions is a direct consequence of the natural function of capitalist economies when unrestrained. Challenging a system that results in these conditions is a no-brainer for growing numbers of people. It's important for progressive activists and organizers to understand socialism in a nuanced way so we can engage with the American people effectively when the question comes up in our work.

Since the 2016 presidential campaign of Bernie Sanders, interest in socialism has grown dramatically in the US, spurred on as a counterpoint to the election of Donald Trump and his racist and hostile policies directed toward working people. The election of Alexandria Ocasio-Cortez, Jamaal Bowman, Cori Bush, and other democratic-socialist congressional candidates in 2018 and 2020 put socialism squarely in the center of practical politics. But what is "socialism"?

Different Meanings of Socialism

Given its long and varied tradition, the word "socialism" has many meanings. It can refer to *a system of thought* that looks at capitalist society from the point of view of the working class and proposes political paths by which the working class can replace the capitalist class as the dominant power in society. This is its meaning in Friedrich Engels's booklet *Socialism: Utopian and Scientific*,[1] in which he contrasts his and Karl Marx's analysis of capitalism with other socialist critics of the time.

Socialism can also mean *a social system* in which the working class is the ruling class, having replaced the capitalist class and gained the power to reorganize society in its own interests. This need not mean that there are no entrepreneurs. It certainly doesn't mean that there will be no managers. But in a socialist society these people will function within the rules established by the working class in power, as workers today function with rules imposed by the capitalist class in power. What that can mean in practice remains to be determined as workers take power in the future.

Socialists have long been divided by differences in opinion about how the working class can come to power. "Democratic socialism" refers to the political process by which the working class asserts its power through the instruments of electoral democracy, insofar as they can be practiced in capitalist society. Some proponents of social democracy seek the end of capitalism and its replacement by a socialist system through democratic elections. In this approach, the working class, the majority after all (as we have seen, over 60% of the population), would rule once in power, again through democratic institutions and norms. Others, more properly called liberals in the New Deal tradition, would settle for a mixed economy in which capitalists respect and protect, at least to some extent, the interests of working people, while retaining ultimate authority. Bernie Sanders's "revolution" is more in the New Deal tradition, while many young organizers in his movement tend to look forward to an ultimate replacement of capitalism, after accomplishing whatever limited reforms might be possible within it.

Revolutionary socialism, on the other hand, typically dismisses altogether the possibility of accommodation with the capitalist class in power. It sees no hope in the possibility of meaningful working class power except through an uprising that forcibly removes the old ruling class and brings to power the political representatives of the working class. This strand of socialist political analysis and organizing is what has been known as communist politics since the Russian Revolution of 1917.

It is a matter of speculation at this point in history how a successful socialist society might be organized to exercise working class rule in its politics, culture, and economic arrangements, and in the political process that would bring it about. But one important task is now available for socialist-minded people that can help to shape that future socialist society: making an honest assessment of actual experience in twentieth-century countries led by communist parties, most notably the Soviet Union, Cuba, and the People's Republic of China. While there are many successes to uphold—for example, land reform and national independence accomplished by the defeat of colonial powers—we will learn more by looking at the lessons to be learned from their failures. Chief among these is the failure to create effective mechanisms and institutions by which the mass of people can hold their leaders accountable. Never having lived in those societies or studied them deeply, I leave this exploration to those who have.

Insofar as socialist politics is concerned, at this moment, as a practical matter, working class politics is unfolding in the arena of democratic-socialist politics. It goes beyond New Deal liberalism in that, in principle, working class politics does not accept the ultimate legitimacy of the capitalist power with which it recognizes it must negotiate and compromise.* But this politics also understands that we do not now live in a revolutionary time.

The programmatic agenda of social democracy in the US advocates such familiar and well-articulated policies as Medicare for All; environmental justice; free education that is nurturing and empowering, from preschool through college, including respect for vocational training; universal food and housing security; defense of workers' right to organize unions and bargain collectively; full employment with living wages and dignity at work; security in retirement; a demilitarized foreign policy; full gender, racial, and ethnic equality; reproductive rights for women; separation of religion and state action; and unrestricted participation in the democratic processes of our politics.

To these I would add the importance of forcing businesses to compete with each other in constructive ways, through product quality, technological advances that increase productivity, customer service, or product price. Employers should be blocked from competing by driving down their workers' wages and working conditions. In short, we need to take wages out of competition.

We can move in this direction by reviving techniques applied in the two decades following World War II. At that time, working class living standards rose significantly, together with corporate profits. Increasing the

---

* "Liberalism" also has several meanings. Modern liberalism in the New Deal tradition refers to a political program and philosophy that enlists the government to regulate aspects of the economy and provide aid to working people, the so-called safety net. This is the opposite of the classical eighteenth- and nineteenth-century concept of liberalism, which champions individual liberty and free markets, originally to challenge the power of feudal institutions. "Neoliberalism," a term in use in recent decades, suggests a return to free markets in the classical tradition, only now in a global context. It signals a turning away from modern New Deal liberalism.

minimum wage to a living wage would set a reasonable floor below which no employer could push their workers. Industry-wide or sector bargaining would set a common wage for a given job that all employers in an industry or trade would agree to pay, arrived at through collective bargaining between unions and employer associations. Each of these methods contributed to increases in working class living standards in the twenty-five years following World War II. But since the late 1970s, corporate power has destroyed those tools, contributing to the dramatic increase, since that time, in the inequality of income and wealth.

Beyond returning to tested methods to take wages out of competition, we need imagination and innovation to bring down the levels of inequality that have recently grown to such grotesque proportions in the US. Writer and educator Sam Pizzigati has proposed an intriguing policy to address this inequality through the imposition of a *maximum* wage. The maximum would not be expressed as a dollar amount. It would be a multiple of the wage of a basic worker in the firm, the ratio set as a matter of social policy.[2] We could decide, for example, to limit top CEO compensation to forty times the wage of production workers in the firm, as was the case (without legislation) in the post–World War II US economy; or twelve times, or seven times as it has been in Japan. We could agree that running a company justifies compensation greater than a basic worker's pay. But by how much? Once we settle on a maximum wage ratio, by law if not by common practice, with shame if not jail attached to any executive exceeding the limit, executives would be free to earn as much as they want, as long as they lift basic worker wages along with their own.

Compensation practices also need to change in another basic way. Capitalists have reorganized production and employment practices during the past fifty years in ways that undermine long-term worker association with a single employer. Yet employers still must hire workers as needed. Since no employer these days even makes a pretense of a long-term commitment to the workers they employ at any given time, we need to increase reliance on the social wage to sustain working class living standards through government programs. This means that workers' claims to their standard of living need to be realized increasingly through public policy that strengthens and extends social "safety net" programs, complementing private compensation with a more robust social wage.

Beyond public provision of education, decent housing, and health care—guaranteed to workers independent of their employment status—the government might provide a guaranteed minimum income, sometimes called a universal basic income, to allow workers to purchase basic necessities in private markets independent of their employment. This would be paid for by taxes on business revenues and government claims on parts of the surplus that now go to unproductive uses. The result would be a system in which the capitalists *as a class* would be responsible to sustain the workforce *as a class*. When worker living standards become meaningfully sustained and improved through the social wage, the pressure to increase private wages goes down, as does the dependence that working people have on direct employment. For example, implementing Medicare for All as part of the social wage would eliminate the premiums private employers now pay for their employees' private health insurance, while guaranteeing continued health insurance for workers no matter what job they have, or if they have no job.

A constantly raised objection to public provision of income or services is that these things undermine the incentive to work. There are several responses to this concern. First, it isn't true. Many studies investigated the effect on work of the extra unemployment benefits the government distributed during the height of the COVID-19 crisis. Critics of the benefits claimed that ending them would result in many people returning to the labor market to find work, thinking that the benefits had caused them to stay home. But the facts did not support that belief. Ending the benefits had almost no effect on labor force participation.[3]

There are two reasons why this is the case. First, people find meaning and social purpose in the work they do. Most people want to work. Second, working class culture values work. It disparages freeloading. Apologists for capital often scoff at the old communist slogan "to each according to his needs," dismissing it as a recipe for laziness. What they forget is the first part of that slogan: "From each according to his abilities."[4]

Before there's any "to," workers understand that there has to be a "from." The culture of work can be much more easily sustained when the "from" that workers contribute to society comes back "to" them in decent living standards and social respect. If workers are treated with respect at work, there is less cause to shirk or stay away.

International Labor Solidarity

Another keystone of socialist-minded, working class politics is international labor solidarity. The foremost example of this in the first part of the twenty-first century was the work of U.S. Labor Against the War (USLAW), in which I participated directly.[5] It was founded in the run-up to the US invasion and occupation of Iraq in early 2003. In the few years following the start of the war, over 180 union locals, central labor councils, state federations of labor, and national unions joined USLAW. In addition to providing material support to our Iraqi counterparts, USLAW affiliates brought eighteen resolutions opposing the war and occupation to the 2005 national convention of the AFL-CIO. The result was that for the first time in history the convention passed a resolution placing the US labor movement in opposition to an ongoing US war.

This work was based on USLAW establishing close working relations with the Iraqi trade union movement, first organized back in the 1920s to resist British capital, which was then starting to invest in oil production there. Repressed by Saddam Hussein in the 1980s and 1990s, these unions reemerged in Iraq after his fall in 2003, as their leaders and activists emerged from prison, exile, or life underground in Iraq.

After Saddam's fall in October 2003, an international labor delegation that included US labor journalist David Bacon and International Longshore and Warehouse Union Local 10 president Clarence Thomas, based in the Bay Area and West Coast, traveled to Iraq and returned to bring news of Iraqi unions to USLAW's founding convention. USLAW took off in 2005 when we brought six Iraqi trade union leaders to the US for a speaking tour of twenty-six cities.[6] The Iraqis in the delegation, some Sunni, some Shi'a, some atheists, some in "mixed marriages," stressed their common interests as workers. They explained that the sectarian religious divisions tearing their country apart at the time were whipped up by US political "divide and conquer" interference and were not characteristic of the Iraq they had grown up in. They spoke of their battles to oppose privatization of government assets that the US was then imposing, their fight for basic rights for all workers to organize unions, and their defense of unions as integral supports for democracy. They called for the end of the US war and occupation of their country, saying that the war and occupation were only complicating their ability to make progress building a democratic, independent, nonsectarian Iraq.

I was deeply affected by the Iraqis' accounts of their experiences and aspirations. They spoke movingly as they addressed US audiences and also during the meetings our delegations had with them when I visited Erbil, Basra, and Baghdad in 2009, 2012, and 2019. Each of their demands struck chords with me, and with US workers in their audiences. We had experience opposing privatization in the US and had also defended the right to organize. We, too, understood the basic role of unions as bulwarks of democracy. We knew as well that the war and occupation of Iraq were draining resources and focus from these questions here in the US, complicating our own political terrain. In the course of three Iraqi tours to the US, workers from both countries came to realize that they were each enmeshed in the same class dynamics, dealing with the same issues. All were workers, fighting in common against the political and military representatives of US capital, seeking to extend their power more thoroughly abroad, as they were doing at home.

US workers saw that they and the Iraqi workers had a common interest in opposing the war and occupation. A victory for one was a gain for the other, as it weakened the power of a common enemy. My union, United University Professions (UUP-AFT Local 2190), representing over 35,000 faculty and professional staff in the State University of New York (SUNY), was one of the first locals to affiliate with USLAW, but only after a sharp debate had unfolded within the union. Some opposed getting the union involved in antiwar activities, arguing that joining USLAW would take the union beyond its function—bargaining over terms and conditions of our employment—and would weaken the union by dividing our members over an issue we had no business addressing. Others argued to the contrary, stating that unions needed to be involved in shaping society in the interest of working people and that the war and occupation in Iraq put our members and students and all working people in danger for no good reason. Furthermore, the huge expense of the war was draining federal money from programs vital to human needs here at home. These arguments carried the day by a wide margin as we voted to affiliate our local with USLAW and engage in its initiatives. The same debates and outcomes were repeated nearly two hundred times in different organizations across the US labor movement.

For example, we in UUP were acutely aware of the austerity the New York State Legislature continued to impose on the SUNY and other social service elements of the state budget as the Iraq and Afghanistan wars continued. Our opposition to these wars heightened when we found out the amount of money New Yorkers paid in federal taxes in 2011 that went to those wars was almost double the entire state budget deficit that year. Returning what New Yorkers paid for the wars that year and applying the money to state government expenses would have entirely wiped out the state's budget deficit. The same was true for thirty-four other states.[7] Such a redirection of funds following new priorities would have eliminated the apparent need for austerity budgets then sweeping much of the country. That year, the AFL-CIO National Executive Council, in presenting its agenda for job creation as the centerpiece of public policy, said: "There is no way to fund what we must do as a nation without bringing our troops home from Iraq and Afghanistan. The militarization of our foreign policy has proven to be a costly mistake. It is time to invest at home."[8]

As capital extends its reach globally, resistance to it arises globally as well. International labor solidarity is not charity work. It is not limited to the fruitful sharing of experiences. As we saw in the case of Iraq, it is undertaken in common struggle. It is a two-way street of mutual learning and respect, across national and language lines.

I saw this most vividly when I was part of a small US labor delegation that traveled to Erbil, in the Kurdish area of Iraq, in 2009, to meet with about 150 Iraqi unionists from all parts of that country. Two US military veterans of the war in Iraq were part of our delegation, the first US soldiers to return to Iraq as civilians promoting peace. At one point in the conference they came to the stage to speak to the assembly. They spoke of their working class roots, how they came to join the army, how they were deployed to Iraq and discovered that the war and occupation were wrong, how they had come back to Iraq as part of the U.S. Labor Against the War delegation, representing our partner organization Iraq Veterans Against the War. They explained that they were not there to issue sentimental apologies but to help make it right in a common struggle to end the war and occupation.

Their talks were given simultaneous translation into Arabic from a booth high above the hall, just as we could hear Arabic speakers translated into English in our earphones. As the veterans closed their talk, an Iraqi man jumped up and ran down the aisle to mount the stage, shouting loudly in Arabic, but without a mic so the translators in the booth could not hear him. We had no idea what he was saying or what his attitude was toward these American former soldiers. It was an extremely tense moment for us, but when he reached the stage and the translators in the booth could hear him, we learned that as he embraced the vets, he was saying: "You are our brothers! You are our brothers for peace! Thank you for coming here again to be with us."

With the winding down of US military operations in Iraq and Afghanistan, the fading away of the national peace movement as a vital social presence, and the coming to the fore of more intense immediate challenges to unions and working people in the era of austerity and broadly recognized racial injustices, it was not possible to sustain USLAW beyond 2020, when the organization came to a close. But USLAW's work provides an example and foundation on which to build, much as foundations have been built for further work in recent years toward advancing racial and gender justice, universal health care, raising the minimum wage, combatting the effects of climate change, and other elements of the progressive agenda.

Boundaries to Political Action

As we undertake political action, whether electoral or movement-building, it is important to reflect on the truly awesome power of the ruling class that we confront. Every political system operates within boundaries established to stabilize and maintain the power of those already in charge. Capitalism is not unique in this. In the United States, where we cherish First Amendment constitutional guarantees of free speech and assembly, these rights have constitutionally permitted limits. The old adage "You can't shout fire in a crowded theater" has its origins in a court case that had nothing to do with theaters or fires. It is a paraphrase of Supreme Court Justice Oliver Wendell Holmes Jr.'s decision in a 1919 case, *Schenck v. United States*, upholding the conviction of a person who agitated against the military draft during World War I. Holmes wrote: "The most stringent protection of free speech would not protect a man falsely shouting fire in a theatre and causing a panic.... The question in every case is whether the words used are used in such circumstances and are of such a nature as to create a clear and present danger that they will bring about the substantive evils that Congress has a right to prevent."[9] The court in this case unanimously found that agitating against the draft during World War I did present a "clear and present danger" to the war effort and so could be prosecuted. This doctrine also sustained the imprisonment in 1919 of socialist labor leader and war opponent Eugene V. Debs.

Abraham Lincoln pursued the same policy as president during the Civil War. In 1863, Union general Ambrose Burnside ordered the arrest of Ohio congressman Clement Vallandigham for "declaring sympathy for the enemy" when he made public addresses condemning the war and calling for Union soldiers to desert en masse. In response to the outcry over the arrest, Lincoln published a letter justifying it "because he [Vallandigham] was laboring, *with some effect*, to prevent the raising of troops, to encourage desertions from the army, and to leave the rebellion [the secession of the Confederate states] without an adequate military force to suppress it."[10]

The breadth of the *Schenck* opinion was narrowed in a 1969 unanimous Supreme Court decision, *Brandenburg v. Ohio*, that upheld the free speech rights of a Ku Klux Klan militant by declaring a two-part test: "(1) speech can be prohibited if it is 'directed at inciting or producing imminent lawless action' and (2) it is 'likely to incite or produce such action.' The [Ohio] criminal syndicalism act [under which Brandenburg had been prosecuted] made illegal the advocacy and teaching of doctrines while ignoring whether or not that advocacy and teaching would actually incite imminent lawless action. The failure to make this distinction rendered the law overly broad and in violation of the Constitution."[11]

The court in this case said: "The line between what is permissible and not subject to control and what may be made impermissible and subject to regulation is the line between ideas and overt acts."[12] In other words, you can think and say anything you want as long as it doesn't matter to the stability of the basic arrangements of power in society. Congress and the court may legitimately seek to preserve these arrangements. Speech, assembly, and political organizing that constitute a true threat to the basic system of class power relations will not find legal protection. That is good news or bad news depending on one's interests in the conflict. It is true in any class-conflicted society, not just in capitalism, although ruling classes will have different tolerances for apparent threats depending on how precarious they believe their power to be.

No Guarantee of a Happy Ending

There is an old saying in the labor movement that "the boss is your best organizer." In the words of Dave Green, president of UAW Local 1112 at the Lordstown, Ohio, GM plant when GM closed it down in 2019, "Unions aren't just about making more money. It's about having a seat at the table. It's about having the ability to talk to your employer and be respected, having some dignity in work, having some dignity and respect for what you do."[13] Unions gain adherents when the boss disrespects the workers and denies them dignity at work. As Bob Dylan put it more trenchantly:

> I ain't gonna work for Maggie's brother no more....
> He hands you a nickel, he hands you a dime
> He asks you with a grin if you're having a good time
> Then he fines you every time you slam the door[14]

The same is true in society, beyond the specific worker-boss relation. In Marx's time, "Prussia's heavy-handed control had the unintended consequence of making 'revolutionaries of very mild reformers.'"[15] As progressive politics in capitalist society get us closer to socialism, we do not know if this turning upside down of power relations will happen through peaceful means in the course of elections in which the working class, the large majority of the population, comes to real power. We do not know if the ruling class will refuse to recognize or allow democratic processes to effect a peaceful transition of class power, or if they will resist it with brutal force and repression. We do not know if demands for deep reforms within capitalism will call forth repression rather than reform. We do not know if it will be reform or revolution. Which it will be depends upon how the ruling class responds to the needs and demands of working people, and on the strength of workers' power as an organized political force.

This is an empirical question yet to be determined by future events. There is nothing preordained about it. Marx and Engels famously wrote in the opening lines of *The Communist Manifesto* that all history is the history of class struggle. What is almost never remembered are the words immediately following that pronouncement, predicting the uncertain outcome of that struggle: "The history of all hitherto existing society is the history of class struggles.... oppressor and oppressed stood in constant opposition to one another, carried on an uninterrupted, now hidden, now open fight, *a fight that each time ended either in a revolutionary reconstitution of society at large, or in the common ruin of the contending classes.*"[16] The rising class can win and reconstitute society. The existing ruling class can beat the rising class back. Or there can follow the "common ruin" of both, out of which may arise the chaos of a "failed state" or some weak truce that restores a semblance of order. We know that change is inevitable, but there is no guarantee of a happy ending.

The structural position in which social democratic politics unfolds is necessarily ambiguous and treacherous. Such politics mobilizes people to oppose capitalist interests, but at the same time progressive organizers, activists, and elected officials must know how to negotiate and compromise while maintaining their opposition. As the saying goes: "If you're not doing politics with people you can't stand, you're not doing politics."

At every turn, capitalists and their representatives will stress their own good will in negotiations, as they seek to minimize any conflict and twist the dynamic to their advantage. At every turn they will seek to reverse any past concession, such as those related to labor rights, women's reproductive health, LGBTQ rights, honest scholarship and educational instruction, and voting rights. This has been the history of reaction we have seen unfold in the fifty years that followed the Powell memorandum, written at the modern heyday of capitalist concessions to anticapitalist power in the US and around the world. What results from this tug-of-war depends upon the focus and organized strength of the working class and its allies, and the flexibility, or ruthlessness, which capitalists exhibit in responding to opposition.

We have seen how this dynamic played out in in the transition from feudalism to capitalism. British historian Eric Hobsbawm described the attitude and practice of European monarchs as they faced the demands of the newly rising capitalist class in the eighteenth century. "[The] monarchy ... was prepared to strengthen its political hand by playing off one estate, class, or province against another. Yet its horizons were those of its history, its function, and its class. It hardly ever wanted, and was never able to achieve, the root-and-branch social and economic transformation which the progress of the economy required and the rising social groups called for."[17] In the end, no matter how clever or repressive, feudal monarchy could not sustain its power.

Sadly, US history provides many stark examples of repressive power applied to domestic mobilizations that challenge capital, even as there have been occasional periods of reform. The US violated hundreds of solemn treaties with Native peoples, robbing them of their lands and forcibly consigning them to desolate reservations. The nineteenth and twentieth centuries are full of examples of the mobilization of anti-union goon squads, private militias, and the National Guard to shoot down striking workers and prevent them from organizing unions. From the late 1930s to the mid-1960s the US Congress harassed and jailed socialist and communist organizers, and others who sympathized with them, through the official hearings of the House Un-American Activities Committee and Senate investigatory committees headed by Joseph McCarthy and James Eastland, among others. Vigilantes and Ku Klux Klan mobs murdered scores of civil rights workers, white and Black, throughout the South with no justice from the legal system. Black Panther Fred Hampton was a charismatic young leader who successfully organized an interracial movement in Chicago. On December 4, 1969, Illinois and Chicago authorities, working with the FBI, organized the murder of Fred Hampton and Mark Clark. Authorities were eventually forced to pay their families $1.8 million in compensation for the injustice done.[18] Los Angeles Panther leader Elmer "Geronimo" Pratt was falsely convicted of murder and only released from prison after serving twenty-seven years, his conviction overturned, with a $4.5 million settlement from state and federal authorities.[19] The National Guard murdered unarmed students protesting the Vietnam War at Kent State and Jackson State universities. The FBI put into place COINTELPRO (the Counter-Intelligence Program) and other programs to sabotage the peace and civil rights movements of the 1960s and 1970s,[20] and it famously hounded Rev. Martin Luther King Jr. for years until his assassination in 1968.

In hindsight, from their positions of victory and continued dominance, the ruling class laments these "unfortunate excesses." Almost no one holds them up as shining examples of the American social system, except for neofascists in and around the MAGA movement. Yet there they are. It would be foolish in the extreme to believe the ruling class would not go back to these techniques as progressive movements rise again to confront their power in meaningful ways that those in power believe present a "clear and present danger," here and around the world. Unfortunately, it is not hard to imagine domestic death squads, armed private militias operating in the US with a wink and a nod from political leaders in service to capital. Donald Trump and his attorney general William Barr went in this direction with their embrace of right-wing paramilitary militias operating in tandem with police forces in cities where antiracist protests unfolded after the murder of George Floyd in the summer of 2020, and their threats to bring criminal charges of sedition against Black Lives Matter activists.[21] Black uprisings against police shootings after the death of Michael Brown in 2014 resulted in the establishment of COINTELPRO 2.0 by the FBI to monitor "Black identity extremists."[22]

We cannot tell what effect severe repression would have. It might be successful and crush progressive politics, for a time. It might result in a jiujitsu effect leading to more militant and radical progressive action that carries the day, either in forced reform or, if more and more people become outraged by the unfairness and brutality, a more revolutionary time. Or, it could result in the mutual ruin of both contending classes and the social chaos that such an outcome implies.

We are living in hard times for working people and marginalized communities in the US. We are still reeling from the implications of an authoritarian-minded president whose outrageous lies of a stolen election tens of millions of people appeared to support. The American Rescue Plan passed in March 2021 provided some relief from the effects of the COVID-19 pandemic, but it was a temporary measure. It will be a difficult road back to circumstances in which a progressive social movement will truly shake the walls of power, as we saw in the 1930s and again in the 1960s. It will take a long time to reverse the more than fifty-year process by which the capitalist class has implemented the recommendations of the Powell memorandum.

But there is always something to do to bend the arc of the moral universe toward justice, as Reverend King envisioned. We know that the constellation of forces is always in flux, that the present is always pregnant with the future. We know that righteous movements for justice are now arising that will again deeply challenge basic power relations in the United States. These are exciting, challenging, fascinating times that give courage to all involved and many who look on, wondering if and how to participate. Knowing what and who we're up against, knowing how society works, facing both entrenched and shifting realities while developing strategies and doing the difficult work of movement building with compassion and mutual respect—we'll need all this and more to shape the future toward progressive ends.

Onward!

Notes

1   Friedrich Engels, *Socialism: Utopian and Scientific*, in *The Marx-Engels Reader*, ed. Robert C. Tucker, 2nd ed. (New York: W.W. Norton), 683–717.

2   Sam Pizzigati, *The Case for a Maximum Wage* (Cambridge: Polity, 2018).

3   Ben Casselman, "Benefit Cutoffs Failing to Ease Labor Shortfall," *New York Times*, August 21, 2021, https://www.nytimes.com/2021/08/20/business/economy/unemployment-benefits-economy-states.html.

4   Karl Marx, *Critique of the Gotha Program*, in *The Marx-Engels Reader*, ed. Robert C. Tucker, 2nd ed. (New York: W.W. Norton), 531.

5   Michael Zweig, "Working for Global Justice in the New Labor Movement," in *Building Global Labor Solidarity in a Time of Accelerating Globalization*, ed. Kim Scipes (New York: Haymarket Press, 2016).

6   The tour is documented in the video *Meeting Face to Face; The Iraq-U.S. Labor Solidarity Tour* (2006), accessed August 30, 2021, https://vimeo.com/51265502.

7   Center for Study of Working Class Life, "Comparing the Costs of War with State Deficits in 2011," March 23, 2011.

8   AFL-CIO National Executive Council, "Fake Political Crises and Real Economic Crises—A Call for Leadership and for Action," August 3, 2011, https://aflcio.org/about/leadership/statements/fake-political-crises-and-real-economic-crises-call-leadership-and.

9   *Schenck v. United States* 249 U.S. 47 (1919), accessed August 29, 2021, https://www.oyez.org/cases/1900-1940/249us47.

10   Lincoln quoted in Doris Kearns Goodwin, *Team of Rivals* (New York: Simon and Schuster, 2005), 524; emphasis added.

11   *Brandenburg v. Ohio* 395 US 444 (1969), accessed August 29, 2021, https://www.oyez.org/cases/1968/492.

12   *Brandenburg v. Ohio*, 456.

13   Latoya Ruby Frazier, "The End of the Line: What Happens to a Factory Town When the Factory Shuts Down?" *New York Times Magazine*, May 5, 2019, https://latoyarubyfrazier.com/news/the-end-of-the-line.

14   Bob Dylan, "Maggie's Farm," track 3 on *Bringing It All Back Home*, Columbia, 1965.

15   Hal Draper quoted in Mary Gabriel, *Love and Capital: Karl and Jenny Marx and the Birth of a Revolution* (New York: Little, Brown, 2011), 19.

16   Karl Marx and Friedrich Engels, *The Communist Manifesto*, in *The Marx-Engels Reader*, ed. Robert C. Tucker, 2nd ed. (New York: WW Norton, 1978), 474; emphasis added.

17   Eric Hobshawm, *The Age of Revolution* (New Yorlu Vintage, 1996), 23.

18   William Lee, "In 1969, Charismatic Black Panther Leader Fred Hampton Was Killed in a Hail of Gunfire: 50 Years Later, the Fight Against Police Brutality Continues, *Chicago Tribune*, December 3, 2019, https://www.chicagotribune.com/news/ct-black-panthers-fred-hampton 50 years 20191203 kbzgzivtlhytp/x4ggtvhncpm-story.html.

19   Douglas Martin, "Elmer G. Pratt, Jailed Panther Leader, Dies at 63," *New York Times*, June 3, 2011, https://www.nytimes.com/2011/06/04/us/04pratt.html.

20   "COINTELPRO," FBI Records: The Vault, accessed August 30, 2021, https://vault.fbi.gov/cointel-pro.

21   Katie Benner, "Barr Told Prosecutors to Consider Sedition Charges for Protest Violence," *New York Times*, September 16, 2020, https://www.nytimes.com/2020/09/16/us/politics/william-barr-sedition.html.

22   Anne Branigin, "FBI Launches COINTELPRO 2.0 Targeting 'Black Identity Extremists: Report,'" *The Root*, October 6, 2017, https://www.theroot.com/fbi-launches-cointelpro-2-0-targeting-black-identity-ex-1819222532.

Acknowledgments

The material in this book has come to me through a lifetime of learning from interactions with thousands of people I've encountered in movement building and academic work. It has come from family history, as I've lived it and as it has been passed down to me from my parents, aunts, and uncles. The material here reflects ideas I've found in books and articles I've gone to for pleasure and for help in understanding the world I've encountered. I feel a great debt to all of these sources and influences. It would be false to pick from this wide array any small number of people or writings for special appreciation. Anyone looking to read further into the topics of this book would do well to start with the books and articles cited in the endnotes.

Still, specific thanks are due to many people who helped shape this book in particular. Christie Launius introduced me to the idea of "threshold concepts," which immediately became the frame I chose for a book that until then had been an inchoate urge to put some thoughts on paper. I've had greatly helpful conversations with Ellen Bravo, Max Elbaum, Gregory de Freitas, Liz Montegary, Paddy Quick, Anwar Shaikh, John Weeks, and the Media Team of the New York State Poor People's Campaign as I've thought about issues that arose in writing. A number of young activists and organizers, older Movement veterans, and fellow volunteers in the Southold Fire Department contributed to shaping this book as well, by reading and commenting on parts or all of early drafts. Their responses were invaluable and often challenging. My thanks go to Gene Bruskin, Keith Cummings, Brandon Forester, Heidi Hoechst, Abigail Lal, Robert Lepley, Martha Livingston, Jay Mazur, Jack Metzgar, Peter Olney, Roz Pelles, John Roslak, Warren Sanderson, Tim Shenk, Erica Smiley, Juliet Ucelli,

Amy Woodward Yi, and Sierra Zweig. Rob Sauté undertook indispensable research that appears in every chapter, and responded with thoughtful challenges over many long breakfasts as we worked to sort out complications in the issues I address.

My thanks go to Mat Callahan for introducing me to Ramsey Kanaan at PM Press, to Ramsey for accepting this book for publication, to the PM Press staff for moving it through to publication with skill and care and for help with arranging publicity. My thanks also go to Abigail Lal for her suggestions for the front cover design.

Kathy Chamberlain was a source of wisdom and insight throughout the process of conceiving and writing this book.

Index

"Passim" (literally "scattered") indicates intermittent discussion of a topic over a cluster of pages.

abortion, 183
Abu Zaid, Nasr, 144–45
affirmative action for whites, 170–71
Affordable Care Act, 82, 133
Afghanistan War, 3, 48, 212, 213
AFL-CIO, 148, 211, 213
African Americans 37–39, 58, 167–79
    passim, 190–204 passim; Black
    liberation theology, 141; Black Panthers,
    217–18; class, 99, 100, 175–76; COVID-
    19 pandemic, 173–74; FBI repression,
    217–18; history, 66, 168–70 passim,
    174–76, 192, 217–18; infant mortality,
    185–86; Lincoln and, 67; lynchings,
    174–75; poverty and, 51; women, 179–80,
    183–85. See also civil rights movement
alienation, 86
All in the Family, 161
American colonies, 114, 115
American Legislative Exchange Council
    (ALEC), 11
Anthony, Susan B., 185, 190
anticommunism, 18, 24, 37, 72, 140, 217
antisemitism, 177, 178
antiwar activists and activism, 3, 161, 212,
    213
arts, 67–69, 155, 159. See also music
Asian Americans, 99–100, 184
astronomy, 64–66
Austin, Scott, 70

backlash, 176; to feminism, 183; white
    supremacist, 192
Bacon, David, 162, 211
Bacon's Rebellion, 168
Baker, Ella, xi, 1, 15
Baldwin, James, 195, 200–201, 204
Bankruptcy Abuse Prevention and
    Consumer Protection Act, 156–57
banks, 104, 108
Baran, Paul, 101
Barber, Rev. William J., II, 16, 136, 141, 149,
    196; foreword, xi–xii
Beal, Frances, 184
Becker, Gary, 156
Belgian Congo, 116
belief and beliefs, 58–61, 66, 69–71 passim
Benedict XVI, Pope, 65, 142
Biden, Joe, 6, 20, 40, 47, 193
Black Americans. See African Americans
Black Lives Matter movement, 8, 26, 218
Black Wave (Ghattas), 144
Black Workers Congress, 22
Boff, Leonardo, 140
Bowman, Jamaal, 19, 206
Brandenburg v. Ohio, 215
Bread and Roses Cultural Project, 162
Brecht, Bertolt: The Rifles of Señora Carrar,
    159–60
Bretton Woods agreement, 118
British in India, 50, 114n, 116
Brooks, David: Bobos in Paradise, 149

Brown, Michael, 218
Brown v. Board of Education, 175
Bruskin, Gene: *The Moment Was Now*,
    190–91
Buddhism, 143, 145
Burnside, Ambrose, 214
Business Roundtable, 40, 98, 124

Calhoun, John C., 169, 202
capital accumulation, 102, 112–14 passim,
    122–30 passim, 179–80; feudal Europe,
    138
capitalist class, 86, 94, 96, 106, 107, 194–96
    passim, 209, 219; class consciousness,
    155; eighteenth century, 217;
    international, 119–20
"capitalist class" (term), 52
capitalist crises, 127–30
capitalist exploitation. *See* exploitation
capitalist production. *See* production
Catholic Church. *See* Roman Catholic
    Church
CATO Institute, 11
censorship, 73, 155
CEO pay, 209
change, 56–58, 64. *See also* reform;
    revolution
Chen, Brian, 100
Chicago School (economics), 129
China, 12–13, 40, 41–42, 73, 207; Belt and
    Road, 121; Cultural Revolution, 12, 152;
    English rule, 116; feudalism, 79; military
    budget, 121
Civilian Conservation Corps (CCC), 49
Civil Rights Act of 1964, 9, 37
civil rights movement, 38, 52, 143, 155,
    159–60, 175
civil servants. *See* public workers
Civil War, 66, 67
Clark, Mark, 217
class action lawsuits, 126, 148
class and classes, 90–111; class
    consciousness, 50–52, 154, 155, 191;
    cross-class communication, 165; culture
    and, 159, 160; gender and, 179, 180, 183,
    189; globalized, 119–20; religion and,
    138; values and, 141, 146–50 passim. *See
    also* middle class; race and class; ruling
    class; upper class; women as a class;
    working class
class conflict and struggle, 138, 194, 216;
    neutrality and, 160
Clawson, Dan, 20

climate change. *See* global warming
Clinton, Hillary, 28
COINTELPRO, 218
COINTELPRO 2.0, 218
Cold War, 18, 37–38, 72, 117
colonialism, 114–17 passim, 199–200
commodities and commoditization, 114,
    130–33 passim
The Communist Manifesto (Marx and Engels),
    216
communist parties, 21–24. *See also* South
    African Communist Party (SACP)
Communist Party of the Soviet Union
    (CPSU), 24, 72–73
Communist Party USA, 21, 36
Cone, James H., 141
Confederate memorials, 66, 67
Congressional Progressive Caucus, 6
Congress of Racial Equality (CORE), 2
consumerism, 82–83
consumption, 87, 131; advertising and
    marketing impetus, 132
contingent employment, 96
contradiction, 57; *see also* unity of opposites
corporate board members, 93
COVID-19 pandemic, 94, 99–100, 123, 125,
    149–50, 173–74, 184; American Rescue
    Plan, 219; unemployment benefits, 210
creationism, 69–70
criminal justice, 21, 40, 175
crises, 127–30. *See also* COVID-19
    pandemic; Great Depression
Crowley, Joseph, 19
Cuba, 207; racism, 197
culture, 158–65; cultural figures
    illuminating the working class, 162; *see
    also* arts; literature; working class culture
Cuomo, Andrew, 6

Daladier, Édouard, 31
Darwin, Charles, 69
Davis, Angela, 176; *Women, Race, and Class*,
    184
Davis, Jefferson, 67
Dazhai Brigade, 12, 13
Debs, Eugene V., 17, 214
debt, student, 156–57
Declaration of Independence, 115
Defense Production Act (DPA), 47–48, 49
defense spending. *See* military spending
demagoguery, 25
Democracy Charter, 23

Democratic Party, 18–20 passim, 40, 148; Jesse Jackson, 198
democratic socialism and social democracy, 207, 208
Depression. *See* Great Depression
"detail division of labor," 131–32
Detroit, 1, 2, 179
dialectics, 55–58 passim, 64, 70–71, 136–37, 190; theory and practice, 61–63 passim, 70–71. *See also* social and private aspects of capitalism; unity of opposites
Dickens, Charles, 153, 162
division of labor, 86, 131–32; gendered, 180
doctors, 93
Domestic Workers Bill of Rights, 182
Domestic Workers United, 182
Dore, Elizabeth, 197
Douglass, Frederick, xi, 33, 41, 190
dualistic thinking, 57, 70, 122, 123, 153
Du Bois, W.E.B., 158, 169, 196
Dylan, Bob, 154, 215

economic growth, 123–24
economic surplus, 45–46, 77–88 passim, 101, 106–8; globalization, 120–21; monetization, 131
economic transition, 49
education, 192, 194; individualism and, 156–58; racism, 173; secondary, 157–58; spending, 48. *See also* higher education; political education
Eliot, George, 158–59
Emancipation Proclamation, 67
empire. *See* imperialism
Engel, Eliot, 19
Engels, Friedrich, 206; *The Communist Manifesto*, 216
environment, 122–26 passim
Errors and Expectations (Shaughnessy), 62
ethics, 30–31, 136–37, 145
European Union, 116
evolution, 69
exploitation, 77–87 passim, 100, 105
externalities, 125–26

"fallacy of composition," 128, 129
Faludi, Susan: *Backlash*, 183
Fanon, Frantz: *The Wretched of the Earth*, 199–200
FBI repression, 217–18
federal government spending, 48
Federalist Society, 11

feminism, second-wave. *See* second-wave feminism
feudalism, 78–79, 85, 88, 104, 106, 113; monarchy, 217
Fight for $15, xii, 6, 8, 26, 82, 96, 186
financial sector, 102–3, 107–9 passim; banks, 104, 108; class composition of labor in, 95; globalization, 119–20
Fitzhugh, George: *Cannibals All*, 97
Fletcher, Bill, Jr., 115, 198
Floyd, George, 5, 40, 192, 199, 218; and other people killed by police, 5
France, Anatole, 148–49
Franklin, Aretha, 12
Frazier, E. Franklin, 173
Freedom Charter, 23
free speech cases, 214
Freire, Paulo, 16
fundraising, 29–30
fusion politics, 18–19

Galileo, 64–67 passim
gender, 179–86 passim; class and, 179, 180, 183, 189. *See also* race and gender
General Agreement on Tariffs and Trade (GATT), 118
general strikes, 36
George III, King of Great Britain, 67
Georgia, 193
Ghattas, Kim: *Black Wave*, 144
GI Bill, 170
Gidlow, Liette, 185
gig work. *See* contingent employment
Glasser, Ralph, 43
globalization, 113–22
global warming, 40, 64, 69–70; Le Guin, 123
Glover, Danny, 198
Goldman, Emma, 43
Goodwin, Doris Kearns: *Team of Rivals*, 158
government workers. *See* public sector workers
Great Depression, 37, 72–73, 118, 125. *See also* New Deal
Great Famine. *See* Irish Potato Famine, 79
Green, Dave, 215
Green New Deal, 40–41
guaranteed income. *See* universal basic income
Guevara, Che, 14, 43
Gutiérrez, Gustavo, 140–41

Hampton, Fred, 217

Harper, Frances, 190
Harrison, Benjamin, 179
health aides, 164
health care and health insurance, 49, 133, 210; racial inequalities, 172, 173–74, 184
Heritage Foundation, 11
higher education, 71–72, 96, 156–57; working people, 158
Hinton, William, 12, 79
Hispanics, 177, 178; class, 99, 100; COVID-19 pandemic, 173–74; poverty and, 51; Unseen America, 162, 163
history, 56–58, 66–67, 113–18, 127, 168–70, 174–79 passim, 190–91; African Americans, 66, 168–70 passim, 174–76, 192, 217–18; religions, 139–43 passim; US internal repression, 217–18. See also feudalism; slavery
Hobsbawm, Eric, 146
Holder, Eric, 175
Holmes, Oliver Wendell, Jr., 214
House Un-American Activities Committee (HUAC), 24; resistance to, 24
Howard, Beth, 193–94

identity politics, 52
IMF. See International Monetary Fund (IMF)
immigrants, American, 1, 177–82 passim, 195
imperialism, 113–14; American, 177–78; Japanese, 143
income, universal basic. See universal basic income
income inequality and wealth inequality, 83, 101–2, 110
India, 50, 114n; military budget, 121
Indigenous peoples, 115. See also Native Americans
individualism, 87–88, 149–55 passim; Ayn Rand, 160; education and, 156–58
Industrial Workers of the World, 178
inequality: in health care, 172, 173–74, 184; in infant mortality, 185–86; in inheritance, 83. See also income inequality and wealth inequality
infant development, 60
infant mortality, 185–86
inheritance, 83
"inside" and "outside" politics, 16, 21, 25, 27
international labor solidarity, 210–14
International Longshore and Warehouse Union (ILWU), 36, 211

International Monetary Fund (IMF), 118–19
International Women's Day (IWD), 158
Intersectionality, 8
Iran, 58
Iraq War, 3, 48, 211–13 passim
Irish Potato Famine, 79
Islam, 144–45
Italian immigrants, 179
I Wor Kuen, 22

Jackson, Rev. Jesse, 196, 198
Jensen, Barbara, 163
Jeong, May, 184
Jesus Christ, 142
Jewsbury, Geraldine, 158
Jim Crow, 2n, 38, 170, 175, 176, 184; new, 38, 199
John Paul II, Pope, 65

Katznelson, Ira: When Affirmative Action Was White, 170
Keynes, John Maynard, 125
Khrushchev, Nikita, 24
King, Rev. Martin Luther, Jr., 13, 143, 196, 204, 218, 219
King George III. See George III, King of Great Britain
knowledge and learning, 55–75
Kondratiev, Nikolai, 72–73
Kuhn, Thomas, 71
Ku Klux Klan, 38, 215, 217

labor, division of. See division of labor
labor, productive and unproductive. See productive and unproductive labor
Labor Party, 17–18
labor solidarity, international. See international labor solidarity
labor unions. See unions
Land, Ray, 12
land dispossession, 115
Latinx people. See Hispanics
Launius, Christie, 12
lawsuits, class action. See class action lawsuits
layoffs: Marriott, 125; racial aspects, 196–97
learning. See knowledge and learning
Le Guin, Ursula K., 123
Lenin, Vladimir, 42–43
Leo XIII, Pope, 138–39
Leondar-Wright, Betsy, 165
Lewis, Penny, 161
LGBTQ movement, 8, 9, 149, 161, 197, 217

liberation theology, 3–4, 16, 140–43 passim
lies, 25, 64, 71; respect for, 31; Trump's, 25, 218
life expectancy: southern states, 172
Lincoln, Abraham, 66, 67, 214
literature, 66, 69, 158–59, 160, 162
living standard. *See* standard of living
Locke, John, 146
Lordstown, Ohio GM plant, 215
love, 14, 66, 149, 207
Lu Xun, 42
Lynch, Loretta, 175
lynchings, 174–75

Mandela, Nelson, 39
Mao Zedong, 41–42
Marshall, Thurgood, 38, 175
Marx, Karl, 13, 50, 72, 76, 83, 101; *The Communist Manifesto*, 216; on religion, 137
Marxism, 58, 72
mass protest, xi, 38, 58, 121, 174, 218
materialism, 55, 59, 63, 69
maximum wage, 209
McCarthy, Joseph, 24, 72
McElhaney, Kellie, 184
#MeToo movement, 6, 8, 26, 198
Medicare for All, 49, 133, 208, 210
memorial statues and monuments, 66–67, 185
Metzgar, Jack, 163, 164
Mexican War, 177
Meyer, Jan, 12
middle class, 51, 52, 90–100 passim, 146, 163–65 passim; gender and, 180, 182, 184
military and militarism, 77, 78, 104–5, 107, 112–18 passim, 213; environmental aspects, 126–27; privatization, 132–33
military-industrial complex, 107, 118
military spending, 48
minimum wage, 6, 43, 170, 186, 208–9
Mishra, Pankaj, 143
Moaveni, Azadeh, 58
The Moment Was Now (Bruskin), 190–91
monetary policy, 129
monetization, 131
monuments. *See* memorial statues and monuments
morality, 3–4, 5, 30, 146–50 passim, 200; moral arc, 67, 219; sumptuary taxes, 46. *See also* ethics
Morning, Ann, 177
Morris, Aldon, 20
Mukherjee, Abir, 50

music, 12, 67–68; Dylan, 154, 215; *South Pacific*, 192; working class, 162
Muslims. *See* Islam
mutual aid, 141, 145–48 passim, 153
Myers, Isaac, 190, 196

National Industrial Recovery Act (NIRA), 34
National Labor Relations Act (Wagner Act), 34–37, 170
National Priorities Project, 48
Native Americans, 5, 77, 115; COVID-19 pandemic, 173–74
natural environment. *See* environment
New Communist Movement, 22
New Deal, 34–35, 49, 170, 208; resistance to, 160
Nisour Square, 133
Nixon, Richard, 9
nurses, 48, 94

Obama, Barack, 88, 133, 168
Ocasio-Cortez, Alexandria, 19, 206
O'Dell, Jack, 23
Omeoga, Oluchi, 26
"outside" and "inside" politics. *See* "inside" and "outside" politics
outsourcing, 132
overproduction, 128–29
overtime, 92

Pareles, Jon, 12
Parks, Rosa, 38
patriarchy, 179, 180, 183
peace movement. *See* antiwar activists and activism
philanthropy, 30
photography: Unseen America project, 162–63
physicians. *See* doctors
Pizzigati, Sam, 209
plunder, 113, 114
Poblet, Maria, 197
police and policing, 42–43, 77, 78, 104–5; militarization, 121; municipal spending, 122; shootings of Black people, 168, 174, 218
political education, 79, 141, 194, 195, 200
political practice, 15–32 passim
political will, 50–52
poor people: stereotypes, 84
Poor People's Campaign: A National Call

for Moral Revival, 3, 16, 26, 136, 141, 149, 198

Pope Benedict XVI. *See* Benedict XVI, Pope

Pope John Paul II. *See* John Paul II, Pope

Pope Leo XIII. *See* Leo XIII, Pope

potlatch, 77

poverty, 51, 141–42; southern states, 172

Powell, Colin, 175

Powell, Lewis, 9–11, 142–43, 147

Powell Memorandum, 9–11, 142–3, 147, 160, 217, 219

practice and theory. *See* dialectics; theory and practice

private aspects of capitalism. *See* social and private aspects of capitalism

privatization, 131–33, high education, 137; US-occupied Iraq, 211

production, 75–89 passim, 107–9 passim; class composition of labor in, 95; commodities, 131; workers' share, 110. *See also* overproduction

productive and unproductive labor, 101–6

productive and unproductive sectors, 46, 108–10

productivity, 80, 132

professionals, 92–93, 98, 164; class composition of labor in, 95; women, 182

protest, mass. *See* mass protest

public sector workers, 169, 170

race, 99–101, 167–72; labor force statistics, 99. *See also* racism

race and class, 51–52, 99, 100, 167–72 passim, 183, 189–205 passim

race and gender, 183–86 passim

race and inheritance, 83

race and poverty, 51, 142

racism, 170–76 passim, 185–86; Cuba, 197; racial stereotypes, 51, 142; Trump presidential election (2016), 203

Rainbow Coalition (1980s), 198

Ramaphosa, Cyril, 40

Rand, Ayn: *Fountainhead* and *Atlas Shrugged*, 160

Ransby, Barbara, 15–16

Ratzinger, Joseph. *See* Benedict XVI, Pope

Red Scare (1950s), 24

Reed, Adolph, Jr., 14, 167

reform, 33–41, 43, 216; criminal justice, 21, 40

"relevant population," 115, 168, 177, 178

religion, 136–46, 191; megachurches, 155. *See also* Roman Catholic Church

Republican Party, 40, 147, 183; Trump and, 25

Rerum Novarum, 138–39

retail. *See* whole and retail trade

revolution, 41–44, 216

Revolutionary Communist Party (RCP), 3, 22–23, 24, 28

Revolutionary Union, 22

Ricardo, David, 101

Rice, Condoleezza, 175

rich people, 44, 123, 131, 148, 169; not capitalist class, 51, 52, 90. *See also* upper class

The Rifles of Señora Carrar (Brecht), 159–60

Roberts, Priscilla, 73

Roe v. Wade, 183

Rohan, Jess, 202

Roman Catholic Church, 138–40; science and, 64–65

Romney, Mitt, 88

Roosevelt, Franklin D. (FDR), 34, 37

ruling class, 52, 98–99, 192, 214–18 passim; African Americans, 175; compromise with, 21, 40–41, 170; division of, 34; feudalism, 146; reform, 30, 34–40 passim; revolution, 42–43, 207; in socialism, 207; South Africa, 39–40; US race relations and, 38, 39; white supremacy and, 192

Rusk, Dean, 38

Russell, Bertrand, 73

safety net, 81, 82, 208n, 209

Said, Edward: *Orientalism*, 28

Salt of the Earth, 181–82

Sanders, Bernie, 41, 48, 206, 207

Schaitberger, Harold, 70

Schenck v. United States, 214–15

Schlafly, Phyllis, 183

Schuller, Kyla, 184

science, 59–66 passim, 69–70, 155; Catholic Church and, 64–65; Russell on, 73

SDS. *See* Students for a Democratic Society (SDS)

second-wave feminism, 182–85 passim

self-service, 154

Seltzer, Michael, 28

seniority rights (labor), 196–97

service sector, 108, 109

settlers, 77, 115, 168

Seward, William H., 158

sharecroppers, 21, 168, 169, 170

Shaughnessy, Mina: *Errors and Expectations*, 62

Showing Up for Racial Justice (SURJ), 193

Silas Marner (Eliot), 158–59

slavery, 66–67, 78, 85, 88, 97, 104, 106; churches and, 138; racialized, 168–69, 176

small-business owners, 91, 92; COVID-19, 174

Smarsh, Sarah, 28–29

Smiley, Jane, 153

Smith, Adam, 81, 83, 85, 101; *Wealth of Nations*, 113

SNCC. *See* Student Nonviolent Coordinating Committee (SNCC)

social and private aspects of capitalism, 86–88, 129–30; social costs ("externalities"), 124–26 passim

social class. *See* class and classes

socialism, 206–20; Catholic Church and, 138, 139; "scientific socialism," 146

Socialist Party of America, 17

social practice, 63–64

Social Security, 82, 169, 170

social wage, 82, 87, 106, 209

Solca, Luca, 92

South Africa, 39–40, 52

South African Communist Party (SACP), 21–22, 23, 39

southern states, 172, 193

Soviet Union, 24, 72–73, 207; Cold War, 37–38, 117; fall of, 118; World War II, 116

Spanish American War, 177

spirituality, 145–46

Stalin, Joseph, 24

standard of living, 45, 82, 106; working class, 102, 181, 208–10 passim

Stanton, Elizabeth Cady, 185

State University of New York (SUNY), 212

statues, memorial. *See* memorial statues and monuments

stereotypes, 194; Italian Americans, 179; racial, 51, 142; white working class, 193–94

strikes, 148, 164, 181–82; strikebreaking, 171. *See also* general strikes

student debt, 156, 157

Student Nonviolent Coordinating Committee (SNCC), 20, 159, 184

Students for a Democratic Society (SDS), 2, 27, 28

subcontracting, 132

subsistence, 130

suffragist monument, New York City, 185

surplus, economic. *See* economic surplus

Sweezy, Paul, 101

Taft-Hartley Act, 72

taxation, 44–47 passim, 210; feudal, 79; sumptuary, 46

teachers, 92–93, 94, 96

Team of Rivals (Goodwin), 158

"technical mimicry," 12–13

Terrell, Mary Church, 185

Thatcher, Margaret, 153

Theoharis, Rev. Liz, 4, 136, 141, 149

theory and theories, 61, 63, 69, 70–71

Thomas, Clarence (ILWU), 211

Thomas, Clarence (Supreme Court Justice), 175

"threshold concepts," 12

Till, Emmett, 2

Tomalin, Claire: *A Life of My Own*, 159

trade agreements, 119

transgender women of color, 184

trial and error, 62, 63

Triangle Shirtwaist Factory fire, 181

triple jeopardy, 184

Trump, Donald, 6, 25, 28–29, 31, 168, 172, 195; antiscience views, 70; presidential administration, 47, 218; presidential election (2016), 190, 192, 193–94, 203, 206; presidential election loss (2020), 218–19

Truth, Sojourner, 185

two-party system, 19–20

Union for Radical Political Economics (URPE), 3

unions, 6, 17–18, 93, 148, 161, 198, 211, 215; anti-union repression, 217; Iraq, 211, 213; seniority clauses and, 196; southern states, 172; Taft-Hartley Act and, 72; university workers, 212; Wagner Act and, 34–36 passim, 170; women, 181–82. *See also* international labor solidarity

United University Professions (UUP), 2, 212

unity of opposites, 57, 186; at heart of capitalism, 87, 130; individual and human society, 152–55; nature and human society, 122, 124; in production, 76, 87; race and class, 167; values and interests, 150

universal basic income, 210

universities, 71–72, 93, 192, 203; tuition and student debt, 156, 157; unions, 212

unproductive labor. *See* productive and unproductive labor
unproductive sector. *See* productive and unproductive sectors
Unseen America project, 162–63
upper class, 42, 149, 169; gender and, 180
upward mobility, 91, 98, 163
US Census: racial counts, 177
US Chamber of Commerce, 9, 40
US Constitution, 66–67
US Declaration of Independence. *See* Declaration of Independence
US interventionism, 117, 177. *See also* Iraq War; Vietnam War
US Labor Against the War (USLAW), 3, 210–14 passim
US military budget, 121–22
US Supreme Court cases, 214–15

Vallandigham, Clement, 214
values, 145–50 passim; progressive, 1, 15, 30, 145, 147; working class, 141, 146
Vatican Council II, 140
Vavi, Zwelinzima, 39
Vietnam, economy, 121; war, 2, 9, 117, 171n, 218
Voting Rights Act, 9, 21, 37
Vuillard, Éric, 31

wages, 81–85 passim, 107, 128, 208–9; maximum, 209; minimum, 6, 43, 170, 186, 208–9
Wagner Act. *See* National Labor Relations Act (Wagner Act)
war and wars, 112–17 passim, 126, 177; Civil War, 214; Iraq, 211; religious faith and, 146; Vietnam, 143, 161
Washington, George, 66–67
wealth inequality. *See* income inequality and wealth inequality
wealthy people. *See* rich people
Weather Underground, 28
Wells, Ida B., 185
White Heritage Month, 181
"white" (label), 168, 176, 178n, 179, 202
white privilege, 170–71, 203–4
whites, affirmative action for. *See* affirmative action for whites
white supremacy, 29, 52, 142, 168–79 passim, 191–98 passim, 202, 203
white workers, 28–29, 142, 167–72 passim, 193–96 passim; in *All in the Family*, 161; stereotypes, 193–94; Trump and, 25, 29, 190–94 passim; Weather Underground and, 28
wholesale and retail trade, 108, 109
Williams, John, 66
Wilmore, Gayraud S., 141
Women, and race, 182–86; in *All in the Family*, 161; in the working class, 99, 100, 179–82, nineteenth-century, 158; Women's History Month, 181; women's movement, 198–99
workers, classified as managers, 91–92
workers' autonomy, 92–93, 94
workers' seniority rights. *See* seniority rights (labor)
workers' share of GDP, 110
working class, 50–52, 84–87 passim, 91–106 passim, 154, 216; in *All in the Family*, 161; cross-class communication, 165; "deaths of despair," 195; economic crises, 128; education, 157–58; gender and, 180, 198–99; globalization, 119–20, 121; in literature, 162; Pope Leo XIII and, 138; presidential election (2016), 190, 193–94; race and, 168–72 passim; religion, 143; slavery and, 168; standard of living, 102, 181, 208–10 passim; values, 141, 146–47, 148, 150. *See also* white workers
working class culture, 162, 163–64, 210
Working Families Party (WFP), 18
Works Progress Administration (WPA), 49
World Bank, 118–19
World Trade Organization (WTO), 116, 118, 119
World War I, 116, 214
World War II, 116, 118; GI Bill, 170
The Wretched of the Earth (Fanon), 199–200

Young Lords, 22

Zaid, Nasr Abu. *See* Abu Zaid, Nasr
Zen Buddhism, 143

About the Contributors

Michael Zweig, emeritus professor of economics and founding director of the Center for Study of Working Class Life at the State University of New York at Stony Brook, received the SUNY Chancellor's Award for Excellence in Teaching. His past books include *Religion and Economic Justice*; *The Working Class Majority: America's Best Kept Secret*; and *What's Class Got to Do with It? American Society in the Twenty-First Century*. From 2005 to 2006, he served as executive producer of the documentary *Meeting Face to Face: The Iraq-U.S. Labor Solidarity Tour*. In 2009 he wrote, produced, and directed the film *Why Are We in Afghanistan?* which won the Working Class Studies Association Studs Terkel Award for media and journalism. In 2014 he received their award for lifetime contributions to the field of working class studies.

Rev. William J. Barber II was elected president of the local NAACP youth council in 1978 at the age of fifteen. He then enrolled at North Carolina Central University and became student government president at age 19. He received his bachelor's degree in political science from NCCU, cum laude, in 1985; a master of divinity degree from Duke University in 1989; and a doctor of ministry degree from Drew University, with a concentration in public policy and pastoral care, in 2003. He is the author of *We Are Called to Be a Movement*; *Revive Us Again: Vision and Action in Moral Organizing*; and *The Third Reconstruction: How a Moral Movement is Overcoming the Politics of Division and Fear*. He is national cochair of the Poor People's Campaign: A National Call for Moral Revival and director of the Center for Public Theology and Public Policy at Yale Divinity School.

ABOUT PM PRESS

PM Press is an independent, radical publisher of books and media to educate, entertain, and inspire. Founded in 2007 by a small group of people with decades of publishing, media, and organizing experience, PM Press amplifies the voices of radical authors, artists, and activists. Our aim is to deliver bold political ideas and vital stories to people from all walks of life and arm the dreamers to demand the impossible. We have sold millions of copies of our books, most often one at a time, face to face. We're old enough to know what we're doing and young enough to know what's at stake. Join us to create a better world.

PM Press
PO Box 23912
Oakland, CA 94623
www.pmpress.org

PM Press in Europe
europe@pmpress.org
www.pmpress.org.uk

FRIENDS OF PM PRESS

These are indisputably momentous times—the financial system is melting down globally and the Empire is stumbling. Now more than ever there is a vital need for radical ideas.

In the many years since its founding—and on a mere shoestring—PM Press has risen to the formidable challenge of publishing and distributing knowledge and entertainment for the struggles ahead. With hundreds of releases to date, we have published an impressive and stimulating array of literature, art, music, politics, and culture. Using every available medium, we've succeeded in connecting those hungry for ideas and information to those putting them into practice.

Friends of PM allows you to directly help impact, amplify, and revitalize the discourse and actions of radical writers, filmmakers, and artists. It provides us with a stable foundation from which we can build upon our early successes and provides a much-needed subsidy for the materials that can't necessarily pay their own way. You can help make that happen—and receive every new title automatically delivered to your door once a month—by joining as a Friend of PM Press. And, we'll throw in a free T-shirt when you sign up.

Here are your options:

- **$30 a month** Get all books and pamphlets plus a 50% discount on all webstore purchases

- **$40 a month** Get all PM Press releases (including CDs and DVDs) plus a 50% discount on all webstore purchases

- **$100 a month** Superstar—Everything plus PM merchandise, free downloads, and a 50% discount on all webstore purchases

For those who can't afford $30 or more a month, we have **Sustainer Rates** at $15, $10, and $5. Sustainers get a free PM Press T-shirt and a 50% discount on all purchases from our website.

Your Visa or Mastercard will be billed once a month, until you tell us to stop. Or until our efforts succeed in bringing the revolution around. Or the financial meltdown of Capital makes plastic redundant. Whichever comes first.

Jackson Rising Redux: Lessons on Building the Future in the Present

Edited by Kali Akuno & Matt Meyer
with a Foreword by Richard D. Wolff

ISBN: 978-1-62963-928-4 (paperback)
        978-1-62963-864-5 (hardcover)
$24.95/$59.95   584 pages

Mississippi is the poorest state in the US, with the
highest percentage of Black people and a history
of vicious racial terror. Black resistance at a time of
global health, economic, and climate crisis is the backdrop and context for the
drama captured in this new and revised collection of essays. Cooperation Jackson,
founded in 2014 in Mississippi's capital to develop an economically uplifting
democratic "solidarity economy," is anchored by a network of worker-owned,
self-managed cooperative enterprises. The organization developed in the context
of the historic election of radical Mayor Chokwe Lumumba, lifetime human rights
attorney. Subsequent to Lumumba's passing less than one year after assuming
office, the network developed projects both inside and outside of the formal
political arena. In 2020, Cooperation Jackson became the center for national
and international coalition efforts, bringing together progressive peoples from
diverse trade union, youth, church, and cultural movements. This long-anticipated
anthology details the foundations behind those successful campaigns. It unveils
new and ongoing strategies and methods being pursued by the movement for
grassroots-centered Black community control and self-determination, inspiring
partnership and emulation across the globe.

"*Jackson is one of the epicenters of resistance for all of us to emulate; this book lays the
scene.*"
—Chris Hedges, journalist, Presbyterian minister, and Princeton University lecturer;
author of *War Is a Force That Gives Us Meaning*

"*Jackson Rising is the rarest of things: a real strategic plan. You will not find a simple
wish list that glosses over the hard questions of resources, or some disembodied
manifesto imploring the workers forward, but a work in progress building the capacity
of people to exercise power.*"
—Richard Moser, author of *The World the Sixties Made*

Strike! 50th Anniversary Edition

Jeremy Brecher with a Preface by Sara
Nelson and a Foreword by Kim Kelly

ISBN: 978-1-62963-800-3 (paperback)
    978-1-62963-856-0 (hardcover)
$28.95/$60.00   640 pages

Jeremy Brecher's *Strike!* narrates the dramatic story
of repeated, massive, and sometimes violent revolts
by ordinary working people in America. Involving
nationwide general strikes, the seizure of vast industrial
establishments, nonviolent direct action on a massive scale, and armed battles
with artillery and tanks, this exciting hidden history is told from the point of view
of the rank-and-file workers who lived it. Encompassing the repeated repression of
workers' rebellions by company-sponsored violence, local police, state militias, and
the US Army and National Guard, it reveals a dimension of American history rarely
found in the usual high school or college history course.

Since its original publication in 1972, no book has done as much as *Strike!* to bring
US labor history to a wide audience. Now this fiftieth anniversary edition brings
the story up to date with chapters covering the "mini-revolts of the 21st century,"
including Occupy Wall Street and the Fight for Fifteen. The new edition contains
over a hundred pages of new materials and concludes by examining a wide range
of current struggles, ranging from #BlackLivesMatter, to the great wave of teachers
strikes "for the soul of public education," to the global "Student Strike for Climate,"
that may be harbingers of mass strikes to come.

"Jeremy Brecher's *Strike!* *is a classic of American historical writing. This new edition,
bringing his account up to the present, comes amid rampant inequality and growing
popular resistance. No book could be more timely for those seeking the roots of our
current condition.*"
—Eric Foner, Pulitzer Prize winner and DeWitt Clinton Professor of History at
Columbia University

"*Magnificent—a vivid, muscular labor history, just updated and rereleased by PM Press,
which should be at the side of anyone who wants to understand the deep structure of
force and counterforce in America.*"
—JoAnn Wypijewski, author of *Killing Trayvons: An Anthology of American Violence*

"*An exciting history of American labor. Brings to life the flashpoints of labor history.
Scholarly, genuinely stirring.*"
—New York Times

Sex, Race, and Class—The Perspective of Winning: A Selection of Writings 1952-2011

Selma James
With a foreword by Marcus Rediker
and an introduction by Nina López

ISBN: 978-1-60486-454-0
$20.00   320 pages

In 1972 Selma James set out a new political perspective. Her starting point was the millions of unwaged women who, working in the home and on the land, were not seen as "workers" and their struggles viewed as outside of the class struggle. Based on her political training in the Johnson-Forest Tendency, founded by her late husband C.L.R. James, on movement experience South and North, and on a respectful study of Marx, she redefined the working class to include sectors previously dismissed as "marginal."

For James, the class struggle presents itself as the conflict between the reproduction and survival of the human race, and the domination of the market with its exploitation, wars, and ecological devastation. She sums up her strategy for change as "Invest in Caring not Killing."

This selection, spanning six decades, traces the development of this perspective in the course of building an international campaigning network. It includes excerpts from the classic *The Power of Women and the Subversion of the Community* which launched the "domestic labor debate," the exciting "Hookers in the House of the Lord" which describes a church occupation by sex workers, an incisive review of the C.L.R. James masterpiece *The Black Jacobins*, a reappraisal of the novels of Jean Rhys and of the leadership of Julius Nyerere, the groundbreaking "Marx and Feminism," and more.

The writing is lucid and without jargon. The ideas, never abstract, spring from the experience of organising, from trying to make sense of the successes and the setbacks, and from the need to find a way forward.

"It's time to acknowledge James's path-breaking analysis: from 1972 she reinterpreted the capitalist economy to show that it rests on the usually invisible unwaged caring work of women."
—Dr. Peggy Antrobus, feminist, author of *The Global Women's Movement: Origins, Issues and Strategies*

"For clarity and commitment to Haiti's revolutionary legacy . . . Selma is a sister after my own heart."
—Danny Glover, actor and activist

Capital and Its Discontents: Conversations with Radical Thinkers in a Time of Tumult

Sasha Lilley

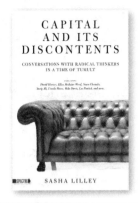

ISBN: 978-1-60486-334-5
$20.00   320 pages

Capitalism is stumbling, empire is faltering, and the planet is thawing. Yet many people are still grasping to understand these multiple crises and to find a way forward to a just future. Into the breach come the essential insights of *Capital and Its Discontents*, which cut through the gristle to get to the heart of the matter about the nature of capitalism and imperialism, capitalism's vulnerabilities at this conjuncture—and what can we do to hasten its demise. Through a series of incisive conversations with some of the most eminent thinkers and political economists on the Left—including David Harvey, Ellen Meiksins Wood, Mike Davis, Leo Panitch, Tariq Ali, and Noam Chomsky—*Capital and Its Discontents* illuminates the dynamic contradictions undergirding capitalism and the potential for its dethroning. At a moment when capitalism as a system is more reviled than ever, here is an indispensable toolbox of ideas for action by some of the most brilliant thinkers of our times.

"These conversations illuminate the current world situation in ways that are very useful for those hoping to orient themselves and find a way forward to effective individual and collective action. Highly recommended."
—Kim Stanley Robinson, *New York Times* bestselling author of the *Mars Trilogy* and *The Years of Rice and Salt*

"In this fine set of interviews, an A-list of radical political economists demonstrate why their skills are indispensable to understanding today's multiple economic and ecological crises."
—Raj Patel, author of *Stuffed and Starved* and *The Value of Nothing*

"This is an extremely important book. It is the most detailed, comprehensive, and best study yet published on the most recent capitalist crisis and its discontents. Sasha Lilley sets each interview in its context, writing with style, scholarship, and wit about ideas and philosophies."
—Andrej Grubačić, radical sociologist and social critic, co-author of *Wobblies and Zapatistas*

Re-enchanting the World: Feminism and the Politics of the Commons

Silvia Federici
with a Foreword by Peter Linebaugh

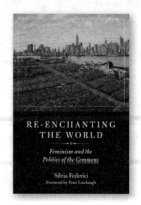

ISBN: 978-1-62963-569-9
$19.95   240 pages

Silvia Federici is one of the most important contemporary theorists of capitalism and feminist movements. In this collection of her work spanning over twenty years, she provides a detailed history and critique of the politics of the commons from a feminist perspective. In her clear and combative voice, Federici provides readers with an analysis of some of the key issues and debates in contemporary thinking on this subject.

Drawing on rich historical research, she maps the connections between the previous forms of enclosure that occurred with the birth of capitalism and the destruction of the commons and the "new enclosures" at the heart of the present phase of global capitalist accumulation. Considering the commons from a feminist perspective, this collection centers on women and reproductive work as crucial to both our economic survival and the construction of a world free from the hierarchies and divisions capital has planted in the body of the world proletariat. Federici is clear that the commons should not be understood as happy islands in a sea of exploitative relations but rather autonomous spaces from which to challenge the existing capitalist organization of life and labor.

"Silvia Federici's theoretical capacity to articulate the plurality that fuels the contemporary movement of women in struggle provides a true toolbox for building bridges between different features and different people."
—Massimo De Angelis, professor of political economy, University of East London

"Silvia Federici's work embodies an energy that urges us to rejuvenate struggles against all types of exploitation and, precisely for that reason, her work produces a common: a common sense of the dissidence that creates a community in struggle."
—Maria Mies, coauthor of Ecofeminism

Understanding Jim Crow: Using Racist Memorabilia to Teach Tolerance and Promote Social Justice

David Pilgrim with a foreword by Henry Louis Gates Jr.

ISBN: 978-1-62963-114-1
$24.95   208 pages

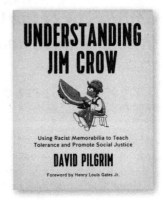

For many people, especially those who came of age after landmark civil rights legislation was passed, it is difficult to understand what it was like to be an African American living under Jim Crow segregation in the United States. Most young Americans have little or no knowledge about restrictive covenants, literacy tests, poll taxes, lynchings, and other oppressive features of the Jim Crow racial hierarchy. Even those who have some familiarity with the period may initially view racist segregation and injustices as mere relics of a distant, shameful past. A a proper understanding of race relations in this country must include a solid knowledge of Jim Crow—how it emerged, what it was like, how it ended, and its impact on the culture.

Understanding Jim Crow introduces readers to the Jim Crow Museum of Racist Memorabilia, a collection of more than ten thousand contemptible collectibles that are used to engage visitors in intense and intelligent discussions about race, race relations, and racism. The items are offensive. They were meant to be offensive. The items in the Jim Crow Museum served to dehumanize blacks and legitimized patterns of prejudice, discrimination, and segregation.

Using racist objects as teaching tools seems counterintuitive—and, quite frankly, needlessly risky. Many Americans are already apprehensive discussing race relations, especially in settings where their ideas are challenged. The museum and this book exist to help overcome our collective trepidation and reluctance to talk about race. Fully illustrated, and with context provided by the museum's founder and director David Pilgrim, *Understanding Jim Crow* is both a grisly tour through America's past and an auspicious starting point for racial understanding and healing.

"One of the most important contributions to the study of American history that I have ever experienced."
—Henry Louis Gates Jr., director of the W.E.B. Du Bois Institute for African American Research

"This was a horrific time in our history, but it needs to be taught and seen and heard. This is very well done, very well done."
—Malaak Shabazz, daughter of Malcolm X and Betty Shabazz

Patriarchy of the Wage: Notes on Marx, Gender, and Feminism

Silvia Federici

ISBN: 978-1-62963-799-0
$15.00   152 pages

At a time when socialism is entering a historic crisis and we are witnessing a worldwide expansion of capitalist relations, a feminist rethinking of Marx's work is vitally important. In *Patriarchy of the Wage*, Silvia Federici, best-selling author and the most important Marxist feminist of our time, asks why Marx and the Marxist tradition were so crucial in their denunciation of capitalism's exploitation of human labor and blind to women's work and struggle on the terrain of social reproduction. Why was Marx unable to anticipate the profound transformations in the proletarian family that took place at the turn of the nineteenth century creating a new patriarchal regime?

In this fiery collection of penetrating essays published here for the first time, Federici carefully examines these questions and in the process has provided an expansive redefinition of work, class, and class-gender relations. Seeking to delineate the specific character of capitalist "patriarchalism," this magnificently original approach also highlights Marx's and the Marxist tradition's problematic view of industrial production and the State in the struggle for human liberation. Federici's lucid argument that most reproductive work is irreducible to automation is a powerful reminder of the poverty of the revolutionary imagination that consigns to the world of machines the creation of the material conditions for a communist society.

Patriarchy of the Wage does more than just redefine classical Marxism; it is an explosive call for a new kind of communism. Read this book and realize the power and importance of reproductive labor!

"Silvia Federici's work embodies an energy that urges us to rejuvenate struggles against all types of exploitation and, precisely for that reason, her work produces a common: a common sense of the dissidence that creates a community in struggle."
—Maria Mies, coauthor of *Ecofeminism*

"Federici has become a crucial figure for young Marxists, political theorists, and a new generation of feminists."
—Rachel Kushner author of *The Flamethrowers*

"Federici's attempt to draw together the work of feminists and activist from different parts of the world and place them in historical context is brave, thought-provoking and timely. Federici's writing is lucid and her fury palpable."
—*Red Pepper*

Surviving the Future: Abolitionist Queer Strategies

Edited by Scott Branson, Raven Hudson, and Bry Reed with a Foreword by Mimi Thi Nguyen

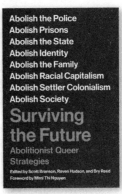

ISBN: 978-1-62963-971-0
$22.95   328 pages

Surviving the Future is a collection of the most current ideas in radical queer movement work and revolutionary queer theory. Beset by a new pandemic, fanning the flames of global uprising, these queers cast off progressive narratives of liberal hope while building mutual networks of rebellion and care. These essays propose a militant strategy of queer survival in an ever-precarious future. Starting from a position of abolition—of prisons, police, the State, identity, and racist cisheteronormative society—this collection refuses the bribes of inclusion in a system built on our expendability. Though the mainstream media saturates us with the boring norms of queer representation (with a recent focus on trans visibility), the writers in this book ditch false hope to imagine collective visions of liberation that tell different stories, build alternate worlds, and refuse the legacies of racial capitalism, anti-Blackness, and settler colonialism. The work curated in this book spans Black queer life in the time of COVID-19 and uprising, assimilation and pinkwashing settler colonial projects, subversive and deviant forms of representation, building anarchist trans/queer infrastructures, and more. Contributors include Che Gossett, Yasmin Nair, Mattilda Bernstein Sycamore, Adrian Shanker, Kitty Stryker, Toshio Meronek, and more.

"*Surviving the Future is a testament that otherwise worlds are not only possible, our people are making them right now—and they are queering how we get there through organizing and intellectual work. Now is the perfect time to interrogate how we are with each other and the land we inhabit. This collection gives us ample room to do just that in a moment of mass uprisings led by everyday people demanding safety without policing, prisons and other forms of punishment.*
—Charlene A. Carruthers, author of *Unapologetic: A Black, Queer, and Feminist Mandate for Radical Movements*

"*Surviving the Future is not an anthology that simply includes queer and trans minorities in mix of existing abolitionist thought. Rather, it is a transformative collection of queer/trans methods for living an abolitionist life. Anyone who dreams of dismantling the prison-industrial complex, policing, borders and the surveillance state should read this book. Frankly, everybody who doesn't share that dream should read it, too, and maybe they'll start dreaming differently.*"
—Susan Stryker, author of *Transgender History: The Roots of Today's Revolution*

We Go Where They Go: The Story of Anti-Racist Action

Shannon Clay, Lady, Kristin Schwartz, and Michael Staudenmaier with a Foreword by Gord Hill

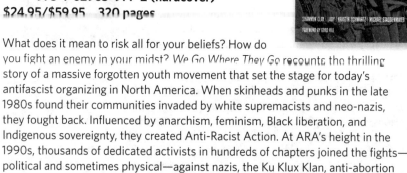

ISBN: 978-1-62963-972-7 (paperback)
       978-1-62963-977-2 (hardcover)
$24.95/$59.95   320 pages

What does it mean to risk all for your beliefs? How do you fight an enemy in your midst? *We Go Where They Go* recounts the thrilling story of a massive forgotten youth movement that set the stage for today's antifascist organizing in North America. When skinheads and punks in the late 1980s found their communities invaded by white supremacists and neo-nazis, they fought back. Influenced by anarchism, feminism, Black liberation, and Indigenous sovereignty, they created Anti-Racist Action. At ARA's height in the 1990s, thousands of dedicated activists in hundreds of chapters joined the fights—political and sometimes physical—against nazis, the Ku Klux Klan, anti-abortion fundamentalists, and racist police. Before media pundits, cynical politicians, and your uncle discovered "antifa," Anti-Racist Action was bringing it to the streets.

Based on extensive interviews with dozens of ARA participants, *We Go Where They Go* tells ARA's story from within, giving voice to those who risked their safety in their own defense and in solidarity with others. In reproducing the posters, zines, propaganda and photos of the movement itself, this essential work of radical history illustrates how cultural scenes can become powerful forces for change. Here at last is the story of an organic yet highly organized movement, exploring both its triumphs and failures, and offering valuable lessons for today's generation of activists and rabble-rousers. *We Go Where They Go* is a page-turning history of grassroots anti-racism. More than just inspiration, it's a roadmap.

"I was a big supporter and it was an honor to work with the Anti-Racist Action movement. Their unapologetic and uncompromising opposition to racism and fascism in the streets, in the government, and in the mosh pit continues to be inspiring to this day."
—Tom Morello

"Antifa became a household word with Trump attempting and failing to designate it a domestic terrorist group, but Antifa's roots date back to the late 1980s when little attention was being paid to violent fascist groups that were flourishing under Reaganism, and Anti-Racist Action (ARA) was singular and effective in its brilliant offensive. This book tells the story of ARA in breathtaking prose accompanied by stunning photographs and images."
—Roxanne Dunbar-Ortiz, author of *Loaded: A Disarming History of the Second Amendment*